The eConsultant

The eConsultant

GUIDING CLIENTS TO NET SUCCESS

Rick Freedman

JOSSEY-BASS/PFEIFFER
A Wiley Company
San Francisco

Published by

JOSSEY-BASS/PFEIFFER
A Wiley Company
350 Sansome Street, 5th Floor
San Francisco, CA 94104-1342
415.433.1740; Fax 415.433.0499
800.274.4434; Fax 800.569.0443

www.pfeiffer.com

Jossey-Bass/Pfeiffer is a registered trademark of John Wiley & Sons, Inc.
ISBN: 0-7879-5629-5

Copyright © 2001 by Rick Freedman.

Library of Congress Cataloging-in-Publication Data

Freedman, Rick.
   The econsultant: guiding clients to Net success / Rick
Freedman.
       p. cm.
   Includes bibliographical references and index.
   ISBN 0-7879-5629-5 (alk. paper)
   1. Internet consultants. 2. Business consultants. I. Title.
   HD69.C6 F738 2000
   650'.0285'4678—dc21
2001000840

Acquiring Editor: Matthew Holt
Director of Development: Kathleen Dolan Davies
Developmental Editor: Susan Rachmeler
Editor: Rebecca Taff
Senior Production Editor: Dawn Kilgore

Manufacturing Manager: Becky Carreño
Interior Design: Claudia Smelser
Cover Design: Blue Design
Illustrations: Richard Sheppard

Printed in the United States of America.

Printing   10   9   8   7   6   5   4   3   2   1

We at Jossey-Bass strive to use the most environmentally sensitive paper stocks available to us. Our publications are printed on acid-free recycled stock whenever possible, and our paper always meets or exceeds minimum GPO and EPA requirements.

For Terri

"Whoso loves
Believes the impossible."

Elizabeth Barrett Browning

CONTENTS

PREFACE

The first five years of the "Internet Economy" have passed, and the initial land grab of the Web's early days are over. The euphoria over such buzzwords as "eCommerce," "first-mover advantage," and "Web-onomics" has faded, as it has become clear that there is more to being successful on the Internet than staking a claim and throwing up a website or storefront. The dot.coms and the established businesses alike realize that success in the new economy requires strategic thinking, innovative marketing, superior technical design, and business process optimization. The Internet may not change everything, contrary to the cliché. It's clear, however, that, whether or not the fundamental rules of business have been repealed by the Web, one industry has been altered irreversibly by the Internet: the IT consulting industry.

The business of advising clients about information technology has seen many incarnations over the past thirty years. The secret priesthood of programmers behind glass doors, feeding cryptic codes to a megalithic machine; the geek in glasses and short-sleeved dress shirt; the "blue suit army" descending on the enterprise to re-engineer everything—these stereotypical images are well-known. The Internet Economy has also spawned its share of stereotypes: the twenty-something with dyed-blond hair who sold his Internet company for $100 million, the profit-less eCommerce IPO and its "record first-day pop," the Web-design consultants who look (and talk) like they just came off their surfboards in Malibu.

Putting these popular images aside, it's clear that both business in general, and the IT consulting business specifically, have undergone an upheaval that's worth examining. A few short years ago, the IT consulting landscape had settled into a recognizable establishment, with EDS, Andersen, IBM, and Computer Science

Corporation at the top of the food chain; Keane, Cap Gemini, KPMG, and a few others in the second tier; and a multitude of smaller players, including many PC resellers that had migrated to services, at the back of the pack. Standardized methodologies for installing networks, implementing SAP or Baan enterprise software, and setting up packaged applications had taken much of the risk out of the consulting business, and the order of things seemed secure.

Then came the Web. Now the giant "Big Five" firms of the IT consulting business have shifted their focus from the ERP, mainframe, and client-server technologies that were their bread-and-butter and are positioning themselves as "eBuilders," architects of the Internet Economy. Upstart consulting firms that were born on the Web, such as Razorfish, Viant, Agency.com, Scient, and a host of others, came from nowhere and earned billion-dollar market valuations, attracting some of the best consulting talent and many of the plum accounts from the established firms in the bargain. Independent contractors and boutique Web design shops are as ubiquitous as dry cleaners, and every small PC reseller or Novell shop is now a "Web architect." Many of the eConsulting firms have fallen just as quickly as they soared as the Internet stock bubble burst in the last months of 2000.

What do all these changes mean to the individual IT consultant? How does our daily work, advising clients on the best use of information technology for business advantage, change based on these new circumstances? Whether we work as independent consultants or are on staff at a large consultancy, whether we work for an old-line "Big Five" consulting firm or a small local Web boutique, what are the foundations of knowledge we need to advise clients well, and what methodologies must we apply to guarantee results? These, it seems to me, are the fundamental questions that the Internet revolution requires IT consultants to answer. These are the issues I'll address in this book.

WHO SHOULD READ THIS BOOK?

Consultants have an exciting opportunity to participate in a world-altering revolution. The new business models and strategies that are developed over the next twenty years will serve as the foundation for a transformation that will change the lives of every worker, from the dock worker on the Brooklyn dockside, to the accountant, to the CEO. In order to add value and have an impact on the development of this new world, Internet consultants need to understand the issues, strategies, and new business models that are rocking the business world. The Internet consultant is no longer simply a technologist with expertise in the IT building blocks of the Internet, such as bridges, routers, and gateways. She can no longer be simply a website designer, creating flashy splash screens and animated home pages in HTML. Both the Internet-born startups and the existing "brick-and-mortar" enterprises are seeking advice on their business models, Web marketing needs, and back-end logistical processes, as well as on IT and site design issues.

This book is my attempt to mentor and guide both novice and experienced IT consultants in the skills and techniques required to succeed in new economy consulting. I've spent the last few years working with clients, from startups to Fortune 500 companies, as they struggle with the strategic and tactical issues involved in designing comprehensive, compelling Internet strategies. I've also interviewed and corresponded with many practicing consultants to gain a broad view of the issues and challenges they face in their real-world encounters with clients. Finally, I've scoured the literature about Internet strategies, Web marketing, eCommerce alternatives, and enabling technologies in order to incorporate the best thinking available (and to point readers to the relevant resources) about Internet tactics.

For clients, too, the game has changed. Business managers trying to craft a compelling Internet strategy remind me of the chess players in Washington Square Park, in my native New York City. As they sit and think through the complex series of moves and countermoves, a chorus of "kibitzers" and advisors stands over their shoulders and suggests their next moves. Is the guy shouting out "rook to E5" an international grandmaster or a drunk? How does the player discern good advice from bad? Likewise in the Internet consulting business, the legion of would-be advisors is overwhelming, the library shelves groan with the weight of Internet strategy manuals, and the listings for "Internet Design Firms" in the Yellow Pages grow exponentially.

Clients need some guidance in the basic background, experience, and techniques that prepare a consultant to offer meaningful advice on Web strategies. Business executives in the midst of the chess game called Internet strategic planning will, I hope, find this book of value in helping identify competent advisors and Internet consulting "best practices."

WHAT THIS BOOK COVERS

In *The eConsultant*, we'll review the basics of business strategy and explore how those strategies are being impacted by the opportunities the Internet provides to reduce friction and to expand business time and space. We'll draw some conclusions about which business fundamentals remain intact and which may be shattered by the new environment. We'll look at the many organizational structures that both new businesses and existing enterprises may invoke, from the entrepreneurial startup to the "spin-up" and the "spin-off." Consultants need to be aware of the different needs, strengths, and vulnerabilities of both the startup and the spin-off. The process mechanics that are necessary to support an Internet business will be explored, as it has become clear that the basics of transactional accuracy and other "off-Net" processes still determine the customer's experience and satisfaction. We'll compare traditional advertising, basically a broadcast model that pushes a brand image to passive consumers, to the possibilities of Web marketing, in which passive consumers become active product researchers, using the search-and-compare capabilities of the Net to seek the brand information that has value for each of them.

Only after we've reviewed all these business issues and outlined some principles of new economy success in each of those disciplines will we address the technology questions related to the building of a Web presence that is based on sound competitive strategies as well as technical robustness. We'll investigate strategies that consultants can use to help their clients through the wrenching changes that this migration will inevitably bring, and we'll explore a personal development program that Internet consultants can apply in order to ensure that they, too, are prepared to grow and change as new lessons are learned and new business truths emerge. Finally, we'll expand on the notion of a "Consultant's Scorecard" to devise an Internet-specific measurement system that clients can use to ensure that they are getting the most value from their advisors, and that consultants can use to demonstrate that they've delivered objective business value, rather than merely billable hours.

I feel like a lucky man, with the chance to participate in the business revolution of the new millennium. I've had the opportunity to work side by side with many of the technologists, business leaders, venture capitalists, and managers who are charting the course for the new economy. In *The eConsultant*, I've tried to present the lessons I've learned from these fortuitous encounters and to present a methodology and a foundation course for IT consultants to help them guide their clients toward success. I've based this book on my experiences while working with a broad spectrum of clients and on substantial research and interviews with practitioners, analysts, and organizations on the critical success factors in the Internet environment. I hope this book positions business managers and corporate IT professionals to get the most from their relationships with their Internet advisors and that it gives IT consultants the tools and knowledge they need to guide their clients to success in the challenging new economy.

June 2001   Rick Freedman

ACKNOWLEDGMENTS

I'd like to thank the following people for their invaluable help and support in creating this work:

Jennifer Recktenwald, Bob Artner, and Paul Baldwin of TechRepublic, the premier informational and community website for IT professionals. They have been kind enough to run my comments and interviews in a series of columns over the past year and have graciously consented to allow me to republish here excerpts from interviews I've conducted for them. I value this relationship with TechRepublic and its reader community greatly.

Thanks to Skip McDonald of Luminant Worldwide, Tuck Rickards of Russell Reynolds Associates, Jim Highsmith of the Cutter Consortium, Seth Neiman and Kelli Tejada of Crosspoint Venture Partners, Chuck Krutsinger of The Interlink Group, Tuck Rickards of Russell Reynolds, and Larry Tanning of Tanning Technology for their kind permission to reprint their comments here and for their insights and mentorship in this ever-changing economic landscape.

Thanks also to Mitchell Chi at Oracle, Steve Porter at Exodus Communications, Marcus Harris at Digex, Doug Sholtis and Murray Hess at Sun Microsystems, Kenn Yancy and Mark Beausir at Cisco Systems, Tony Ahillas and Blair Rundell at Portal Software, Mike Fox at Competitive Communications Group, Susan Goldenberg, Craig Kaminer, Keith Yahl, and Cindy Mahoney at influence, Gretchen Gregory at Extreme Networks, Ken Harrington at Worknet, Robert Hilsinger at Siemens, Paul Kincaid-Smith and Steve Roper at Software.com, Stephanie Millette at Razorfish, Bill Perry and Alan Warms at Participate.com, David Rye at Atlas Ventures, Mark Dreher at InterVentures, Kevin Owens and Bob Mater at Nevik Networks, and Bob Sands at SandCastle for their kind assistance with the research on this project.

Matt Holt, Kathleen Dolan Davies, Josh Blatter, Jeanenne Ray, Adrienne Biggs, Susan Rachmeler, Dawn Kilgore, Ocean Howell, and Samya Sattar from Jossey-Bass/Pfeiffer and John Wiley and Sons for their encouragement and confidence. Every book is a collaboration.

As always, Shawn, Leila, Danny, Dalia, Jeremy, Josh, Abby, Ellie, Katie, Patrick, Mikey, and Emily.

The New IT Consulting Model

chapter ONE

THE INTERNET CHANGES EVERYTHING!

Does the Internet change everything, as the cliché asserts? Or does it only change certain things, and do certain truths remain? Is it a whole new world, or just a new slant on the old one? Which fundamental rules of business remain inviolate, and which have gone through a space warp and been altered forever? And which current business models are about to spin beyond the event horizon and sink into the black hole, never to be seen again?

These are the questions that every business leader and executive must answer. From the most stable and predictable of old-line enterprises to the startup basing its future on a revolutionary new technology or a surprising new twist on an old business model, all businesspeople are strategizing, evaluating, and meditating on the possible outcomes of their encounter with the new economy. There is no doubt that, for some, this encounter will mean dominance and prosperity. For others it will mean doom.

What will differentiate the dominant from the doomed in this new world? Organizations at all points of the spectrum, from the Fortune 500 industrial giants to the "two-guys-in-a-garage" startups, are traveling many different paths as they seek the answer. Some are trying internal "skunkworks," covert projects with unique measurements and objectives, made up of talented technicians and "intrapreneurs." Others are trying spin-offs, entirely separate companies tasked with the goal of developing compelling Internet strategies that can then be brought back into the "mother ship." Some companies have created task forces or committees to research the options and report to the board. Some, alas, have even turned the development of an Internet strategy into just another IT project to fit into the already insurmountable backlog of projects on IT's heaping plate.

Whichever strategy and organizational structure they ultimately choose, many of these enterprises have one thing in common: They will engage consultants to help them navigate this sea change. They will enter into engagements with consulting firms hoping that, through their expertise, exposure, and experience, their advisors will jump-start their efforts to craft Internet strategies and will protect them from the blind alleys and "gotchas" that can derail them on their path to a successful Web initiative. New consulting organizations and agencies, with specialties ranging from Internet infrastructure to creative design and Web branding, are established weekly to great fanfare. And many consultants formerly focused on technical fields, such as mainframes, client-server systems, networks, or application development, are migrating their practices to concentrate on—and capitalize on—the Internet and the new economy.

For consultants wishing to migrate to this new era of IT services, there are risks and challenges. Consultants wonder how to expand their skill sets from the purely technical to the strategic, marketing, and logistical arenas on which their clients so urgently need counsel. How can I, as a talented and experienced technician, develop my abilities in areas that were never before central to my success? How can I evaluate the hundreds of different Internet-related books, articles, research reports, checklists, and business cases that are published daily to glean those points of wisdom that will apply to my clients' needs so that I can help them vault over their competitors? Do I have to become a graphic designer, an advertising agency, a management consultant, a researcher, and a process re-engineering guru just to compete in this new IT services marketplace?

Consulting firms are also struggling with these questions. Many of the former "Big Five" firms are on acquisition sprees, purchasing everything from advertising agencies to network security firms, all in a bid to offer "one-stop shopping" to their corporate clients. Yet there are significant questions regarding the "agency" model, in which consultants attempt to provide the complete range of Internet advisory services, from branding to Web-hosting. In fact, some of these marriages are now turning into messy divorces, as the principals and partners realize that the difficulty of merging the creative, unstructured advertising agency with the methodology-driven management consulting firm can be a real distraction in this speed-driven marketplace. If you're a partner in a consulting firm, which model is right for you? And what criteria do you use to choose among partnering, outsourcing, alliance, or specialization models?

For those enterprises that are setting out on the journey to their new economy destinies, too, there is fear and trepidation as well as excitement and challenge. Will the consultants they select to guide them bring valuable insight and help them achieve the vaunted "first-mover advantage," or will they lead them down a dead end? Will their consultants have the full range of talents required to be strategic advisors, such as technical, business, process, branding, and project-management skills, or will they be narrowly focused and technically biased? In short, will they add value to the search for competitive advantage or merely generate billable hours? I hope to answer those questions in the chapters ahead.

Most of us become consultants, rather than corporate IT professionals, because we savor the chance to experience new challenges, to work with new teams and meet interesting, talented individuals, to tame new technologies, and to invent new combinations and permutations of IT that solve unique problems. For the adventurous consultants willing to elevate their games and expand their knowledge, the transformation to the new Internet economy creates a golden moment of possibility—the chance to participate in, and shape, a revolutionary migration; to architect the new business models, technical designs, and customer experiences that will become the norm of daily interaction over the next century. For all the difficulties and challenges that face the pioneers of this new economy, there are equal rewards and satisfactions. Apart from the financial compensation and the sheer joy of learning and growth, we each have the chance to collaborate with our clients to build something innovative and new, something that we can point to with pride.

THE NET CHANGES BUSINESS

In the following chapters, we'll examine the basics of business strategy as they've been delineated by pioneers of strategic thinking such as Michael Porter and C.K. Prahalad. In preparation for that discussion, however, let's examine some of the basic elements of all business strategies and how the Internet impacts them.

Whether your business is a local shoe store, a car dealership, or a toy manufacturer, there are certain elements that drive profitability, that allow you to charge more for your goods or services than you pay for them. In the "brick-and-mortar" world, the elements of geography, informational superiority, and the dynamics of supply and demand are key determinants of your ability to command profitable prices. Let's explore how these basic elements work in the current economy, and then we'll see how they are changed by some of the new capabilities of Net-based business.

Geography

The old cliché about "location, location, location" points to one of these key elements, geography. Your ability to charge a premium for your products is regulated by the size of your local market, the competition that is convenient to that market, and the local supply and demand for your product. If you own the only shoe store in an isolated village, you can pretty much charge what you like for your shoes. If, however, there's a discount shoe store across the street from your full-price store, you may be in for a disappointing earnings outlook. If the closest discount store is forty miles away, your ability to charge full price isn't absolute, but it looks a lot rosier. Some highly price-sensitive shoppers will make the trip to save a few bucks, and even those who are willing to travel are taking a chance that they may reach the discount store and not find the style or size they want. Enough consumers will value the convenience of your location to spend the extra money and avoid the trip.

Informational Superiority

Information about your products and services is also a distinct advantage. The classic case is the car dealer, who typically has a lot more information about the cars she's selling than the buyer. She knows what the dealership pays for the car, which options significantly enhance her margins, which service packages are winners for the dealership, what the trade-in is really worth, plus a lot more information about what local competitors have on their lots, what they're charging, and what rebates and incentives the manufacturer is offering. Educated buyers may be armed with the latest ratings from the Consumers' Union and the latest prices from the Edmunds *Blue Book,* but the information imbalance is still in the dealer's favor. This imbalance is central to the profitability models of car dealerships today and is also responsible for the contentious and uncomfortable relationships most car buyers have with their dealers.

Supply and Demand

Anyone who has witnessed the craze over Beanie Babies® or the Christmas toy de jour has observed the effects of an imbalance of supply and demand. The impromptu black market for Beanie Babies® that developed, with sellers hawking the cute little beanbags at inflated prices out of their homes or from the trunks of their cars, illustrates another key economic law: Price is the instrument for mediating supply and demand. In other words, when demand exceeds supply, prices will rise, and vice versa. Pre-Internet dynamic marketplaces, such as the NASDAQ stock market, clearly demonstrate the imbalance of supply and demand and its effect on prices. These imbalances offer sellers an opportunity for significant profits. When the demand for Dell shares goes up, sellers can instantly respond by asking for a higher price. If TY, the maker of Beanie Babies®, were able to determine the demand for its toys as instantaneously and accurately as sellers on the NASDAQ, TY's ability to obtain the best price for its products would be enhanced. Unfortunately, in the brick-and-mortar world, there is no dynamic mechanism for gauging supply and demand and instantaneously modifying prices, as NASDAQ traders can.

So how do these fundamental elements of business change in the new economy? Let's examine each of them again, but this time through the lens of the Internet.

How the Internet Impacts These Elements

The shoe buyer who turns to the Internet, rather than to the local retail outlet, for his footwear needs experiences a dramatic broadening of his options. No longer subject to the tyranny of *geography,* he has visibility into a selection of shoes, not only from his local village, shop, or mall, but from every shoe supplier on Earth (theoretically). He can peruse the sites of shoe manufacturers, select the style, color, and price range he desires, then visit the sites of both full-price and discount dealers, and select the mix of price, value, style, service, and convenience he feels comfortable with. Maybe he'll go ahead and purchase his shoes from the local store's website, because they have a relationship with him, know his special needs, and will deliver and repair his shoes as needed. Maybe he'll buy his shoes directly from the Italian designer's factory outlet on the Web, or from the giant discount mall's site (which is located in a data center in Winnemucca, Nevada). Whatever his decision, the geography of the supplier has ceased to be a competitive advantage. His supply has expanded from the local retail outlets to the entire catalog of shoes available worldwide. His local supplier may still have competitive advantages, but they are based on customer service and relationship, not on geography.

The car buyer also has gained advantage by the introduction of the Web. She can access sites designed specifically to provide her with the information she needs to be on an even playing field with the dealer. She can go directly to the Consumers' Union website and compare and contrast the safety record and durability of car models dynamically. The dealer invoice price and the dealer cost of various options are all totally exposed to the inquiring purchaser. The trade-in value of her current car can be calculated based on a simple input form available on multiple sites. Advice on accepting or declining service options and extended warranties is available, along with analyses of the costs and benefits of each. The local supply of cars in each style, color, and model is aggregated by certain sites, based on the zip code supplied by the buyer. In short, those car dealers who base their business model on one-sided information, rather than on value, relationship, and service, are playing in a whole new game, with rules that favor the purchaser rather than the seller.

As anyone who has visited eBay knows, the selling of Beanie Babies®, for example, has been revolutionized by the Net. The lively, dynamic meeting of buyers and sellers that has characterized the securities markets—and resulted in superior liquidity and responsiveness to the pressures of supply and demand—has now been extended to any item that has an active market. Items as varied as guitars, baseball cards, toys, fine art, and lawn furniture have all been transformed into commodities that are globally visible and whose prices can instantly respond to changes in the supply and demand of the marketplace. We haven't reached a state of perfect competition yet, as issues of item condition and authenticity are still being arbitrated and government regulation of pricing still limits many companies' ability to participate in dynamic pricing. However, the example of eBay demonstrates that worldwide communication and access make markets (and prices) much more responsive to the demands of buyers and sellers.

This short introduction to the metamorphosis of the marketplace by the Internet is meant to lay a brief foundation for the discussion on business strategy to follow. The tendency of universal supply to drive prices lower (in many cases to zero!); the availability of price-sniffing "bots" that can search the Web for the best price, thus turning many items into commodities; the ability of Internet-based businesses to measure customer demand and price sensitivity in real time, rather than having to extrapolate from past data; the ability of Net-based businesses to exploit "infinite shelf space"; all of these competitive issues will be explored in depth in later chapters. This discussion is meant to highlight one simple proposition: The rules have, without a doubt, changed! Consultants, in order to add value in this new economy, must grasp these basic principles and must be able to apply them to every engagement they undertake.

THE NET CHANGES CONSULTING

International Data Corporation (IDC), the respected IT industry analyst, publishes annual reports that describe the growth and financial results of the IT services industry. In 1996, IDC categorized the IT services industry into twelve components so that it could size each market and compare the growth and revenues of each segment. At that time the twelve categories were:

- Information Systems Consulting
- Information System Outsourcing
- Processing Services
- Business Process Outsourcing
- Systems Integration
- Custom Application Development and Maintenance
- Software Installation and Support
- Hardware Installation and Support
- Network Consulting and Integration
- Network Operation Outsourcing
- Desktop Management
- Information Technology Training and Education[1]

Within two years, the Internet had changed the IT services world so drastically that these categories needed to be revised. The category of "IS Consulting" was too technology-focused, as many consultancies were now providing business strategy, branding, graphic design for websites, change management consulting, and other non-technology consulting services. So that category was changed to simply

"Consulting." A new category of service, "Application Outsourcing" was added to reflect a completely new business model that the Net had made possible, the "Virtual Data Center" or Application Service Provider (ASP). The network operations category was also revised and was renamed "Network Infrastructure Management Services" to reflect the central role that the network and its associated Internet connectivity play in the enterprise.

IT consultants and professional services firms have been as deeply impacted by the new economy as have our clients. Like our clients, consultants are searching for the right business models to meet the challenges of the Internet economy. The face of the consulting business has mutated concurrently with Internet technology. In the early days of the Web, many corporate Web presences were static brochure-ware, typically consisting of a reproduction of the company's ads and marketing materials, with some catalogs and users' manuals occasionally thrown in. Most companies looked at the Web as a one-way broadcasting mechanism, another way to blast out company image messages to prospects and customers. The corporate website was seen as a marketing opportunity, and so companies went to their advertising agencies for advice. Ad agencies hired or acquired the technicians and Web designers they needed to provide Web services and to retain their exclusive client relationships.

As Web technology migrated toward a more interactive experience in which communities of interest were encouraged and surfers became participants, and as Web presentation technology advanced to provide more animated and engaging images, the Web started to look more like a content medium. So clients turned to film and video specialists and high-end Web developers for assistance. There was a rush among both technical consulting firms and ad agencies to recruit and groom promising film and video talents and to turn them into Internet "content providers." The consulting firms that specialized in this arena started calling their consultants "producers" instead of project managers.

The next big buzzword in the Internet explosion was "intranet," as companies realized that the standardized protocols and browser software that was emerging as a standard for Net access also allowed the creation of internal networks for the exchange of information with employees and partners. Everything from employee phone directories and 401(k) lookup applications to extensive partner networks for the exchange of sophisticated specifications and component orders were migrating to the Net. In this iteration, those consulting firms that had experience in electronic data exchange, such as EDI and Lotus® Notes specialists, and those with expertise in mapping internal work and data flows had their phones ringing off the hook. Those firms without this expertise sought again to recruit or acquire it.

As Amazon.com, eBay, and Dell demonstrated that the Web was a catalyst for entirely new business models and even new industries, clients sought advisors with strategic and business acumen, with understanding of supply chains and value chains, channel strategies and product strategies, to help them redefine the nature of competition in their marketplaces. The traditional management consulting firms, with excellent reputations in the strategic disciplines, once again began to dominate as they started to "get the Net," and as they allied with or absorbed partners that could help them provide the broadest set of new economy services. Because the underpinning of this revolution was the technology itself, a superior understanding and delivery capability in Internet protocols and infrastructure remained the price of entry for consultants wishing to compete in this explosive and lucrative market.

Consulting firms have been scrambling to keep their service offerings in sync with the needs of the market. Razorfish, a born-on-the-Web consultancy that started as an "anti-ad agency," began with a focus on unconventional interactive media and branding projects and has grown into a worldwide full-service firm with thousands of employees and a market capitalization in the billions of dollars. Other "anti-agencies," such as Agency.com, have followed a similar growth path.

Other firms that came from the same milieu have taken entirely different paths: Digital Pulp, for example, another firm that started as an alternative to the traditional ad agencies of Madison Avenue, has stayed small and independent by choice. Lee Nadler, the firm's president and CEO, is not interested in "growth at all costs" or jumping into the IPO market. More interested in the creativity of the work than with grabbing every account, Nadler says his firm often works with clients because of their innovative strategies and their ability to see beyond brochure-ware. "We're not about popping out websites. We're interested in growing businesses,"[2] he states. With only $2.7 million in 1998 revenues, they're tiny compared with their exploding agency competitors, but Digital Pulp has managed to generate a profit from the beginning and to snare prestigious clients such as 1–800-Flowers, DoubleClick, and Egghead.com.

Some firms have decided to narrow their focus to one area of the Internet consulting arena and become the recognized specialist there. Tanning Technologies, a

Denver-based IT services firm, is pursuing a different strategy than the full-service agencies: They've decided to stick to their core competency, Internet infrastructure technical integration. It's been a successful strategy for them: They generated $19.6 million in revenue for the first quarter of 2000, up from $11.3 million in the same time frame the year before, a 57 percent growth rate. "It's one thing to understand a simple client-server application with straightforward transactions. It's something entirely different to go into the kind of companies that are looking for differentiations and breakthrough technologies that must meet service levels that are complex and require large quantities of data," says Larry Tanning, the founder and CEO.[3]

Other companies have decided that bigger is definitely better. Witness March-First, the firm that has resulted from the merger of two giant Web consultancies, USWeb and Whitman-Hart. Prior to this recent merger, USWeb absorbed CKS to become USWeb/CKS, which then acquired 700-person strategic business consultancy Mitchell Madison Group (MMG). Mitchell Madison had the reputation as a strategic business advisor, but needed the technical expertise and Web-savvy of USWeb, and USWeb likewise needed MMG to round out its offerings. In all, March-First has absorbed over forty separate consulting, marketing, or Web-design firms. iXL, another Web-focused firm, has acquired over thirty-five firms in its short lifetime. The ability to absorb new firms became such a critical aspect of their growth strategy that iXL created a boot camp for acquired employees, called iXL101, designed to communicate the corporate vision and to build consensus among the recruits. Based in Cambridge, Massachusetts, Sapient, one of the fastest-growing and most respected Internet consultancies, has also been acquiring companies. Sapient has acquired firms across the spectrum, from advertising agencies to technology specialists. Like iXL, Sapient has instituted a training program, SapientStart, a five-day "new-hire experience" that introduces employees to the Sapient work culture.

The merger strategy has its disadvantages, however. Many of the acquired firms are entrepreneurial startups whose teams experience a sense of loss, both of autonomy and of culture, when acquired. Many of the "Gen-X" creative developers who started or joined these firms chaff at the corporate atmosphere of the giant consultancies. If they decide to leave, they take a large part of the original justification for merging with them. Wall Street has not been thrilled with many of these mergers either. USWeb, for instance, saw its stock plunge from 54 to 34 after the merger with Whitman-Hart was announced. Whitman-Hart's shares went from 58 to 32.

The eConsultancies, which were subject to the same Internet euphoria that lifted the stocks of companies like Priceline.com and Pets.com to unsustainable heights in 1999, have become subject to the same gloom and disillusionment that have come with the bursting of the Internet bubble in late 2000. As I write this (in December 2000), the news on Wall Street is about the announcements from two of the leading players in this space, Scient and Viant, that each will be laying off over 30 percent of their workforce and closing offices. The crash of the dot.com stocks has set off a chain reaction that has placed new pressures on the Internet-focused consultancies. The very public failure of hundreds of dot.coms had an effect on both the eConsultancies and the Fortune 500 companies. For the new consulting firms, dependent on the dot.coms' free-spending ways, many lucrative contracts just disappeared. At the same time, the traditional Fortune 500 companies, no longer subject to the fear of being "Amazoned" by some revolutionary Internet startup, no longer feel the pressure to develop Internet strategies in Internet time and so have taken a step back and are reconsidering their investments, and their timetables, for launching Web-based businesses. This confluence of factors has hit the eConsultancies between the eyes, and few firms in the sector have been left untouched by negative announcements affecting earnings or staffing. All of the publicly traded Internet consulting firms have seen their share prices eroded by the unrelenting bad news; many have lost 95 percent of their stock market valuations or more in the past six months.

These events in the stock markets do not mean that the opportunities for Internet consultants are going away. Both investors and analysts may have been optimistic, or even hallucinatory, in their expectations of the quickness of change in the gigantic and fundamentally conservative American economy. The fact remains that the Internet and its associated technologies will have a profound effect on the business environment that will leave few organizations untouched. It may not happen overnight, as some analysts and investors might have expected, and the effects may not be obvious or predictable, but Internet-inspired change is inevitable.

For those consultants with an entrepreneurial bent, the dream of starting a small, full-service agency in a loft or basement and growing it into a billion-dollar, publicly traded powerhouse is attractive. Independent consultants who wish to migrate from technically focused IT services to strategic Internet consulting need to make some of the same decisions that the companies profiled above had to make: To select a niche or to broaden their service offerings (sometimes called the "go broad or go deep" dilemma); to remain independent or to merge or create alliances with partners who can help provide the full range of services clients need; to go for a low-growth strategy focused on choice assignments or to pursue a high-growth strategy that necessarily includes taking both the plum and the routine projects.

I've found, as an independent consultant trying to provide value to my clients, that my choices are a bit more limited: I discovered from my daily practice that I have no choice but to develop a wide grounding in all the disciplines in which clients look for advice—from technology to strategy and from marketing to metrics. I also discovered that I could never be deep in all of these areas, and so partnerships and alliances have become a central part of my modus operandi. Finally, I learned that there are some constants of the consulting business that still need to be observed, even in the warp-speed environment of the Internet. Let's review some of the fundamental practices of project management, client relationships, and communications that haven't been altered by the Net.

SOME THINGS NEVER CHANGE: THE CONSTANTS OF IT CONSULTING

In an April 17, 2000, report to its clients, Giga Information Group, one of the top IT analyst firms, announced that, although "the new breed of Internet consulting firms barely resembles its systems integrator predecessors, . . . there is one consistent factor among the strong consultants: investment in methodology." They go on to state that "not only are the Internet consultants investing heavily in organized development methodologies; they are heavily marketing the fact that they exist and that they demonstrate the consultant's ability to deliver in this new world of Internet-based architectures."[4]

This opinion from Giga reinforces a contention that I will make throughout this book: Although the high-speed world of Internet consulting requires consultants to deliver value more quickly than ever before, this circumstance must not be misinterpreted to mean that we can throw structure and methodology out the window. The lessons that have been learned in the forty years of IT evolution, in which we went from ad-hoc, "spaghetti-code" programming practices to structured and disciplined project management and system development practices, cannot be disrespected.

This is not to say that the methodologies of the past must be applied as is. The system development lifecycles crafted in the early days of IT were experiencing significant re-engineering even before the Internet took off, as IT professionals realized that the strict "define-design-build" techniques were too inflexible and slow to satisfy user needs. As IT projects grew from back-office automation to strategic applications, new development disciplines such as Rapid Application Development (RAD) and Joint Application Development (JAD) were developed to help put these business-critical IT systems on a fast track. The PC and network revolution created an upheaval in user expectations, as IT's traditional customers grew weary of waiting months or years for applications and embraced tools such as Lotus 1–2–3® and Dbase to develop their own applications in days. The use of methodologies that focused on iterative prototypes instead of huge "all or nothing" development projects moved IT even further from the traditional "waterfall" methods of development, in which each phase, from definition to design through implementation, needed to be completed before the next phase could begin.

So how do the methodologies employed by the new Internet consultancies differ from those of the traditional IT services giants? Xcelerate, a Florida-based full-service consultancy with over three hundred employees, calls its methodology "Velocity Discipline," further described as "a fusion of workshops and proven techniques that unite creativity, interactive marketing, eBusiness strategy, and technology teams in the design and development of your eBusiness." Starting with a half-day "discovery workshop" at which clients have a chance to "share their vision," Xcelerate then follows a four-step process that includes a Strategy Roadmap, a Solution Roadmap, a Solution Design, and a Solution Launch phase. They project that the entire process, from engagement to launch, will take between ten and twenty weeks.[5] Scient, the San Francisco based eBusiness services giant, also employs a four-stage methodology that offers clients "compressed time to market." The Scient methodology includes phases to Conceive, Architect, Engineer, and Extend eBusiness strategies.[6] Their Conceive phase includes both a strategic and a technical component, and their Architecture phase focuses on clearly defining scope and responsibilities, as well as technical architecture, in the client relationship.

Although some of the language and the names of the phases are different, these leading eBusiness consultants are applying methodologies that enforce the same disciplines of client collaboration, scope management, communication, and project management that the "Big Five" firms apply. The concentration on "speed to value" has been a constant driver to the adoption of more streamlined techniques, and the Internet has accelerated that; but the Web was not the sole genesis of these methodologies. At the core, these less bureaucratic, more collaborative, and more iterative methodologies solidify the gains that have been made in system development disciplines over the last twenty years.

In fact, some of these new practices are now being codified in a movement that has picked up the designation "light methodologies." New project lifecycles and techniques, with names like Extreme Programming, Lean Development, and Adaptive Development, are gaining acceptance as appropriate methods for dealing with the time constraints and experimental nature of eBusiness projects. These methodologies are described as "heavy on skills, light on process," and make the assumption that, after the collective experience of thirty years of system development, the IT community doesn't need ten-volume methodologies in order to create robust applications and systems and that perhaps we've learned enough to be able to make project-specific decisions as to how much process and structure we need to apply. Analogies are made between these light methodologies and the lean manufacturing techniques that the Japanese used to revolutionize the automobile business. Both assume that workers are motivated experts who know how to do their jobs without intensive oversight; and both focus on the discovery of defects throughout the process and on rectifying their cause rather than just their symptoms. These light methods are also focused on customer satisfaction and participation and incorporate continuing customer interaction to ensure that what is being developed and delivered actually meets the client's expectations, even as those expectations change in the dynamic Internet environment. Stalwart proponents of process-driven, highly structured methodologies, such as Ed Yourdon and Ken Orr, authors of some of the seminal texts in these areas, have endorsed this movement toward quicker, less bureaucratic, and more collaborative and iterative development techniques. Tom Demarco, the author of such system development classics as *Peopleware* (1999) and *Controlling Software Projects* (1982) said recently in support of these methodologies, "The key to achieving the kind of mobility [in system development] this new century requires is to move away from time-consuming inspections and document-intensive approaches. The focus of investment needs to change from the organization (investing in process) to the individual (investing in skills)."[7]

The key point here is that, as the Giga report quoted above concludes, clients still look at the methodologies and practices that their consultants apply as a critical assurance factor when selecting an advisor. Although methodologies are changing, consultants migrating to the Internet arena still must resist the temptation to view the need for speed as a license to disregard the basic rules of the road.

A Conversation
with Skip McDonald

In a recent interview with Skip McDonald, director of knowledge management for Luminant, I asked Skip, a veteran of Ernst and Young, how the methodologies of the "eBuilders" differ from the "Big Five" style of IT consulting to the new economy consulting companies.

"One area where we differ from a typical Big Five project," Skip told me, "is that we don't have deliverables that are purely technical. Our deliverables incorporate strategy, marketing, creative, and technical elements, so what we deliver is multi-disciplinary. Our technical guru is sitting across from the creative consultant who's doing multimedia design. Our technical folks understand that we're trying to hit not just technical targets but also emotional and usability targets. Those cross-functional teams are a lot different than you see in a typical IT consultant engagement. They can see that if they compromise a technical detail they may be compromising a business strategy."

When I asked Skip what a typical client engagement at Luminant looks like—how the project process flows—he told me, "We look at the whole scope, the overall goal, and tell the client, if we were to build this as we've got it defined today, here's the benefit you're going to get. But we all know that goal is going to move. So we take the piece that gives the most important benefit, the biggest hit from the business standpoint and also the highest risk, and we tackle those. It's a way of taking the risk out of the project. We'll implement three quick releases. The first release is to get a base functionality out. The second release is going parallel with the first; it's the base functionality with the addition of some things that we knew would take a bit longer technically to implement. We do some learning based on what we've done so far, because we can now measure the market. One thing that's great about the Internet, you know you're successful or not almost immediately. Then you can add the details that will make it more effective. And you're not two years into it—you're months into it, and you've got 80 percent of the functionality and you've only spent 50 percent of the budget. Now you can measure what you've done and make decisions about how to effectively spend the other 50 percent of the money. The scope will change based on what you've learned, so you spend some time revisiting the strategy. So we've done two things. We've delivered increasing functionality over the life of the project, while spending half the money you would have spent on a waterfall project. We've got 80 percent of the functionality and we can now respond as the market moves. We can tell the client that this is not the end of the game. Let's talk about where the market is now. Maybe you'll need to spend some more money to stay in the game; but the client is in the game, perhaps making money, certainly learning what they need to do to be successful in their Internet marketplace."[8]

End Notes

1. Winthrop, P., Hoffman, C. IDC's IT Services Segmentation: Definitions and Methodology. *IDC Analysis Report,* March 2000.
2. Werner, B. Zen and the Art of Interactive Advertising. *The Industry Standard,* Nov. 1, 1999.
3. DeMarzio, R., Doyle, T. Q & A with Larry Tanning. *VarBusiness,* Feb. 16, 2000.
4. Internet Consultants Promote Methodology as Key Success Factor. *Giga Information Group Research Report,* April 17, 2000.
5. Methodology © Xcelerate Inc. *www.xcelerate.com.*
6. Methodology © Scient Inc. *www.scient.com.*
7. Highsmith, J. *Business Technology Trends and Impacts: Light Methodologies.* The Cutter Consortium, 2000.
8. Interview with the author, published as "Conversation with a Knowledge Management Guru," July 21, 2000. © TechRepublic, Inc. *www.techrepublic.com.* Reprinted by permission. All rights reserved.

chapter TWO

A Methodology
for Internet Consulting

SIMILAR MODELS IN PLACE

I find it ironic that, as often as the new Internet-focused consulting organizations insist that the Internet changes everything and that the old-line consulting giants like EDS and Andersen "just don't get it," the methodologies of the new economy consulting firms look surprisingly similar to the standard IT lifecycle. Many of the new firms, such as Scient, Razorfish, and Luminant, publish overviews of their methodologies on their websites, and a quick review of those illustrates my point. From Razorfish's "Clarify, Architect, Design, Implement, Enhance" methodology[1] to Scient's "Conceive, Architect, Engineer, Enhance" process,[2] and through Luminant's "Strategy, Development, Operations" approach,[3] the tried-and-true structured development techniques still hold sway even after the revolution.

A peek under the hood of these methodologies does show some significant differences, however. Because each of these firms follows the "agency" model of Internet consulting, in which the consultants take on strategic, marketing, and technical duties, their methodologies address branding and business process issues more thoroughly than any standard IT lifecycle would. As Luminant states in their methodology document *Maximizing Your E-Business Potential*,[4] "Don't mistake an eBusiness initiative as just another technology project." This Luminant white paper then goes on to instruct clients to create an eBusiness plan that addresses the following areas:

- Strategic Business Models
- Marketing

- Processes

- Information

- Technology

Although many IT consulting projects will have elements of information, technology, and process embedded in them, rarely are pure IT consultants called on to advise on business strategy and marketing. Yet, this sort of strategic advising is core to the Internet consulting practice. So how should Internet consultants construct a personal methodology for engaging with clients on Internet projects? Which elements of the standard "waterfall" IT lifecycles still have value, and which elements need to be revisited? How can consultants balance the need for quick results and for more strategic and less technology-centric advice with the need to apply a structured technique that leads us and our clients through the engagement and that can guarantee results?

After extensive conversations with practice leaders at many of these firms, I've found that each takes the best from the established methodologies and applies some new twists. The changes in technique are attributable to the main differences between standard IT consulting and new economy consulting:

- New economy consulting is multi-disciplinary. Not merely focused on designing and building IT systems, the new consultants must deliver business strategy, creative design, customer relationship strategies, marketing and branding, as well as technology.

- Speed is a key project driver. Rapid development techniques, which have been gaining in popularity and acceptance over the past decade, are de rigueur in the Internet world, and the ability to deliver quick but robust results is a hallmark of a successful Internet consulting practice.

- Prototyping and iterative design are also central elements of Internet development. One of the keynote pieces of advice to Internet entrepreneurs is "Ready, Fire, Aim!" In a famous quote, Marc Andreesen, founder of Netscape, remarked, "Keep building systems. If they buy it, it's a product. If they don't, it's market research."[5] As the Y2K dilemma demonstrated, many IT-centric projects result in systems that are extremely persistent and that become ingrained in corporate processes and subsequently remain in place for decades. Internet strategies and systems, at least at this stage of the development cycle, change and improve continually, and methodologies must reflect that fact.

- Finally, change management is a central element of Internet consulting. I don't mean the kind of change management that project managers typically handle with change control forms, but am referring to the psychological and cultural issues involved with wrenching organizational change of the type that migration to Internet business models causes, especially for established enterprises. Internet consultants need to have skills that will allow them to guide clients through major organizational change. These skills include organizational communication, consensus building, training, and team facilitation techniques.

The eConsulting Framework that I'll present here is meant as a guideline, not a rulebook. Many of the Internet practice leaders I've interviewed agree on one thing: The old "waterfall" methodologies are too constricting and bureaucratic for the Internet economy. As Skip McDonald of Luminant Worldwide told me, "If you look at a typical waterfall methodology project, you've got a box that contains the requirements definition, a box that contains the detailed scope, another box that contains the implementation, and then the consultants come in and build the thing, the client turns the handle, and you're done. Luminant's methodology instills the idea that it's not a project and then you're done, you walk out and leave. It's a series of releases that you develop over time to meet that overall business goal, because that business goal hasn't been met by the very first release of the very first website."[6]

The phases of the eConsulting Framework are illustrated in Figure 2.1. They appear as a straight path from beginning to end, but, as we've discussed, Internet consulting is an iterative, prototype-driven process. There are many points within the framework where the specifics of the engagement will cause a consultant to go back to a previous phase to revise, optimize, or simply throw out a design element based on test results or client reaction. Rather than attempting to depict a convoluted process with arrows pointing in all directions, I've taken the road of clarity, with the hope that, as we review each stage, I can clearly articulate the circumstances in which we may want to go back and revisit earlier decisions. The phases of the eConsulting Framework are described on the following page.

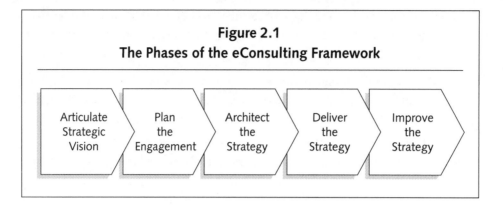

Figure 2.1
The Phases of the eConsulting Framework

Articulate Strategic Vision → Plan the Engagement → Architect the Strategy → Deliver the Strategy → Improve the Strategy

ARTICULATE A STRATEGIC VISION

Working with your client to articulate an Internet strategy is the key success factor for any Internet consulting engagement. Whether the client is a Fortune 500 company hoping to use Internet technology to optimize its communication with vendors or a startup hoping to knock off that Fortune 500 company with an innovative business model, a complete assessment of the client's current status and vision for the end result is the starting point. The issues that need to be addressed in this phase include the following:

- *Overall Business Strategy:* What is the core business? Is it a product business, a service business, an information business? Is it targeting consumers or other businesses? What are the organization's vision and mission?

- *Problem or Opportunity:* What problem is it solving for customers, or what opportunity is it exploiting?

- *Value Proposition:* What is the compelling reason for users or customers to buy or select our product or service?

- *Competitive Advantage:* Who else is in this marketplace? How is this offering similar? How is it different? What is its sustainable competitive advantage?

- *Enabling Technology:* What's the technology required to realize this vision? Is it existing, or does new technology need to be developed?

- *Customer Relationship Strategy:* How will this initiative attract customers? What's the marketing and promotional strategy? How will customers be supported? How will their satisfaction be measured? How will it develop long-term, personalized relationships with them?

- *Revenue Streams:* Where does the revenue to support this initiative come from? If this is an eBusiness, do the numbers add up? Have incremental revenue streams, such as advertising, licensing, or data mining, been considered?

- *Management and Organization:* How will this enterprise be managed? Is this a spin-off of an existing company, an internal effort, a "skunkworks" project, a startup? What management roles and skills are required to make this a success?

The deliverable from this phase of the engagement is, at minimum, an executive summary that articulates all the elements we've just described. For clients who are expecting to take their concept to outside investors, whether venture capitalists, banks, or "friends and family," they will need to also create a business plan and a presentation. Entrepreneurs who aren't willing to take the time up front to develop a compelling mission statement and to think through these fundamentals of business strategy are certainly not prepared to wrestle their concept through the hurdles of funding, building, and operating a growing concern. Those who understand the importance of agreeing on these basic strategies are much more likely to have the wisdom and persistence to create a real business.

PLAN THE ENGAGEMENT

Many of the planning disciplines will be familiar to any IT consultant who has participated in a structured IT project before. As with any consulting project, clear definition of the scope and boundaries of the engagement, and of the client's expectations, can make or break the effort.

Define the Scope

When defining the scope of your engagement, it's important to focus not only on the scope of services you'll be delivering, but also on the extent to which you'll be involving separate departments of the organization, partners and suppliers, and managers and teams. Internet initiatives are driven very differently in different organizations and cultures, and the implications for the project are formidable. Is this project being led by the board of directors, from an executive level, or by marketing or IT? Also define the scope of your deliverables in each of the planning areas we defined above: strategic business models, marketing, processes, information, and technology.

We'll explore each of these components of a comprehensive Internet strategy in detail in subsequent chapters. Depending on the needs and expectations of the client, your particular areas of expertise and practice, and the requirements of the specific engagement, you may be asked to participate, or not, in any of these areas. We'll talk later about how to handle issues such as client neglect of required planning decisions, but at this stage it's critical that your scope of action be clearly defined to protect both you and your client from mistaken assumptions.

Define the Deliverables

No scoping process is complete without a clear definition of the concrete deliverables that the project will produce. One of the primary causes of customer dissatisfaction and of rework or unbillable time by consultants is unclear expectations of the tangible outcome of the engagement. Again, protect yourself and your client relationships by taking the time to think through and document the deliverables.

Define the Roles and Responsibilities

Internet consulting projects, due to their interdisciplinary nature, are inherently collaborative team efforts. Strategic decisions will occur at one level of the organization, branding and imaging conversations will happen with a different team, and technical discussions with yet another group. Each will have different deliverables, schedules, milestones, and objectives. It's critical to negotiate and document all expectations regarding the participation, roles, responsibilities, and deliverables from each group of participants.

Create a Preliminary Project Plan

Just as the scope, deliverables, and roles will differ across a great range, so will the level of detail in the project plan at this point. In some projects, you will have spent a significant amount of time with the client in strategic and technical planning. In others, you will be implementing a technology that you understand well and have delivered before. In these cases, you may be able to prepare a plan to the detailed task level. Other projects will require you to participate in the invention of wholly new business models and technical architectures. In those cases, the detail of the effort required will not be visible at this stage. Whatever the case, you should prepare a project plan that at least identifies key participants, their required skills, and your planned project approach and gives an indication of the events that need to take place so you can prepare a more detailed plan. Always remember that the client is insecure and nervous, even in the best of circumstances, when embarking on an IT project with its inherent risk and intangibility. How much more uncomfortable is the client about to undertake a journey into the new economy, where fortunes and careers go up and down with the gyrations of the NASDAQ and even the most well-informed CEO knows only how little he knows. Anything you can do to reassure the client that he's in the hands of an experienced professional, such as demonstrating that you have a robust project methodology, will be a plus for the project.

Create a Communication Plan

All the reasons already cited—from the multi-disciplinary nature of Internet projects, through the probability of significant organizational change, to the nervousness of the client—should incline us toward a forceful communication program from the beginning. In this environment of uncertainty and fear, your clear and thorough communication of the vision, status, issues, and results will be the guiding light that assures the client that the effort is sailing in the right direction and that the result will be as expected. Your ability to help your client develop consensus around the strategy will be the dividing line between success or failure. In short, communication is critical to the success of your client's Internet strategy.

Create a Preliminary Estimate

One of the clearest guidelines I've ever heard about estimating is also one of the simplest: Estimate what you know. If you've developed detailed plans and strategies and your team has the expertise to estimate the time, effort, and cost of implementing those strategies, then estimate them. If you haven't, don't. Estimate to the level of detail you have uncovered, and present all other estimations of time, effort, or cost as "order of magnitude" estimates with clear disclaimers that help the client understand that you will estimate in finer detail when you've planned in finer detail.

ARCHITECT THE STRATEGY

The architecture phase of an Internet project is the core creative process, the stage where business strategists, technologists, marketing experts, visual artists, process engineers, and information modelers collaborate to draft a customized solution to the client's problem or opportunity. It's important to note that architecture, like implementation to follow, is an iterative process that will deliver options and prototypes to the client, which will then be reviewed, tested, and approved or revised. Even during the implementation process, we need to look at the implementation as a process of iteration in which layers of refinement, additional functionality, and lessons learned will be applied to the creation in the pursuit of the most competitive result. After the "visioning" and the project planning process, we now have our chance to create the detailed plans for each of the following areas.

Business Modeling. This is the stage in which the business model that was visualized earlier is now laid out in detail, the stage in which business plans, those strategic overviews that describe our concept for a business, become organizations, policies, and procedures that can actually be used to run a business. Management and reporting structures, corporate roles and responsibilities, ongoing strategic planning processes, performance assessment and compensation programs, and all of the other nuts-and-bolts governance issues move in this phase from concept to documented reality. This is where strategy meets tactics, and where broad five-year plans meet daily measurable results.

Marketing. In marketing, broad strategies also become tactical plans of action in this phase. Branding, image, and creative design now move from concept to prototype, and detailed decisions about media, message, customer relationship management, and tools and techniques all move to the drawing board and then to the client's desk for review and revision.

Processes. Of the lessons that have been learned in the pioneer days of Internet commerce, one lesson stands out above all: The critical importance of excellence in off-Net processes. Logistical, fulfillment, accounting, and customer support procedures, not merely the website, define the customer's experience with the company. eConsultants can add great value by helping clients stay focused on the business processes that will identify their company in the customer's mind. Shipping, billing, supply-chain management, returns and credits, and customer service may not be as sexy as flashy websites, but, in the quest for competitive advantage and customer brand awareness, they're a lot more lasting. Again, the architecture phase is where consultants will help clients utilize the Internet to streamline all the processes I just mentioned, so the client can present the most consistent, efficient, and responsive experience possible.

Information. The advantages of conducting business on the Internet all come down to information. The power to present enhanced product information and to create virtual "shelves" with unlimited supply options; the ability to capture customer information, both in the aggregate and in the particular, that can be used to personalize the relationship, enhance the experience, and refine the business strategy; the capability to offer products based on digitization, such as Web-based content, video, audio, or telephony services; all of these capabilities represent information that needs to be managed, analyzed, and acted on. The development of a robust information management policy, and the security and privacy concerns that go with it, are a central element of any Internet business model. In this phase, we work with our client to develop detailed blueprints for the management of the information that will flow to and from our website.

Technology. Of course, without the underlying technology, there is no Internet business. I've emphasized repeatedly the non-technical elements of an Internet strategy. I do this because I assume my audience is composed of IT professionals, whose natural inclination would be to focus on the technology. Now that we've reviewed the importance of the non-technical elements in depth, let's talk about the technical infrastructure. Just as we would for any technology project, we need to create a detailed design that addresses each of the layers of the Enterprise IT Model, as illustrated in Figure 2.2. As I described it in *The IT Consultant* (2000), this layered model allows us to look at the infrastructure, data, application, process, and business aspects of the IT infrastructure separately, to "divide and conquer" so as to ensure a complete and thorough solution to the technical problems presented. Whether we are developing enabling technology for a client-server accounting implementation or an eCommerce website, the discipline should be the same. We must examine and analyze the performance requirements, the security and stability needs, and the customer service level expectations and then evaluate and recommend the infrastructure and applications we'll need to deliver on those requirements. Even though the Enterprise IT Model depicted in Figure 2.2 was not designed for

Internet applications, it's clearly as applicable to that use as it would be for any other IT scenario. It reinforces the need to resist the urge to tunnel in on the technical aspects we're most comfortable with and to look at the project in the context of the business strategy in which it's placed.

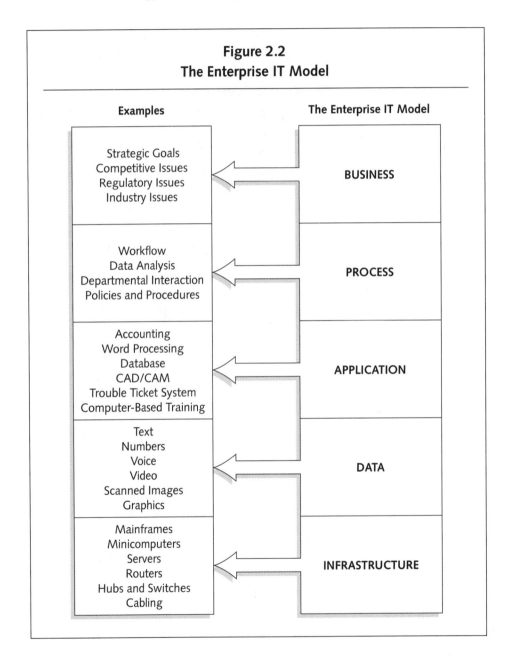

Figure 2.2
The Enterprise IT Model

Examples	The Enterprise IT Model
Strategic Goals Competitive Issues Regulatory Issues Industry Issues	**BUSINESS**
Workflow Data Analysis Departmental Interaction Policies and Procedures	**PROCESS**
Accounting Word Processing Database CAD/CAM Trouble Ticket System Computer-Based Training	**APPLICATION**
Text Numbers Voice Video Scanned Images Graphics	**DATA**
Mainframes Minicomputers Servers Routers Hubs and Switches Cabling	**INFRASTRUCTURE**

One final comment on architecture: The architecture process is a process of presenting options to the client and then helping the client decide which options fit their culture, objectives, budget, schedule, and strategies. After investing all the creativity and teamwork in creating a set of blueprints, it's human nature to become emotionally attached to those designs. Consultants must remember that they are counselors and advisors, and that their greatest successes come when they guide the client to the right choice, rather than making that choice themselves. I emphasize this because it's my personal approach to avoid making recommendations, but to instead present a series of options from which the client can construct a solution. This does a couple of things: It puts the client in the position of having made the decision herself, and so she can't come looking for a "blame agent" when the inevitable problems pop up. More importantly, it results in the best solution, because it requires the client's participation in the final decision process and doesn't allow delegation of the key strategic judgments.

DELIVER THE STRATEGY

After all the planning and decision making, this is the phase in which we use our project management and development skills to actually deliver on the blueprints we've spent so much time creating. This book is not intended to teach project management or system delivery skills; there are plenty of great mentors and books available that can guide those readers who need direction in those disciplines, and I refer to many of them in the Bibliography. I merely want to emphasize again the iterative nature of this phase of the engagement and remind Internet consultants that this effort is never finished. As anyone who regularly surfs the Web or shops at sites like Amazon.com or eBay will attest, even the biggest names on the Net revamp, revise, and experiment continually to find the best mix of usability, clarity, and customer experience.

Remember to deliver complete results, by which I mean the training, documentation, maintenance and support plans, and security that your client will need to keep his site and business operational.

I also want to reiterate one more point: The implementation phase is also the phase in which the reality of organizational change hits home for the users, managers, partners, and customers of your client, so it is critical to include communication and training as part of your implementation strategy. Consultants who build communication plans into their methodology from the beginning and who consistently help clients and stakeholders understand the process, the expected results, the benefits, and the steps along the way will consistently deliver the best outcomes and the most customer satisfaction. Empathy with the client, and assistance in integrating the rapid and far-reaching change that Internet initiatives generate, is a quality of the most trusted and effective advisors.

IMPROVE THE STRATEGY

The final phase is the ongoing activity of continuous improvement. I don't mean to imply that projects in the Internet arena go on and on: Like any project, defining an end point and getting client acceptance is crucial. Where Internet consulting differs from many IT projects, however, is that consultants are often asked to help define an ongoing strategic planning process, to help define measurements that can be used to refine and optimize the site, and to participate in periodic review sessions to help the client integrate new ideas and lessons learned. As we learned from the comments of Skip McDonald, the first release of a website or an eCommerce strategy often doesn't deliver the complete business benefits expected. Help your client understand this, and help her feel secure that you'll be there as her Internet strategy unfolds to help her build a business that will be successful over the long term.

I've included an interview here with Jim Highsmith, president of Information Architects, Inc., and director of The Cutter Consortium's eProject Management Advisory Service, that I conducted recently for TechRepublic. Jim, author of *Adaptive Software Development* (1999), is a leader and advocate of the light methodologies movement. This movement and some of the other innovative development disciplines associated with eBusiness development, such as extreme programming and lean development, are illustrative of the changes sweeping the IT community as a result of the Internet. Every eConsultant should be familiar with these new development disciplines in order to counsel our clients on the appropriate approach for every project.

An Interview with Jim Highsmith[7]

Rick: Jim, give us a flavor for the kinds of projects that would be appropriate for using the light methodologies.

Jim: I define eProjects as extreme projects, and these are the targets for these light methodologies. These are large projects. Web projects that used to be four- or six-week projects are now getting larger because they deal with legacy systems and have to be delivered rapidly. They are research-like and mission-critical. A lot of these projects are things that we haven't done before, so they're projects in which you're exploring as opposed to planning and doing. You're deciding on what you'd like to have and then exploring how to get there.

Rick: More of a creative approach than one of taking a tried implementation and doing it again?

Jim: That's right. These projects tend to be very innovative, because just coming up with the same old thing is not going to work. At the same time, they're still mission-critical. I have clients who work in the financial district in New York, and they can't be dropping transactions! We have to manage these projects in a turbulent business and technology environment, because the technology is changing and business models are changing. If you look at that as the project definition—large, rapid, research-like, mission-critical, turbulent environments—the risk is inherent to the project, as opposed to how you approach it.

Rick: Help me understand how these light methodologies would be applied to bring up the success rate of these complex, high-turbulence projects.

Jim: Let me start by saying that the light versus heavy debate has been in the wrong dimension. In the process or formality dimension, the discussion revolves around things like how much documentation you have; and I think that's only one axis of the debate. The other is the collaboration, the decision making, the adaptability, the skills. You just can't reduce documentation without increasing collaboration practices or skill-building practices. There've been some studies recently about the difference between documentation and understanding—just because I've documented something doesn't mean I understand it!

Rick: As evidenced by much of the documentation that's produced today!

Jim: That's right. Understanding comes from interaction between people, from discussions and asking questions, so that, whether it's heavy or light methodologies, if you don't have the collaboration neither process is going to produce effective documentation. There is a balancing act. We're not likely to do away with documentation, but we need to understand that documentation has a limit in terms of the understanding it can convey. You need to have practices like collaboration or peer programming—putting programmers together to develop something in a collaborative practice—and with that shared understanding you may not need so much documentation. You want to have a life cycle in which there's an exploratory mindset. In my life cycle I've substituted the word "speculate" for "plan." What I'm trying to convey is that we don't necessarily do less planning, but we don't necessarily expect the plan to work out as we originally envisioned. We expect the plan to change over time. We expect the project to change and evolve over time as we uncover new things.

Rick: As we go through discovery and uncover things that we could not have seen up-front . . .

Jim: That's an important point—things that we could not have seen up-front. It's not that we did a poor job on requirements; it's just that things happen that we couldn't foresee, a change in the marketplace or in the business model. So we need to have this evolutionary mindset. The other thing is that these light methodologies are focused on the business features, as opposed to the task approach in which we say, "OK, I need to do the requirements, then the definition, then programming." These light methodologies are made up of iterative cycles every three to six weeks, at the end of which we demonstrate to the client that we were actually able to accomplish something.

Rick: In the new consulting firms, folks are very focused on collaboration and team effort, everything from the setup of the office to the cultural atmosphere enhances that image, and the old image of the programmer as lone samurai is being replaced by the tightly integrated development team, where everyone has a chance to contribute and be creative.

Jim: That brings up two things. All the light methodologies are very dedicated to advocating the people aspect, that it's people and their skills that are going to dominate, and that process is the support. It used to be thought that if we had a great process we could get the job done, and now we're focused on the idea that the people and their skills are going to make us successful. They need a little bit of support, as we provide with the light methods, but the people and their skills are going to carry the day. We sometimes perceive computer folks as geeks who want to go off in the corner, but in reality we geeks want to be with other geeks and have a community, and I think the light methodologies really speak to that sense of community and the various ways that people want to work together. I would include the whole open source movement as an example of this. It's an example of the kind of community that technical people want to build.

Rick: These methodologies have been criticized because they de-emphasize the need for documentation. How do you respond to that?

Jim: I've been in situations recently where I had project managers and methodology people and developers in a room talking about the need for some very specific kinds of documentation, and I would turn to the programmers and say, "These people have just said that you need these kinds of documentation so you can do maintenance more easily. How much of this documentation do you actually use?" The programmers, to a person, said either never or virtually never. All the managers looked at them incredulously and said, "You don't ever look at the documentation?" and the programmers said, "No, we look at the code!"

Rick: Do you see the migration to these light methodologies as a competitive issue, in the sense that a lot of consulting organizations use the robustness and detail orientation of their methodologies as selling tools, and customers have been trained to look for that highly structured methodology when they're selecting consultants?

Jim: The speedup in competition is working its way back from the dot.coms to the IT organizations, and it hasn't made it all the way back to all of the IT organizations yet. I'm working with three large systems integration firms, one from the U.S., one from India, and one from Japan, who have all come to me and said, "From two years ago to this year our business has changed from 80 percent legacy to 80 percent eBusiness, and we understand that our CMM* approach isn't going to work on these type of applications."

Note: CMM Level 4 is the widely accepted Software Capabilities Maturity Model, a framework for software engineering developed by the Software Engineering Institute at Carnegie Mellon University, www.sei.cmu.edu/.

It [CMM] can be a handicap, so my IT services clients are saying, "For our legacy stuff, we'll continue to use our CMM methodologies; however, we want to put in place these agile light methodologies for stuff we take on in the future." They see that as a competitive advantage move for the future. There are three levels to the migration to light methods: How do we manage projects differently? How do we measure them differently, because the management and the measurement are very different? and How do we deliver differently? There's another element: How do we sell this to our clients?

Rick: The more sophisticated the client is in terms of understanding CMM and structured methodologies, the more difficult it may become to sell these new approaches to them.

Jim: In one of my engagements there were some salespeople, and the sales guy was actually the most enthusiastic. He said, "We're running up against clients who are sophisticated enough to understand that the old ways aren't working, and they want a new model, and we want a new model to sell to those clients." I think part of the selling issue is understanding what kind of project we have at hand. These light methods are best used for higher risk projects, and therefore you tend to need more skilled people—in particular more skilled project managers. You don't want to run one of these light methodology projects with beginning project managers. If you've got a critical project, you don't want to run it with inexperienced project managers no matter how you run it!

Rick: This is where the concept of "heavy skills, light process" comes into play, because the experienced project manger can almost instinctively assess the project and the client and make decisions about which pieces of the methodology are pertinent to this project and which are not.

Jim: Right, and a lot of this comes from the scientific realm. Things like creativity and innovation emerge from the interaction, from putting a bunch of creative people together. These things occur at what scientists call "the edge of chaos." You've got to maintain that critical edge; and if you have too much process, it weighs that down and you lose the creativity.

Rick: So as the pendulum swings from overbearing structure to the edge of chaos is there a risk that this light methodology movement could be misunderstood and end up swinging the pendulum too far toward chaos?

Jim: The risk is that these methodologies appear to be ad hoc, so some people may use them as an excuse to go back to ad hoc methods. Some people will try to use them without the requisite skills, or they'll look at it as a panacea. Some may just start cranking the stuff out, lightening up on the documentation or lightening up on the process without supplementing that with more skill training or mentoring. They'll take away the formality, but they won't add back the collaborative piece. Actually, I think these light methods are the swing to the middle. I think that the rapid application development [RAD] stuff was the swing the other way. The RAD stuff of the early 1990s was a complete divergence from the heavy information engineering theories of the early 1980s. In the 1990s we got away from the mainframe into client-server, and I think that was really the move to ad hoc. The light methods combine the essence of the software engineering disciplines with the iteration and the speed of rapid development; because of that we've created a robust methodology that really scales up, because the RAD stuff didn't scale.

Rick: So for our readers who are used to working within the more structured methodologies, how does this change the approach on a day-to-day level? What stays? What goes away?

Jim: If I know that something has to be delivered four weeks from today, and I know the features that need to go into that, I'm not as likely to have a detailed task list that says, "Here are all the things you need to do." I'm more likely to say to my development team, "Here's the objective; you go to it." It's more oriented to discipline on the back end and exploration on the front end. The requirements definition might be minimal, but the programming will be more disciplined about the programming standards, the testing, and the configuration control. It's definitely much lighter in terms of documentation. The practices are more collaborative. Some people already use some of these like joint application development sessions, but we also specify things like customer focus groups on the back end so that we actually demonstrate what we've done in each development cycle.

Rick: So the pervasive theme in all of this is really customer focus?

Jim: It's customer focus, customer value. If what you're attempting is an exploration into how a business is automated, it's virtually impossible to do that without customer involvement. So there's a higher emphasis on customer involvement throughout the entire process.

Rick: So with your adaptive development, and with some of the other light methods like lean development, extreme programming, and crystal methods, what are the common themes and what are the differences?

Jim: With all of these methods, there are some common principles and values they all revolve around. They're exploratory as opposed to predictive, and they're oriented toward people and supporting their unique skills. Extreme programming and lean development are very similar. They're focused on small teams of programmers, and they've got a short list of the minimum things you need to do to guarantee that you deliver a project. What I've tried to do in adaptive development is show how you can scale these collaborative approaches so that they're useful for larger projects. People in the XP [extreme programming] community say that XP is for small teams, but if you need to use large teams or distributed teams then you should add some of the practices from adaptive development. The value of all of these methods is simplicity. What's the simplest thing you can do to get the job done? The XP folks have an acronym called YAGNI, which stands for "You Aren't Going to Need It." Someone will be talking in a discussion group, and someone may yell out "YAGNI." You take a hard look at everything you're doing in a project and ask yourself, "Do I really need to do this?" Another thing that I think is a common thread between these light methods is that they focus on how we incorporate change. A lot of the traditional methodologies look at rework as the result of a broken process. What the light methodologies are saying is that change comes from the environment. So rework is not a result of a broken process, but the result of a change in the environment; and we have to get better about responding to change. A lot of the traditional practices are change resistant. The light methodologies say, "As long as the project stays within the boundaries, let's incorporate these changes."

Rick: In our rapidly changing business and technical environment, we're uncovering things that are going to significantly enhance our deliverables, so that's an advantage of these methods.

Jim: One of the metrics that I keep track of is the disposition of all the change requests, and I report back on that. Clients are not used to software development organizations being responsive to them, so when we say that we delivered 230 of the 280 changes you requested, it shows a responsiveness. Most customers are very happy about that.

Rick: So will these new approaches take over the world in the next few years?

Jim: I think they'll have a very significant impact because they go beyond software development and project management. They're about how organizations are managed. The collaborative mindset behind light methodologies reflects the kinds of organizations that people want to work in and the kinds of development teams that people want to work in. This is not a movement that's going away unless the Internet and eCommerce go away.

Rick: How do consultants and developers prepare mentally to make this migration?

Jim: Without innovation we have no eBusiness. These light methodologies really speak to the idea of innovation and creativity, and we have to have that. It's too hard to do these eBusiness things without innovative groups and organizations. These approaches create the kinds of communities that people want to work in. To me, it really boils down to innovation and community.

Now that we've laid out the outline of a methodology for delivering Internet business results, let's look at some basic business strategic concepts. We'll review some of the fundamental theories and beliefs that have driven business thinking over the last century, and then we'll look at how these theories have been transformed by the capabilities of Internet technology.

End Notes

1. *www.razorfish.com.*
2. *www.scient.com.*
3. *www.luminant.com.*
4. Montz, A. *Maximizing Your E-Business Potential.* Available on *www.luminant.com.*
5. Marc Andreesen, as quoted in Hartman, A. *Net Ready.* New York: McGraw-Hill, 2000, p. 160.
6. Interview with the author, published as "Conversation with a Knowledge Management Guru," July 21, 2000. © TechRepublic, Inc. *www.techrepublic.com.* Reprinted by permission. All rights reserved.
7. Interview with Jim Highsmith. © TechRepublic, Inc. *www.techrepublic.com.* Used by permission. All rights reserved.

Basics of Business Strategy

STRATEGIC THINKING

In an interview in *The Industry Standard*, Chris Lochhead, chief marketing officer for Internet consultancy Scient, described a brainstorming process that Scient engages in with clients: "One of us gets up in front of the executives, and we say, 'You're all fired. Now, you're all part of a startup, and we want you to come up with three ways to take away your former employer's market share.' And in five minutes, these guys come up with a zillion ways to kill their companies."[1]

This story is revealing in a number of ways. Brainstorming with clients on ways to kill their own company is an activity that few IT consultants would have engaged in a few years ago, yet sessions like the one Lochhead describes are common in Internet engagements. It's also critical to note that this type of activity is not at all focused on technology; it's a conversation about business strategy. These types of sessions are exercises in creative destruction; in helping clients look at their existing businesses and ask questions about their competitive advantage, strategic assets, core competencies, the value their company brings to its customers, the chain of suppliers, distributors, and partners they rely on to deliver that value; and then in helping clients imagine how those elements might change to take advantage of new opportunities. As Yobie Benjamin, chief of global strategy at Ernst & Young, states, "We force executives to rethink their core competencies and assets, and how to re-leverage them in this new eBusiness environment."[2]

By helping clients engage in this type of business deconstruction, consultants can guide clients toward new and creative business opportunities. In order to do this effectively, however, consultants must have a basic understanding of business strategy and the drivers of competitive advantage. For those consultants who work for the traditional management consulting firms, such as Ernst & Young or McKinsey & Company, strategic business planning is a central tool in their bag of tricks. Other consultants have taught themselves these lessons, or learned them through experience, by helping clients work through competitive issues during a lifetime of engagements. Many IT consultants, however, have been technically focused throughout their careers and have never had the opportunity to expand their repertoire from the technical to the strategic. This is not a value judgment, as many IT consultants have been driven by their aspirations, circumstances, and talents to concentrate on the technical aspects of consulting, and many have achieved great success doing that. For those who want to migrate to the Internet consulting field, however, a strictly technical focus turns into a handicap. Although it's true that many Internet consulting teams are multidisciplinary and include experts from the creative to the strategic to the technical, each consultant on a team needs to apply strategic thinking to his or her personal piece of the puzzle. For those consultants who are not part of a large organization or a team, a strategic foundation is even more critical for successfully guiding clients, as solo consultants don't have expert comrades they can turn to. Whatever their core competencies, all consultants increase their value to clients in direct proportion to their grasp of business strategic concepts.

In this section I'll present a brief foundation course in business strategy, drawing on the concepts and principles developed by pioneer thinkers in the field, such as Michael Porter, C.K. Prahalad, and Adrian Slywotzky. Because it's been my experience as a trainer of consultants that most can benefit from a review of the basic tenets of strategic thinking, I'll present this material with the assumption that the reader has a limited background in these concepts. By doing so I run the risk of alienating those readers who have had exposure to these theories before, so if this includes you, please look at this as a chance to refresh your basic understanding of these issues. This foundation is central to the more advanced principles we'll examine later, when we'll take the conventional wisdom of strategic planning and turn it on its head in order to engage in the creative destruction that makes Internet consulting so exciting and challenging.

SUCCESS BY STRATEGY

The classic case study of successful business strategy is that of General Electric under the stewardship of Jack Welch, called by *Fortune* magazine "The Greatest CEO in History."[3] From its founding by Thomas Edison in 1879, through its popularization of the light bulb, toaster, electric fan, refrigerator, clothes washer, steam iron, jet engine, and nuclear power plant, GE has been the most influential industrial products company in history. When Welch became CEO in 1981, he inherited a company worth $12 billion in market capitalization. Its major competitors, such as Westinghouse and United Technologies, were each worth about $3 billion.

By 1997, Westinghouse and United Technologies had grown to be worth about $17 billion each. Impressive results, until we note that, over the same period, GE had grown to a market capitalization of $260 billion! Based on some simple rules of business and a few well-placed and well-executed strategies, Welch had succeeded in out-growing his competitors by $243 billion. His success was based not on esoteric "ivory tower" econometric studies and complex scenarios designed by a team of MBAs, but rather on a simple set of ideals, no less strategic because of their simplicity and straightforwardness. His personal set of rules included such simple tenets as:

- Face reality as it is, not as it was or as you wish it were;

- Don't manage; lead;

- Change before you have to; and

- If you don't have a competitive advantage, don't compete.

His strategy for growth was also based on some clear-cut rules:

- Be number one or two in every global market you choose to compete in; and

- Fix, sell, or close any business that is not in that position.

Welch eliminated 125 businesses, including businesses that defined the GE name to millions of American households, such as TVs, radios, and small appliances. He restructured 350 separate businesses into thirteen operating units. He reduced head count from 420,000 to 280,000.[4] Until upstaged by the technology juggernauts of Microsoft and Cisco in the late 1990s, GE was the most highly valued company in the world, and it's still number three at this writing. When contrasted with its peer group of dominant American industrial giants, from General Motors to U.S. Steel, its performance is even more miraculous.

Each of these actions was based on the simple set of strategies Welch developed to help GE compete in the new global marketplace. When I call these strategies simple, I'm referring to their ability to be clearly and plainly stated and communicated, not to ease of execution. Each of Welch's simple tenets was executed ruthlessly and unsentimentally, with total focus on the long-term plans and objectives for the business. Although they meant wrenching changes for many employees, customers, shareholders, and partners of GE, they serve to illustrate the fact that simple vision- and values-based strategies can have extraordinary results.

In the world of high-tech business, too, simple strategies can rocket one competitor ahead of the pack. In 1993, Bay Networks, the entity formed from the merger of Wellfleet and Synoptics, the pioneers, respectively, of routing and networking, had a market capitalization of $2 billion. Bay's chief competitor, Cisco, wasn't far ahead, with a value of around $4 billion. The highly competitive and fragmented networking market also supported dozens of smaller players, such as 3Com, Newbridge, Cabletron, Madge, Chipcom, and others.

By 1998, however, the market had changed significantly. Bay had been absorbed by Nortel and ceased to exist as an independent player. 3Com, Cabletron, and Madge were struggling to retain their market share and customer base. Astride the networking world stood Cisco Systems, with a market capitalization of $76 billion (grown to $531 billion by May 2000!) and with wide recognition as the de facto standard for network hardware and routing software. What was the strategic break-through that facilitated Cisco's rise to dominance? According to a recent *Fortune* magazine article on Cisco CEO John Chambers, "Chambers has put together an impressive list of how-to's, from open systems to seamless acquisitions, blanket option packages, closeness to the customer, and superior Web management." Or, as Chambers himself has said, "When it comes to customers, we will do whatever it takes to win them. 'No' to us just means we have to come back. I have no love of technology for technology's sake. . . . Only solutions for customers."[5] It's clear from Chambers' comments that customer focus is one of Cisco's core strategies.

Another is acquisition, or "buy instead of build." The routing technology that started the company in its march to dominance was innovative, but only for a moment. In 1993, companies such as Kalpana and Crescendo were offering a competing technology, switching, that threatened to upstage the router at the core of corporate networks. Switches were cheaper and easier to configure and manage than Cisco's complex routers. So, much to the derision of the computer and business press at the time, Cisco spent the unbelievable sum of $293 million to simply buy Kalpana and Crescendo and thus to build switching into its product set. Since then, Cisco has bought more than sixty companies and spent over $40 billion on acquisitions. It has bought its way into the market for high-end switches that the giant telephone companies and Internet service providers need to run their networks and into the optical networking market. It has bought software companies and service companies. "End to end" is one of Chambers' most famous phrases.

The drive to dominate shown by companies such as General Electric and Cisco are not accidents, and they are not based merely on the personalities of their mythical CEOs. Neither are the less-stellar results of General Motors and U.S. Steel. Some of these companies thought long and hard about their futures, the global marketplace they'd be competing in, and the actions they needed to take to rule that marketplace. Then they executed those strategies despite the pain and dislocation they caused. Others became complacent or bureaucratic or were immobilized by labor politics, technological change, or ineffective management. The point is simply this: Strategic thinking is a critical factor in the success of businesses.

Strategy began as a military pursuit, but its application to business is natural and logical. The military analogy helps us understand the difference between strategy and tactics. Strategies are focused on the long-term battle plans designed to give armies a superior position before the battle begins. They are more likely to be focused on selecting the battles, objectives, and areas of attack than on the formation of troops on the battlefield. Once the battle begins and the "fog of war" descends over the field, tactics come into play. A marketing campaign is strategic, and the decision to air a certain commercial on a certain radio station is tactical. The design of a new automobile line is strategic, and the decision to offer a certain dealer a special deal on that model is tactical. Strategy is long-term, global, and resource-intensive, while tactics are short-term, local, and require fewer commitments.

Like military strategy, business strategy is focused on the competitive battle. As Michael Porter, considered by many the pioneer of modern strategic thinking, states, "The essence of strategy is coping with competition."[6] Because all competitors in a particular marketplace are surveying each other's actions and creating their own strategic thrusts and counter-thrusts, strategy becomes a complex and interdependent exercise. Robert Grant, in his *Contemporary Strategy Analysis*,[7] breaks strategy into three easily understood components:

1. Long-term, simple objectives;
2. Profound understanding of customers and competitors; and
3. Objective appraisal and effective use of resources.

Although there are other, more complex analyses of the elements of strategic planning, for our discussion Grant's components are most helpful. When we think about GE's Jack Welch or Cisco's John Chambers and the strategies they used to become dominant competitors, Grant's three components can guide us to a deeper analysis and can serve to help us, as consultants, guide our clients to success. After all, that's the point of this whole discussion!

Jack Welch's principles, such as "Don't manage; lead" or "Be number one or two in every market you choose" are simple, straightforward, easily communicated objectives. They contain elements of both hard-nosed pragmatism and value-based inspiration. By giving his management team the incentive to be leaders instead of foremen, Welch created an environment in which values and vision could cascade through the organization and create a culture of achievement. The very language used in communicating strategies is a key indicator of their effectiveness. The mantra of "Be Number One!" is a lot more inspiring than "Maximize Shareholder Value." In the same way, John Chambers' exhortation to the Cisco troops to "Do whatever it takes to win" is internalized by the Cisco sales teams more than any appeal to "Achieve 12 percent gross margin before taxes" would ever be.

The absolute need to understand customers and competition can best be illustrated by the fate of those who ignored this imperative. The industrial giants of the 1950s that failed to understand or respect the competitive changes created by the rise of Japan, the globalization of commerce, and the information revolution paid the price in lost market share and opportunity. U.S. Steel and General Motors are the poster boys of the asleep-at-the-wheel complacency and arrogance that were caught napping by the changes of the 1970s and 1980s; and they paid for it in eroded market share and near-death experiences. The new power of the customer, the consumer activism movement, and the dramatic increase in customer choice created by global competition also caught many industries, such as the American consumer electronics industry, by surprise. Try to buy an American-made radio or television and the effects become obvious. Finally, many of the pioneers of information technology, who should have known better, were overwhelmed by the speed and velocity of change in their business, as Wang Laboratories, Digital Equipment, and Data General illustrate. Most strategic thinking today is focused on developing and executing strategies that gauge customer requirements and beat the competition in meeting those needs.

The objective appraisal and effective use of resources requires sober analysis of your own strengths and weaknesses, a discipline not every businessperson can execute. Welch's rule to "Face reality as it is, not as it was or you wish it were" is easier said than done, but it's central to the competitive struggle. The essence of this component of strategy is to "know thyself." Whatever your politics, the guerrilla struggles of North Vietnam, in its battle against the French and the United States, demonstrate that bigger is not necessarily better, and that, by understanding and utilizing your resources effectively, you can craft a winning strategy whatever the size and apparent strength of your opponent. When Dell went up against the powers that be in the PC marketplace, such as Compaq and IBM, it used those companies' channel affiliations against them by selling directly to customers at a time when Compaq and IBM had entrenched relationships with resellers that were difficult to break. Dell took an apparent weakness, its lack of reseller relationships, and turned that into a strength by creating a new set of rules. As startups everywhere know, insurgency has its advantages and incumbency its weaknesses. Those strengths and weaknesses only translate into competitive advantage when you can honestly assess your position and strategically deploy your forces. When we dig deeper into some winning Internet business models, we'll explore these strengths and weaknesses in depth.

PROBLEMS WITH STRATEGIC PLANNING

Despite the clear successes we just explored, strategic planning is a discipline in serious disrepute. Henry Mintzberg, well-respected author of the foundation text in strategic planning, *The Strategy Process,*[8] and former chairman of the Strategic Management Society, contends in his book, *The Rise and Fall of Strategic Planning,*[9] that strategic planning can actually be a detriment to a company's competitiveness, that the process can straitjacket an organization by stifling innovation. He builds a strong argument for a reassessment of the entire strategic planning process based on his assertion that forecasts become obsolete too quickly to be of much value, that long-term plans can often lock companies into vulnerable positions when markets shift, and that strategic planning departments often become political fiefdoms or debating societies rather than sources of business advantage.

The strategic planning process, as it has been implemented since its introduction in the 1950s, has been seen by some as the only viable method to create competitive advantage for the enterprise and by others as an ivory-tower exercise in number manipulation and academic debate. Some of the common complaints about strategic planning follow:

- It is an exercise in analysis that does little to drive measurable results;

- It has been too susceptible to the latest management fad, so that it has become an incomprehensible hodgepodge of theories;

- It is an elitist exercise that fails to involve or gain commitment from those who must implement strategies on a day-to-day basis;

- It is inward-focused, concentrating on the needs of the enterprise rather than the needs of the customer; and

- It creates complex plans and forecasts but neglects to create a vision or mission that people can believe in.

Some recent commentary about strategic planning illustrates these problems. Mintzberg asserts that "Strategic planning often spoils strategic thinking, causing managers to confuse real vision with the manipulation of numbers."[10] John Byrne, in a *Business Week* article addressing the controversies around strategic planning, notes that "In its heyday, strategy-spinning was the ultimate left-brain exercise for the corporate elite. Thousands of B-school-trained thinkers sat high in the climate-controlled aeries of bloated business empires, crunching numbers and spinning scenarios. . . . You could plot a strategy that would safely steer your company to triumph if only you *thought* hard enough."[11] In the words of William Finnie, a former director of strategic studies for Anheuser-Busch, strategic planning "Has become more concerned with the quality of the rain dance than with producing rain."[12]

With all this negative commentary about strategic planning, why bother to review it or utilize it as a consulting tool at all? The most obvious answer is that just because strategic planning *can* be subject to the ills enumerated above doesn't mean it *must* be. New planning techniques have been developed to specifically counter these problems, such as:

- Democratized planning, in which teams of associates from all levels of the organization are invited to participate in the process;

- Customer-focused planning, which involves customers in the planning function and seeks above all to answer the question, "What does the customer need and want?";

- Value planning, in which managers focus more on developing a core set of values and a vision for the company in the belief that with a consistent vision in place everyone will use his or her best judgment and efforts toward a common goal; and

- Strategy implementation models, in which strategies are designed with built-in communication, consensus building, and measurement methods to ensure that they actually achieve results.

In the discussion to come, we'll examine some successes of strategic thinking, some of the fundamental ideas and concepts, and these new twists on strategy as well. Many of the new strategic concepts, especially democratized and customer-focused planning, are central to the work that the successful Internet consultancies and independent advisors are doing with their clients. Before we examine these innovations on the traditional strategic planning model, though, let's dig down a bit into some of the basic concepts of business strategy.

STRATEGIC FUNDAMENTALS

Value Propositions

"Value proposition" is a complex term for a simple concept: What value is the company selling? What problem are you solving for your customers? How are you enhancing your customers' lives and happiness (if you're a business-to-consumer enterprise) or your customers' competitiveness (if you're a business-to-business enterprise)? To illustrate this concept more clearly, let's look at a typical business-school diagram, known as the competitive triangle, in Figure 3.1.

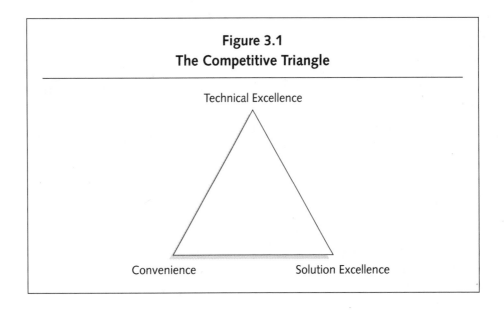

Figure 3.1
The Competitive Triangle

Technical Excellence

Convenience   Solution Excellence

The three points of the competitive triangle indicate three strategies for providing value to customers, and thus achieving competitive advantage. Before we examine each of these elements, however, it's important to make a couple of points. First, although many enterprises will focus on one or the other of these competitive strengths, that doesn't mean that the others can be ignored. No matter how convenient it is to do business with you, if your product is technically inferior or difficult to integrate into a complete solution, any competitive advantage your convenience brings will be short-lived. Likewise the other elements. While many strategic experts agree that focusing on one competitive element and being the best in your market space at that element is a winning strategy, competence in the other elements is also required. Also, notice that price is not one of the competitive elements. Price is often the most apparent attribute of a product or service, but in the competitive markets of the 21st Century, consumers and corporate customers alike are sophisticated enough to understand total-cost-of-ownership issues and will analyze their needs for state-of-the-art technology, an integrated solution, and convenience, match those requirements against available prices, and come to a balanced decision—rather than just checking the price. Price may be one element of the decision, but it is rarely sufficient for creating a strategic advantage.

Technical Excellence

It would seem obvious that the technical superiority of your product would be an overriding competitive advantage, yet experience shows us that many of the market leaders in that most technical of pursuits, information technology, are not necessarily the technical leaders. Dell, Microsoft, and Cisco have products that are technically competent, but are not so overwhelmingly superior that they are the choice of buyers who seek state-of-the-art technology. Conversely, companies such as Digital Equipment, with its Alpha servers, Lotus, with Notes®, and Bay Networks, considered an innovator in network routing, all discovered that technical superiority was not an automatic advantage.

That being said, many companies, especially in the manufacturing sector, rely on technical superiority as their key differentiator. Many customers actively seek the best technology—whether it's in television, audio, automobiles, or computer equipment—and are willing to forego convenience and low price in order to find it. Whether it's the automotive technology of Saab or BMW, the consumer electronics of Sony, or the audio products of Bang and Olufson, a certain segment of the customer base will go out of its way to procure the most technologically advanced and innovative products.

Those enterprises that decide to focus on technological superiority as a competitive strategy have a tough row to hoe. They must build a culture that is capable of consistent innovation and creativity, that can manage quality better than their competitors, and that can provide the premium level of service, support, and information that their elite customer base demands. Not many companies have been able to sustain the level of research and development, creativity, and commitment to quality that this competitive choice requires.

Solution Excellence

The progression from product to solution has overtaken many industries. This migration up the value chain was one of Jack Welch's core strategies as he built sales and support teams that were focused on helping their customers get the best use—and the most value—from the GE products they purchased. Let's look at another example of value chain migration in the PC industry.

For PC resellers in the 1980s, the ability to accurately stock and ship PCs, printers, and peripherals at a reasonable price was enough to sustain a business for many so-called value-added resellers (VARs). By the 1990s, however, many customers were wondering where the added value was and were demanding more of a concentration on service and less on product. Product margins were slipping from over 25 percent in the early days of the PC revolution to between 2 percent and 5 percent for most VARs. Competitors with more efficient business models, such as Dell and Gateway, were hijacking the VARs' most profitable customers and squeezing the margins out of the hardware business. Like many industries before and since, the PC resellers discovered that the way to stay in business and retain their competitive advantage was to migrate from selling "boxes" to selling solutions.

This migration in customer value has become so prevalent that the word "solutions" has become an overworked marketing cliché. When razors become "shaving solutions" and trash haulers become "waste management solutions," it's pretty clear that the wave of a marketing trend is cresting. Marketing hype aside, however, those companies, from Nordstrom to Federal Express to Cisco to General Electric, who have made the commitment to providing complete solutions for their customers have attained positions of business advantage that their competitors envy. They've discovered, through customer interaction, focus groups, market research, and customer intimacy, how their customers actually use their products and how they struggle to get the best value from them. And they've devised strategies for enhancing usability and solving problems.

Just as competitiveness based on technical excellence depends on a total commitment to creativity and research, solution-based advantage requires customer focus and excellence in support services such as training and technical support. And, like technical excellence, it ain't easy! The ability to build a large-scale enterprise in which every individual who has contact with the customer is uniformly friendly, courteous, informed, helpful, and responsible is an extraordinary achievement, as those who compete with Nordstrom will attest. The investment into a support organization that can afford to take the time to train and mentor each customer in the best uses of the product, to answer any and all questions they may have, and to gauge their satisfaction with the product throughout its lifecycle and fix any problems that arise can drain the enterprise if not managed closely.

Convenience

When we think of convenience, the first factor that typically comes to mind is location. It's a lot more convenient to go to the full-price shoe store on our block than to drive to the discount superstore twenty miles away. Consumers will weigh the extra cost against the inconvenience, and some proportion will decide to pay the price and avoid the hassle.

Convenience has other components, however. How easy is it to use the product? How easy is it to return if it's not what was expected? What's my comfort and security with this supplier versus its competitors? How easy is it to do business with the company? I personally do an informal calculation every time I decide to make a substantial purchase before I even decide where to look for an item. Is that new lens for my telescope going to be cheaper at the camera store or on the Internet? Which will have the better selection? Which will be easier to return if it's wrong or defective? How much time will it take to perform the transaction? Which supplier will give me advice so that I select the right product the first time?

Different companies rely on different parts of the convenience equation for their competitive advantage. Catalog vendors and Internet storefronts rely on the convenience of doing business, day or night, from the comfort of home. Successful ones like Amazon and J. Crew will also make it easy to return merchandise, since the consumer is relying on a picture and a description rather than on the chance to touch and evaluate the product personally. Department stores competed against the mom-and-pop local retail outlets by making customers feel secure—knowing that the giant resources and stability of the company would back up their purchases with service and support. In the same way, the big financial service companies, such as Schwab and Fidelity, transformed personal investing from an intimidating exercise for the elite into an understandable and comfortable activity for the many. Savvy consumers and businesses, as I stated before, will weigh all the factors involved in the use of their potential purchase and calculate a total cost, including travel time and expense, the risk involved in the possible need for service or to return the item, and ease of use (as well as price), and make a decision based on their personal priorities.

Before we leave the topic of basic competitive advantages, I want to make one crucial point. Competitive advantage doesn't happen because a team of planners decides to focus on one of the three points in the competitive triangle described above; it grows based on the ideals, talents, desires, and skills of the organization and the needs of the marketplace. Companies founded by a team of leading-edge silicon wafer designers who've invented a new way of fabricating microchips will have a different orientation than companies started by seasoned executives in the retail business. In the retail business, convenience may be the overriding requirement, while in the chip fabrication business technical excellence may be the key differentiator. These strategic decisions are not as clear or obvious as they may seem, however. Few would have predicted in 1980 that a company like Intel, focused on the design of complex and specialized microchips, would find competitive advantage from pasting a little "Intel Inside" sticker on the PCs that used its chips. Intel's need for technical excellence and solution excellence may have seemed obvious, but the convenience factor of a branded and trusted name in microchips would have seemed far-fetched. The experience and personality of a company's leaders are also critical strategic factors an organization decides to focus on. When Bruce Nordstrom of Nordstrom's department stores states, "We were raised kneeling in front of the customer"[13] and Jim Nordstrom tells employees, "I don't care if they roll a Goodyear tire into the store. If they say they paid $200, give them the $200"[14] they are reflecting deeply held personal values more than a calculated strategic choice.

I dwell on this at length because, as a consultant advising on strategic business matters, you will need to evaluate the personalities and values of your clients as much as the competitive landscape. Strategies must be devised that are in sync with the aspirations and talents of the human beings as well as with the direction of the marketplace. Conventional wisdom aside, many entrepreneurs are not in business simply to bring their company public and cash out, as evidenced by the many high-tech entrepreneurs who keep working long after they've amassed huge personal wealth. Many are actually in it to have an impact, to change the world, to achieve personal goals beyond money. Your ability to measure the needs and talents of the individual and to collaborate to create strategies that will advance that person's goals—both business and human—will be a central contributor to your own success as an advisor.

Now that we've laid the basic groundwork for your understanding of competitive advantage, let's delve into some other strategic business issues in which Internet consultants must be conversant. In this section on the basics, we'll focus mostly on definitions and some illustrative examples of each of these strategic elements. In the next chapter, we'll look at the ways the Internet economy has "flipped the script" on these strategies and on the creative thinking Internet consultants can apply to help their clients win.

Supply Chains

The global economy is an interwoven chain of links between suppliers and customers. Every enterprise in that chain is both a supplier and a customer at some point. The pencil manufacturer must purchase wood, graphite, rubber, and metal to make each pencil, cardboard to package those pencils, and shipping services to bring them to market. The shipper must buy trucks. The truck manufacturer has his own chain of suppliers. Even the professional services firm that advises the pencil manufacturer, the shipper, and the truck company must buy pencils so their consultants can take notes. For the pencil manufacturer, the sequence of interactions with suppliers, either of hard products like wood and metal or soft services like shipping, makes up the pencil supply chain.

Early in the industrial age, many manufacturers found significant competitive advantage through their ownership of many of the links in their supply chain. When General Motors owns the rubber plant and the tire company, the steel smelter and the body works, the dealerships and the service organization, that integration of the supply chain creates powerful efficiencies, which create insurmountable advantages and barriers to entry. Unfortunately for GM, it also creates anti-trust problems, and this scenario and many others like it were addressed by the anti-trust division of the U.S. government. Many integrated industrial companies were ultimately forced to divest themselves of some of their suppliers or dealers. Many other companies found that the huge, aggregated enterprise was simply unmanageable. Transferring excellence in managing the production of automobiles, for example, to excellence in harvesting rubber or smelting steel was more difficult than it looked.

The pendulum of strategic thinking has swung in the other direction in the recent past. Many organizations now believe that, rather than trying to aggregate all of their suppliers under a huge conglomerate, strategic advantage can be better built by concentrating on core competencies and outsourcing all other activities and processes to partners, who can then gain competence in their areas of concentration and pass along the savings and efficiencies. This is a strategic debate and a pendulum that is in motion and will continue to evolve; many permutations and combinations of insourcing, outsourcing, co-sourcing, and internal integration will be evaluated and accepted or rejected in the coming years.

Many of the new competitive wrinkles of the 1980s and 1990s were focused on efficiencies in the supply chain. The Japanese inventory management techniques that created the just-in-time inventory model have forever changed the way manufacturers handle product procurement, warehousing, and production. The application of standards to the supply chain was one of the key ingredients in McDonald's rise to dominance, as they taught their suppliers how to provide the raw materials for the perfect French fry. As McDonald's has migrated around the world, its standardization of its local supply chain has gone with it, allowing the company to provide consistent French fries in Memphis and Moscow.

IT is a significant driver to efficiency in the supply chain. Many of the largest IT projects of the past fifteen years have been focused on the implementation of manufacturing (or materials) resource planning (MRP) and enterprise resource planning (ERP). These products, provided by software developers such as SAP, Baan, Oracle, and JD Edwards, are designed to allow large enterprises to coordinate, track, and control the myriad steps in a modern production environment and to offer their partners in their supply chain electronic links into their activities. Other technologies, such as electronic data interchange (EDI) and advance shipping notice (ASN), although often called cumbersome and overly complex, have been used to great advantage by that master of supply chain optimization, Wal-Mart.

These technologies, although they have brought terrific incremental gains in productivity, are tactical solutions, achieving efficiencies but seldom changing the strategic landscape of the industry. They have served an important purpose, however, by preparing managers for the revolution in supply chain management that the Internet makes possible. It's important for Internet consultants to remember that interactions between members of a supply chain are governed by a complex set of processes that include credit, invoicing, shipping, receiving, inventory control, returns, quality control, and a plethora of other procedures that change significantly industry to industry. By forcing managers to examine the underlying processes that drive supplies through their chain and to re-engineer and optimize those processes, this first generation of IT tools has set the stage for the quantum leap to Internet supply chain management and its higher-value sibling, value chain management. IT consultants assisted their clients in the selection and implementation of MRP and ERP software products in the pre-Internet days; eConsultants will be asked to help clients examine, re-engineer, optimize, and migrate their core supply chain processes to the Web.

The benefits of an optimized supply chain are not trivial. According to research performed by the Supply Chain Council,[15] companies rated "best in class" achieve advantages in their supply chain management costs equal to 3 to 6 percent of their total revenue and turn supplies into cash 45 to 65 percent faster than their competitors. These results are impressive and can make the difference between profit and loss for many companies in today's low-margin environment. Even more impressive are the results shown by companies that go beyond supply chain management to value chain management, which we'll review next.

Value Chains

The difference between supply chain management and value chain management is critical to our discussion of Internet business strategies. While supply chains typically are focused on the raw materials and logistics that allow an enterprise to create and deliver its product, value chains extend the strategic thought process to include the entire design, production, and delivery process of a manufactured good from beginning to end, regardless of which firm owns any particular value-adding step. The value chain encompasses not only the suppliers and the suppliers' suppliers, but the customer and the customers' customers as well. Supply chain optimization requires managers to think about the movement and delivery of materials in the most efficient ways, but value chain management requires that strategists evaluate the opportunities for adding value at every step—for linking the enterprise with other partners in the chain, creating extended organizations that share planning, inventory, human resources, information and IT systems, and even corporate cultures. Value chain thinking, rather than simply squeezing inefficiencies out of the delivery of materials, naturally leads to such concepts as collaborative design and mutual forecasting.

Value chain activities can be moved in both directions of the value chain, as Wal-Mart shows by migrating stocking and inventory operations to its suppliers and as Amazon.com illustrates by moving sales activities to its "associates" and unpaid reviewers. "The traditional supply chain is very internally focused," says Vijay Govindarajan, professor of international business at Dartmouth College's Amos Tuck School of Business. "In this value-chain approach, the emphasis is on an external view: Is value being created at every step of the process?"[16] In value chain thinking, the concentration is on creating value by applying disciplines such as collaborative design, in which value chain partners all have input into the design so all can contribute their knowledge and expertise, or mass customization, in which partners work together to create individually configured products as customers are ready to purchase them rather than building standard products to sit on a warehouse shelf.

One of the key concepts for strategic consultants to understand is that, as supply chain and value chain management takes hold of corporate planning, competition moves from company-to-company competition to chain-to-chain competition. Cisco Systems is a stronger competitor not because its routers are inherently better or cheaper, but because Cisco has developed, through alliance, partnerships, and acquisition, a chain of companies that can provide a complete, integrated, locally supplied, and individually configured product to customers globally. When the Italian government looked for a provider of network and telecommunications gear, Cisco beat rivals Bay, Lucent, 3Com, and Ericsson primarily because Cisco quickly created a joint manufacturing venture with an Italian supplier and so instantly became a local, rather than a foreign, corporation. This was not an isolated incident, but part of Cisco's core strategy, internally referred to as the "single-enterprise" system. With every partner in the value chain having access to Cisco's Internet-based applications that allow them to forecast, design, build, and deliver Cisco products as a single entity, Cisco uses its entire chain to create a competitive enterprise that is bigger than any one company and clearly creates more value than its competitors. As one of Cisco's key suppliers, Paul Esling at Avnet, explains, "For all practical purposes, we *are* Cisco."[17]

One last key point regarding value chains: They mark a migration from mass production to mass customization. Since the advent of the industrial revolution, there have been manufacturers who concentrated on designing and building standardized products for the mass market, and there have been job shops that worked directly with individual customers to create individual, customized products that fit exactly the client's budget, schedule, and requirements. In the industrial age, some products, such as televisions and automobiles, were well suited to mass manufacture, and some, such as buildings and specialized machine tools, were not. Even in the age of mass manufacture, however, the rich always had access to custom manufacture, ranging from the "bespoke" tailors of Saville Row to the society architects of New York. In a model popularized by Dell, however, the advent of value chain management and modern information technology now makes custom manufacture possible for the many, as Web-based configurator software allows customers to design and configure their own products and Web-based value chain applications enable manufacturers to build to order efficiently. Value chain strategies allow manufacturers to become less like industrial age mass producers and more like specialized job shops. Because value chain management includes the supplier and the ultimate consumer of products in its strategies, it encourages those companies that practice it to migrate to "pull" manufacturing, where the customer configures his own product and forecasts the need to manufacture, and away from "push" manufacturing, where the producer builds products based on historical data and often inaccurate forecasts, pushes them out to the warehouse, and hopes they meet the customers' needs and schedules.

Revenue Streams

The timing of this book is, I believe, a real advantage for the reader who wants to become an Internet advisor. Rather than being caught up in the initial euphoria of the Internet craze, we can look at the successes and failures of the Web pioneers with a clear eye and learn the lessons of success and failure. One of the clearest lessons to me is something that should have been obvious from the beginning: Revenue matters! In commentary that, with the benefit of hindsight, seems ridiculous and hallucinatory, CEOs, founders, and venture capitalists talked about the overriding importance of building "market presence" and "brand" or of "capturing eyeballs" and scoffed at the idea that, to have a business, you needed money flowing in. "We'll capture the eyeballs first, and then figure out how to monetize that later," a bit of Internet doublespeak that CEOs, with a straight face, intoned into the CNBC cameras day after day. We now know, as we watch startups that burned brightly (and expensively) whither and die, that "monetizing" your enterprise is not an afterthought; it's the sole purpose of creating a business!

The strategic consultant, when advising a startup or an existing enterprise about Internet strategies, must help the client think through the revenue opportunities that their strategy affords. It is, I believe, an exercise in pure hucksterism to tell clients to just get out there and grab some land and worry about how to "monetize" it later. Internet strategic advisors need to examine the client's proposed business model, whether it consists of e-retailing to consumers or hosting a business exchange and collecting transaction-based revenue, to ensure that there is in fact a reasonable expectation of sufficient revenue streams to make the enterprise viable.

It is not ridiculous, however, to realize that the Net creates many new revenue streams that were not available pre-Net. While the advertising model has been used by weak business models to cover many sins, there are opportunities for advertising revenue when the business model includes a website that will attract a wide audience, especially if that audience has a desirable demographic profile. The analysis of transactional data also has some revenue possibilities. The ability to capture useful information about your customers' behavior, preferences, and demographics as an inherent part of the shopping process—and to then rent, sell, or analyze that data—is taken to a new level by the shopping experience on the Internet. The mountain of data that is generated by Internet activities is staggering, as every click, purchase, login, and checkout creates a trail that can be collected, followed, and analyzed. While the use of this information raises privacy and appropriate use questions, which we'll examine later, it's clear that it also creates a new opportunity to understand what motivates or inhibits customer behavior, how that behavior differs or syncs up based on factors of grouping, demographics, age, or income, and how everyone from marketers to public servants can use these behavioral insights to perfect their appeals to the marketplace. The commercialization of collective data on consumer behavior is just one example of a revenue opportunity that is uniquely enabled by Internet technology.

We'll explore other unique Internet revenue possibilities as we proceed, but the point here is that consultants who hope to advise their customers well on Internet strategies need to blow past all the smog of "eyeballs" and "brand" and help clients concentrate their efforts on real business models that produce real, sustainable, profitable revenue.

COMPETITIVE ADVANTAGE

So what is the point of all this analysis of business strategies? Why does an IT consultant who wants to become an Internet advisor need to wade through all this material about supply chains and revenue streams? Isn't our role to help clients select the best Web-design software or the most secure firewall?

Whether we are working with clients to evaluate Adobe Pagemill® and Microsoft FrontPage® or to review Hewlett-Packard versus Sun hardware or whether we are acting as strategic consultants to help clients design an Internet auction site, our activities are focused on one result: Helping our clients attain sustainable competitive advantage. Elegant IT architectures and stunning website graphics are nice, but only competitive advantage attracts venture capitalists and investors and delivers the profitability and growth that create a strong and prolonged enterprise that grows in value and that creates opportunities and satisfied customers. Those consultants who can develop a track record of helping customers devise a proprietary market advantage will be assured of projects and billable revenues for years to come.

So what is sustainable competitive advantage? One of the pivotal business articles of the 1980s, "Sustainable Competitive Advantage—What It Is, What It Isn't," by Kevin Coyne, presents this definition: "Sustainable competitive advantage is a consistent difference in product attributes that are a direct consequence of a capability gap that endures over time."[18]

In the Internet gold rush of the last five years, many startups believed that the concept of sustainable competitive advantage was an archaic holdover from the industrial age and that only "first-mover advantage," market presence, and a catchy domain name were required for business success. Many companies with identical concepts, minimal barriers to entry, and no special core competencies or market insight were rushed to market by eager entrepreneurs and flush venture capitalists. Luckily, with the benefit of hindsight we have the opportunity to learn that, even in this revolutionary time of business deconstruction, some fundamental things do still apply.

As ethical and conscientious professional advisors, we owe it to our clients always to bring them back to the concept of competitive advantage in every discussion about Internet strategy. Does that flashy graphic give us an opportunity to beat our competition and create customer value, or does it merely appease the creative instincts of our Web-design team? Does that new firewall really give us a security advantage over our competitors that can translate into customer reassurance and convenience, or is it merely the latest "whiz-bang" technology that our engineers have fallen in love with? Does that wacky domain name give us an opportunity to create a distinctive brand image in the minds of our customers, or does it serve to make the marketing team feel really clever? By always going back to Coynes' defining concepts of "consistent difference" and a "capability gap," we ensure that easily duplicated elements like flashy graphics and goofy domain names do not become the central components of our clients' strategic plans. By working with each client company to understand its unique core competencies, its competitive marketplace, the competencies and strategies of its competitors, and the unique combination of convenience, technology, logistical excellence, and customer relationships that makes up its competitive advantage, we can migrate up our own personal value chain and become strategic advisors, rather than website designers or infrastructure integrators.

End Notes

1. Ward, J. Scient to Go Public and Take on the Big Boys. *The Industry Standard,* March 25, 1999.
2. Wilder, C. What Business Are You In? *VarBusiness,* May 29, 2000.
3. The Greatest CEOs in History. *Fortune,* December 1999.
4. Finnie, W. *Hands-On Strategy.* New York: John Wiley & Sons, 1994, pp.1–4.
5. Serwer, A. There's Something About Cisco. *Fortune,* May 15, 2000.
6. Porter, M. How Competitive Forces Shape Strategy. *Harvard Business Review,* March/April, 1979.
7. Grant, R. *Contemporary Strategy Analysis.* Cambridge, MA: Blackwell, 1991.
8. Mintzberg, H., & Quinn, J. *The Strategy Process: Concepts, Context and Cases.* Upper Saddle River, NJ: Prentice Hall, 1995.
9. Mintzberg H. *The Rise and Fall of Strategic Planning: Reconceiving Roles for Planning, Plans, Planners.* New York: Free Press, December 1993.
10. Ibid.

11. Byrne, J. Strategic Planning. *Business Week,* August 1996.

12. Finnie, W. *Hands-On Strategy.* New York: John Wiley & Sons, 1994.

13. Itow, L. Nordstrom: Shopper's Delight. *San Francisco Examiner,* Feb. 15, 1987.

14. Yoshihara, N. Chain Sets Itself Apart with an Old-Fashioned Service Policy. *Los Angeles Times,* Sept. 30, 1984.

15. The Supply Chain Council's 1997 Integrated Supply-Chain Benchmarking Study. *www.supply-chain.org.*

16. Liegs, S. Getting Your Company Ready: How to Prepare Your Organization to Adopt a Value Chain Model. *Industry Week,* Sept. 6, 1999, p. 54.

17. The Cisco value chain case study is based on material presented in Tapscot, T.D., Lowy, A., & Ticoll, D. *Digital Capital.* Cambridge, MA: Harvard Business School Press, 2000, pp. 93–118.

18. Coyne, K. Sustainable Competitive Advantage-What It Is, What It Isn't. *Business Horizons,* Jan. 1986, p. 27.

chapter FOUR

Strategies for
the New Economy

INDUSTRY TRANSFORMATION

The basics of business strategic thinking, which we reviewed in the previous chapter, serve as both a *preface* and a *warning*. A preface, because it's critical to understand the competitive issues and constraints that lead managers and planners to select their business strategies. A warning, because every strategy has its day, and every strategy can wobble and fall under the pressures of events, technology, innovation, and customer desire. The vertically integrated behemoths of the industrial age had tremendous competitive advantage from their ownership of resources, refineries, design facilities, manufacturing, and dealerships—until the craze for diversification reached absurdity and unmanageable entities started to collapse of their own weight and bureaucracy. Huge conglomerates, such as Gulf and Western, were built of unconnected collections of enterprises, from sugar plantations in the Dominican Republic to the movie factories of Paramount Pictures, under the theory that the business you're in doesn't matter, because competent managers can manage any enterprise. They can't, and the over-diversified conglomerates went into crisis when leaner and hungrier competitors from Japan and Europe recovered from their wartime disasters and began to compete aggressively.

The business revolutions of the 1970s and 1980s, like many revolutions, were responses to unavoidable crises. The quality of Japanese manufacturing forced American management to embrace the quality theories of W. Edwards Deming and Phillip Crosby, theories invented here but mostly ignored until the Japanese used them to eat our lunch. The development of just-in-time supply chain management in Japan and the standardization of quality processes led by the Europeans, resulting in ISO

9000 quality certifications, were *process* innovations that optimized the internal value-creation mechanisms within corporations. The business process re-engineering movement of the 1980s encouraged organizations to free themselves from the outmoded processes of the past and to re-examine their beliefs and procedures with a fresh eye. As is the case in many revolutions, however, some participants got overzealous and turned re-engineering into wholesale downsizing, thus demoralizing organizations and sabotaging the very loyalty and commitment organizations need to survive. Michael Hammer, the consultant credited with inspiring the business process re-engineering (BPR) movement,[1] stated in a *Wall Street Journal* article, "I was insufficiently appreciative of the human dimension. I've learned that's critical."[2]

Competitive pressure also forced organizations to examine their very structures. The process innovations of the BPR movement led strategists to search for the core value in the enterprise, and that led naturally to the concept of focusing on that core and finding an outside source for non-core processes. One of the key buzzwords of the re-engineering movement was the admonition for companies to "stick to their knitting," to do those things they did better than anyone and spin off or outsource those functions that were not at the heart of their value proposition. The outsourcing movement, like vertical integration and BPR before it, had its abuses, in which outsourcing, rather than a search for world-class partners, became a search for problem functions that could be dumped to outsiders who could then be browbeaten into providing commodity services at unprofitable prices. In its highest form, however, it evolved into the business ecosystem, in which first-rate companies band together around a standard, such as Microsoft Windows®, Cisco routing products, or the Linux operating system, and together contribute to creating the best value for the customer.

Each of these strategic business movements, from the disaggregation of the industrial giants to the optimization of internal processes to the creation of virtual ecosystems in which each participant adds unique competencies, was a critical and necessary precursor to the Internet economy. Creative business leaders were ready for virtual organizations, networks of suppliers, designers, builders, and marketplaces that would work together to construct value for customers. In the 1990s the technology caught up with the visions of those creative strategists. Finally, through the use of software like ERP and customer relationship management (CRM), virtual organizations could obtain a unified view of the pieces and parts that together created a thing of value for the customer. Once these elements were in place, the availability of a worldwide network that could bring it all together electronically was inevitable. If the Internet wasn't there, we would have had to invent it.

The elements for a revolution were in place, as we've reviewed so far. The catalyst, the event that accelerated the momentum toward the flood of new business models, was the discovery by businesspeople of the Internet, especially its popularization by the creation of the World Wide Web. We all recognize that the capabilities of this communication medium will change the way businesses develop and maintain competitive advantage. For consultants, the question is "How do I guide my clients so they can successfully exploit the new business models that the Internet enables?" To answer that question, we must first look at those new capabilities in a structured way so we can then apply our analysis to each client's situation and propose the best strategies.

As we discussed earlier, the Internet demolishes the three most common competitive weapons of the offline world: geography, information, and supply and demand. Through our example of the local full-price shoe store, the discount superstore, and the selection of shoes available on the Internet, we examined how each of these elements of competitive advantage is impacted by the Internet's geography-independent, information-rich, and infinite supply dynamics. Let's now explore some of the less obvious implications of the new economic realities imposed by the Internet.

THE END OF LOCATION

The demise of geographic limits that the Internet enables does more than weaken the competitive advantage of the local retail store. It creates business complications for managers and business owners globally. For instance, in Italy a Xerox copier may cost 25 percent more than that same device costs in the United States. Part of the difference is due to tariffs, but some proportion is also based on local market dynamics of supply and demand. When the copier is available on Xerox's website at the U.S. price, how does the Italian reseller maintain his profit structure? For us as consultants, we also have to help our clients think through the implications of competing in a global marketplace. Forrester Research, the IT analysis firm, estimates that business websites get about 30 percent of their traffic, and 10 percent of their orders, from non-U.S. customers. Yet this same study indicates that 46 percent of all orders placed by eShoppers outside the United States in 1998 went unfilled due to process failures. IDC, another respected IT analyst, estimates that, by 2003, 67 percent of Internet users will log on from outside the United States, and the foreign share of eBusiness transactions will go from 26 percent in 1998 to 56 percent in 2003.[3] Both the potential for profit—and for problems—are exponentially increased by global accessibility.

For those clients who want to create a worldwide business presence (which is the point of the World Wide Web, isn't it?), global issues of culture, currency, and process must be learned and integrated into the business model. The cultural issues of globalization aren't trivial. As AOL has discovered in its competition with local players such as Freeserve in the U.K. or Tiscali in Italy, local knowledge and presence can be powerful benefits. Jim Rose, chairman of QXL, the British auction site that has successfully kept eBay from dominating the auction space in his country, puts it simply: "Sensitivity to the cultural and national distinctions will separate success from failure."[4] Finally, the global nature of the Net makes it easy for eager entrepreneurs across the world to usurp any business model and, with the benefit of hindsight, optimize it and put their name on it. Clearly, running a business with instantaneous global exposure is a complicated and risky enterprise. Just as clearly, the potential payoff for those who do it right is enormous.

INFORMATION MIGRATION

Information, the second element in our competitive threesome, is changed by the Internet in some obvious ways—and in many ways that are not so apparent. One of the key points about this medium is that it changes the viewer as much as the material being viewed. Many companies make the mistake of focusing on the content only and on changing it to fit a more interactive and dynamic medium. What they miss is that, in the words of McCann-Erickson, an ad agency recognized as a leader in eMarketing, the Internet customer is "leaning forward" whereas the TV viewer is "leaning back."[5] The Internet customer, far from being a passive "couch potato," is in fact active, engaged, and emotionally charged. She's participating in a community, searching for personally relevant information. And sometimes she's actively disparaging the companies that don't live up to her expectations or their marketing slogans.

Interactive information changes the marketing dynamic. Customers can instantly research a vendor's claims and find out for themselves whether Volvo is safer or Wheaties are more nutritious. If a company's products actually are safer or healthier, the Web can be a powerful tool for getting that information out to interested prospects. If, however, the marketing and the reality don't quite sync up, the Web can be a dangerous place. Customers have access to detailed product information that was previously hidden, and they have a forum for expressing their opinions, good and bad, about product and brand experiences. As any surfer who's checked out StarBucked.com, the unofficial Starbuck's consumer site, can attest, these sites can be revealing, damaging, and disturbing. In typical old economy style, many organizations' first impulse is to sue, or attempt to control, these critical voices. Internet consultants need to help their clients understand that these voices are a permanent part of this new medium and that they must develop strategies for opening a dialogue with their critics in order to gain from their critiques. We'll dig deeper into this in our marketing chapter, when we'll discuss strategies for helping our clients, who hope to weave successful Web strategies, become more customer-focused and open.

One of the most obvious migrations from the old to the new economy is the often-used image of "atoms to bits." First popularized by Nicholas Negroponte of the MIT New Media Lab,[6] this concept illustrates the fact that many information-based products that formerly required "atoms," meaning physical presence, such as CDs, books, or newspapers, can now be transmitted as "bits," in the form of digitized data. This has an enormous impact on the marketplace for intellectual property such as the latest release by Pearl Jam, the classified ads in the newspaper, or this book. As the controversy over the digital download of copyrighted music has shown, this new marketplace for digitized products and services is still in its genesis, as engineers, lawyers, and business strategists try to figure out how to exploit its commercial potential while protecting the rights of content providers. The digitization of information impacts many industries in unique ways. The ability to convert voice traffic into standard Internet data traffic, as an example, opens a world of possibilities for new communications services and creates a world of threats for the existing telephone companies. Some industries, notably the newspapers, have already been hurt by the move to digital information. As the help wanted, cars for sale, and local movie and television listings move to the Web, many newspapers have been hit with a double whammy, losing both their most lucrative advertising clients and many of their readers as well.

There are strategies, however, by which innovative newspapers—and others threatened by the digitization of their information products—can fight back. Many old-line newspaper companies, such as the Tribune Company, have become Internet powerhouses by buying or building competitive offerings before upstarts take away their core advertisers and readers. Others, like *The New York Times* and *The Wall Street Journal,* have expanded their franchise onto the Web by offering innovative new services and content that isn't available in the daily paper. The point is, Internet consultants need to understand the competitive threats that the "atoms to bits" movement represents and to have a background in some of the actions established companies have taken to ensure their survival. Only through a deep understanding of the strategic decisions Internet winners and survivors have made can we add value to our clients' search for answers.

One additional complication of this information element of the competitive landscape is this: As companies join Internet-based exchanges to facilitate "frictionless" supply chains, the migration from private to public information creates cultural upheaval. The recent announcements of cooperative exchanges, such as the Covisint automobile supply chain exchange co-owned by GM, Daimler-Chrysler, and Ford, seem to make a lot of sense on the surface. By banding together, enterprises can quickly gain the size and scale that can lead to dramatic cost savings and efficiencies. They can also create barriers to entry that protect their turf from the voracious dot.com startups eyeing their lucrative markets.

These giant marketplaces also raise a series of interesting questions. How will the fiercest of competitors learn to share their secret information in order to cooperate in a single Web marketplace? Transora, for instance, the exchange created by General Mills, Coca-Cola, Kraft Foods, Unilever, and Proctor & Gamble, will have fifty owners, each with a stake of less than 5 percent. Any consumer who understands the power of Coca-Cola's "secret formula" will recognize that this sort of cooperation signifies a real change. And any consultant who has worked through the decision process at one of these major enterprises will feel a shudder up her spine when she thinks about the decision process at a conglomerate like this. These exchanges also operate under the watchful eye of the antitrust regulators. Walking the fine line between cooperation and collusion in this uncharted environment will make the success of these exchanges a challenge, even with their extraordinary resources and market presence. The strategic, cultural, and regulatory issues around the use of confidential competitive information is one more aspect of the information revolution on which consultants must be prepared to advise.

TOWARD THE PERFECT MARKETPLACE

Economics professors like to hypothesize a world of perfect competition in which sellers and buyers can meet in a neutral marketplace, where supply and demand are not limited by the constraints of time or location, and where the friction of tariffs and taxes, search costs, and government regulation were all squeezed out of the bargain so that only product features and price determine the buyer's selection. Although we're still far from that ideal world, many observers believe that the technology of the Internet brings us a step closer, "greasing the skids" by eliminating time, distance, and search costs from the transaction.

In our discussion of supply and demand, we imagined a shoe buyer whose choices had suddenly expanded from the corner shoe store or the discount chain at the mall to all the shoes available from stores, manufacturers, and designers on the Internet. The immediate expansion in apparent supply is well-known to any shopper who has compared the selection available at their corner bookstore to the choices at Amazon.com. Automobile shoppers, who previously were limited to the local dealers with their exclusive sales areas strictly controlled by the manufacturers and powerful dealer councils, can now use Net-based services such as Autobytel.com or CarSmart to compare prices, options, deals, and availability in a much wider marketplace of dealers. The supply of cars hasn't changed, but the window of availability to the average shopper with Internet access has broadened exponentially.

To illustrate some of the ways the Internet has changed the dynamics of supply and demand, let's take a look at the financial information industry. Ten years ago, giant organizations such as Reuters, Bloomberg, Telerate, and Quotron charged both professional stockbrokers and active investors high prices to get real-time transmission of live market data and analysis. This was a true indication of the law of supply and demand, as these information dealers had built huge, private networks to receive, interpret, and transmit that data and, because of its value in making investment decisions, were able to charge fees that ranged from $300 to $2,000 a month for their proprietary data feeds. The supply was constrained due to the huge costs involved in setting up these networks, hiring analysts to make sense of the data, and then selling and supporting these networks of data lines and user work stations. The demand was controlled by the competitive environment, in which performance-conscious investment professionals couldn't afford to be without the latest market knowledge.

Now that this data has migrated from closed, private networks to the public Internet and many financial services firms wish to offer this data as a value-added feature of their other services, the supply has increased tremendously. Now, rather than having to build proprietary infrastructures and huge sales and support organizations, new competitors can purchase this information from the exchanges, post it to a website, and make it accessible to anyone with a Web browser. The cost to users has dropped in concert with the rise in supply to the point where investors who are willing to deposit $500 in a brokerage account can get real-time quotes and expert analysis for free.

The supply side is not the only part of the transaction that has changed. Priceline.com is a primary example of the changes in the demand side of the equation. At a standard auction, sellers advertise their desire to supply a good or service and then buyers declare their willingness to pay a certain price for that product or service, until they reach a price that fairly compensates both. Priceline has turned the tables on that standard scenario by setting up a marketplace in which buyers can advertise their desire to purchase a good or service at a certain price, and sellers can then determine whether they are prepared to offer their products at that price. In the case of inventory that expires or loses its value at a certain moment, such as empty seats at flight time, event seats at game time, and hotel rooms after last check-in, this buyer-centric marketplace redeems lost value. The Priceline "reverse auction" business model illustrates some important new business realities. Astute entrepreneurs can create tremendous shareholder value through their creative design of business models, as the billion-dollar market value of Priceline demonstrates. Priceline owns no aircraft, no hotels, no stadiums, yet achieved a market value similar to those old-line enterprises that own and operate these assets. Priceline's value is based solely on its strategy. Perhaps more telling is the shift in the balance of power between the buyers and the sellers. No longer can sellers expect to set a price with a comfortable profit margin built in and then thrust it out in the marketplace with a take-it-or-leave-it attitude. In this instantaneous, dynamic Internet business environment, buyers are prepared to leave it and go looking for the seller who's more realistic about his own pricing power.

Another demand-side phenomenon is the aggregation-of-demand model in which sites offer to create a buying cooperative of individuals and aggregate their demand to get better pricing from the supplier. In the small business market, for example, this model has been popularized by companies such as BizBuyer.com and

DemandLine. These small business buying services offer members the opportunity to aggregate their demand for standard-issue office items such as printers and copiers and then use that demand to negotiate volume discounts with suppliers that are greater than the individual consumer could get. In other markets, such as the market for energy or bandwidth, mass markets enabled by the reach and access of the Internet are changing the supply-and-demand equation and driving prices down.

As we discussed earlier, price is a symptom of the balance between supply and demand. As the phrase "seller's market" indicates, when the seller of goods has the upper hand, prices will rise, and vice versa. And in the Internet marketplace, vice is versa all the time. As anyone who passed Economics 101 knows, competition in open markets will drive prices down to their lowest possible level and—in some cases—will drive them to zero. You don't have to be an economics major to know that, with the advent of automated price-comparison engines or "bots" that can surf the Web for the best price on any standardized item, prices will be driven to the low end of their feasible range. Some Internet strategists even see a market for goods priced below break-even. Buy.com sells items such as books, CDs, and consumer electronics below cost, with the strategy of selling advertising on its site to provide a revenue stream. At this point the "lose money, make it up in advertising" model has been discredited, as only the largest sites, such as Yahoo and AOL, have been able to attract sufficient ad revenue to build a business on. Whether or not these experiments in miniscule or negative margins result in success for their founders, however, they have succeeded in one thing: They've driven prices to the floor. As a study by Forrester Research, in which they used shopping bots to research prices on CDs, blenders, and Palm PCs, shows, prices on the Net undercut retail store prices by an average of 15 percent.[7]

The ability to forecast demand accurately is one of the most powerful of competitive weapons. For those who do it well, the payoff is tremendous; and those who fail can pay the ultimate price. Apple Computer is one example of a company that nearly lost its life due to its inability to accurately forecast the demand for its products. Apple was famous, during the dark days following the departure of John Sculley, for being stuck with inflated inventories of products and components that nobody wanted, even at fire-sale prices, and for never being able to deliver the hot models. Apart from his ability to articulate the vision and mission of Apple, Steven Jobs was able to turn the company around based on simple execution: He put in place some stringent disciplines for analyzing customer requirements, and he began to communicate again with the community of Apple loyalists to get some real-world feedback on the needs and desires of the customer. The missed opportunity can be enormous for those who can't manufacture to meet a meaningful forecast of demand, whether they are marketers of the newest computer model or the latest Christmas toy. In our section on Internet marketing, we'll discuss the use of customer data, gathered from actual transactions, to drive forecasting.

BEYOND THE BASICS

So far we've discussed some of the basics of competitive strategy, such as geography and information. These elements have been turned on their heads by the new competitive world of the Internet, but at least they are familiar aspects of the competitive landscape. There are some factors that are less familiar to the old economy strategist, but central to understanding and succeeding in the new economy. The ability to harness a community of customers with similar interests, the designation of marketing affiliates who can help grow your business, and the migration of some of the actual business development activities to the consumer are all phenomena that have been invented or accelerated in the Internet economy.

The concept of network-based community is not new. Even before the popularization of the Internet, many of the early commercial computer networks, such as CompuServe and Prodigy, were in large part based on their ability to create online communities of interest, where groups as diverse as computer consultants and cat lovers could gather in virtual chat rooms and discuss their interests. At the beginning of the Internet explosion of the 1990s, the newsgroup communities that covered every topic from gardening to bestiality were sources of media fascination with this new communication tool. These early experiments in community building proved one thing: People with similar interests and tastes will form virtual neighborhoods with bonds that are extremely powerful. Many successful websites are designed around this concept of community. iVillage, the women's Internet community, for example, was developed based on the success of an AOL-based community called Parent Soup. This site, dedicated to parenting issues, has grown into a valuable set of Web properties that include sites focused on health and fitness, relationships, and personal finance, all oriented toward women's needs and preferences. This collection of sites is consistently rated among the top fifty Web properties in number of unique visitors. As Candice Carpenter, co-founder, puts it, "We strive to help women navigate through increasingly busy lives and maximize their potential in their various roles as parents, friends, spouses, partners, career women, breadwinners, employees, and individuals. We provide the supportive and nurturing environment . . . where women can find sound advice and practical solutions from experts and each other."[8]

The desire to build community is, ironically, one of the key drivers to Internet acceptance. From the investment opinion boards to the sports chat lines, from the public movie-review sites to the pop-star fan sites, Internet surfers with similar interests seek one another and will develop loyalty to those sites that enable them to connect. Smart Internet businesses capitalize on this drive by creating an environment that fosters connection. Smart Internet consultants know that the possibilities for utilizing community to drive customer loyalty are endless. Customers of the shoe store who buy hiking boots every winter contain the nugget of a community with an interest in winter hiking, which can be addressed with offers and information that provide real value and enhance the recipient's life, rather than simply hawking gear. Bookstore customers can be segregated into communities of interest, as Amazon has done with its "purchase circles," that can become areas of reference for like-minded readers. I personally check the consulting purchase circle every week or so to see which books are being read by my peers and competitors. Offline bookstores can review my transactions and gauge my interests, but it would be very difficult for them to reproduce the value I get from my ability to review the popular titles in any area of interest at my leisure. Consultants who can help their clients think beyond the simple eCommerce possibilities toward developing strategies that take advantage of unique capabilities such as online community will differentiate themselves and their clients from the run-of-the-mill.

One of the reasons America Online has been able to maintain its status as the top destination on the Internet, even with its $21.95 monthly fee, has been its focus on the creation of structured communities that are well run and that provide value and meaning for their participants. One of the reasons these communities offer a better experience for the user is AOL's use of moderators, unpaid volunteers who are members of the community and offer their time and effort to organize and guide the community's activities. This concept of transferring some of the work to the customer is another important key difference in Internet commerce with which consultants must be familiar. From the community guides on sites such as AOL and iVillage to the book reviews posted by Amazon visitors, all the way through the open source software movement in which the community becomes its own software developer, participation and active involvement are permanent dynamics of the new economy. Consultants need to work with their clients to help them understand the opportunities for involving the customer in more than simply pointing, clicking, and buying. By creating a forum for their community and opinion, by involving them in the administration of the community and site, and by allowing them to participate in the shaping of the site and software itself, new economy entrepreneurs can create an environment in which the customer has real ownership and involvement in the relationship, rather than being a passive receptacle for broadcast "buy now" messages.

One of the ultimate uses for this customer involvement is to turn customers into partners. Through the use of affiliate programs that allow customers to post links on their own websites, companies such as Amazon, barnesandnoble.com, CDNOW, and many others are creating networks of partners who drive traffic and prospects to their sites and who participate in the revenue they generate. In a recent study, Forrester Research found that affiliate networks are the most cost-effective method of marketing, ahead of advertising, public relations, and targeted e-mail.[9]

Fogdog, an e-commerce company focused on selling sporting goods to consumers, has created an affiliate network of over fifty thousand sites. A perfect example of a spot where community, consumer involvement, and affiliation converge is the Fogdog affiliate, The Running Network. An Internet-based community of running enthusiasts, this site combines content from many local publications such as *Michigan Runner* and the *Washington Running* report. Much of this content is contributed by community members. Members also offer reviews of running gear. Finally, The Running Network also offers community members the ability to purchase gear online through its affiliation with Fogdog. This program combines all the elements we've addressed in this discussion: Online community, active participation, and the commercial power of affiliation. Creative consultants who bring their knowledge of the power of community to their client engagements can help clients bring one more competitive weapon into the mix.[10]

INTERNET BUSINESS MODELS

"Business models," like "eyeballs" and "first-mover advantage," is one of those Internet clichés that has moved from the jargon of Silicon Valley insiders to the public discourse. The business press compares the business model of Amazon.com to that of barnesandnoble.com, and the commentators on CNBC ascribe the latest dot.com flare out to a weak business model. Before we begin to analyze the factors that make a business model weak or strong, let's agree on a definition. I'll present a couple of definitions because I think they complement each other. Paul Timmers, head of sector for the European Commission's Information Society, presents this description: "An architecture for product, service, and information flows, including a description of the various business actors and their roles, a description of the potential benefits for the various business actors, and a description of the sources of revenue."[11] This explanation is meaningful to us because of its presentation as an *architecture,* a framework that all IT consultants should find familiar. Another clear definition comes from Adrian Slywotzky, a vice president at Mercer Management Consulting: "The totality of how a company selects its customers, defines and differentiates its offerings, defines the tasks it will perform itself and those it will outsource, configures its resources, goes to market, creates utility for customers, and captures profits. It is the entire system for delivering utility to customers and earning a profit from that activity."[12]

Experienced IT consultants are accustomed to thinking in terms of systems, and so Slywotzky's definition, which emphasizes a total system conception of the business, should be comfortable to us. As we examine Slywotzky's definition in more detail, a few more aspects come forward. Let's dissect his description a bit and discuss in more detail what it means to us as business advisors.

- *The totality:* With all the emphasis on "brand" in the Internet and general business press, the one aspect that defines a brand in most consumers' minds is lost—the sum total of experience with that provider. The McDonald's brand is built around consistency, cleanliness, value, and speed. If any of these elements is missing, the brand gets tarnished, as many formerly loyal McDonald's customers have demonstrated in the past few years. As we progress through this discussion of strategy, we'll return to the concept of total and consistent experience for the customer as a critical success factor.

- *of how a company selects its customers:* In the early days of the Internet, many startups followed the mantra of "if you build it they will come," as if any old surfer who happened to stumble on the site was good enough to build a business on. The selection of customers, however—otherwise known as target marketing—is one of those fundamentals of offline business that is even more critical in the online world. One of the key metrics often quoted in the Internet press is that of customer acquisition costs, pegged by the Boston Consulting Group at an average of $82 per customer for Internet retailers.[13] This means that a customer must generate $82 of profit before the typical e-tailer breaks even. Targeting customers who will stick around long enough to generate those returns is just a small part of the equation. Online enterprises need to be sure that their offerings are targeted to the right technical demographic, since many groups of customers who would have great potential offline aren't even online yet—and may never be. Loyalty and rewards programs, pioneered by the airline and credit card industries to segment customers by profitability, are also critical to the success of the Internet business, but they are not enough. Commentators and research analysts, who frequently disagree on everything, are unanimous on one point: The customer is king in the Internet business world, and those businesses that can figure out how to personalize their service and create real loyalty built on individualized value, rather than on the bribery of traditional loyalty and rewards programs, will triumph. Industrial age businesses hope that the customer selects the mass-produced products they've stuck on the shelf; Internet age businesses target and select their customers with every move they make, from the domain name to the service mix.

- *defines and differentiates its offering:* As we discussed in the last chapter, the definition of products and services, and their differentiation, is the essence of strategy. In the Internet marketplace, however, it isn't only products and services that compete, it is business models competing against other business models. Will techies buy their technical books from a specialized store such as Fatbrain or will they go to a general purpose bookstore such as Amazon? Will neutral market exchanges dominate or will company-affiliated marketplaces win? Will business travelers go to an online aggregator such as Priceline to get the best price or will they go to the website of their favorite airline to keep their frequent-flyer miles coming? As you can see, the concept of a company's "offering" takes on a whole new meaning, expanding from the narrow definition of product or service to encompass the total interactive experience and relationship between client and provider.

- *defines the tasks it will perform itself and those it will outsource:* Only 74 percent of orders arrived on time. Storefronts were unavailable 10 percent of the time.

8.8 million orders showed up after the holiday was over.[14] As these dismal statistics from the 1999 Christmas season illustrate, many online businesses have a long way to go in developing the back-office logistical systems to support their Web storefronts. The rush to the Web has also sparked a rush to disaggregation of the processes and activities that make up a business event. From returns to incentive programs, from the measurement of website metrics to the hosting of the site itself, the provision of outsourced services to Internet businesses is a robust business model all its own. With all the opportunity to divide the processes and functions of the business into independent modules and to farm them out to niche service providers, Internet businesses must make some hard choices about which processes are really core to their competitive strategy and which pieces can safely be outsourced. This exercise is deeper than merely making partnership choices; it forces entrepreneurs and managers (and their consultants!) to ask themselves where they really add value. Are we a marketing company, an operations company, or a technical company? Can we afford to outsource customer service, or is that a key differentiator that we need to control? Can we allow someone else to host our servers, and if we do, how do we ensure the quality and availability of our services? The definition of process tasks often leads to a deeper discussion of core roles and values.

- *configures its resources:* As I write this, the dot.com backlash is in full swing, as the NASDAQ tumbles and Internet startups either liquidate or lose 80 percent of their market value. The Internet magazines such as *The Industry Standard* and *Business 2.0* are full of articles about the frivolous and wasteful spending of startups, some of whom spent millions on lavish IPO parties or undifferentiated Super Bowl® advertisements. While the venture capital (VC) funds were flowing and every IPO soared, naïve entrepreneurs acted as if the laws of gravity had been repealed, even as experienced observers warned of a bubble about to burst. In the recent crash, many unfortunate entrepreneurs learned that the business rules were still in effect, as the reality of basic economics brushed aside the idea that "this time is different." This latest shakeout illustrates again that the judicious and effective use of limited resources is what business is all about.

- *goes to market:* Of all the elements of business that are changed by the Internet, marketing is perhaps the most significantly impacted. This is one area where the old rules *have* been made obsolete; only those who can grasp and capitalize on the new rules will prevail. That Marketing 101 construct, *the "four Ps" (product, price, place,* and *promotion),* is dead and about to be buried by the Net. The *product,* as we've discussed, has migrated from a manufacturer-knows-best, forecast-driven "pushed" product to a customer-demand-driven "pull" product that is different for each customer. *Price* has moved from a one-price-fits-all model to a dynamic model of interactive buying and selling that sets prices in the instant as supply and demand ebb and flow. The added variant of versioning adds even more dynamism to the Internet-based pricing mechanism. The *place* is no longer Main Street, Mall Street, or Wal-Mart, but a digital marketplace that is always open, available from anywhere (that has Internet access), and always competitive. *Promotion* is perhaps the most endangered of all the marketing fundamentals, as informed, savvy consumers demand individualized and relevant product information and disdain untargeted, one-size-fits-all broadcast marketing. Customers have extraordinary access to real product information from impartial sources on the Web in every form, from product reviews by their peers to durability statistics from independent analysts. So when marketers tout their products as better, safer, faster, and cheaper, customers can easily surf through to a review site and see whether those claims are true. Just as product manufacturing is moving to a pull model, so is product information, and the old "advertising push" will never be the same.

- *creates utility for customers:* Customer value is what it's all about, and what many of the ashtrays.coms forgot about. The central conversation between an Internet consultant and a client must focus on customer value.

- *and captures profits:* Profitability matters. Enough said.

- *It is the entire system for delivering utility to customers and earning a profit from that activity:* Just as a competent IT consultant will look beyond the obvious task of configuring a server to consider the associated activities that make up a client's IT strategy, including security, backup, documentation, support, and training, so must a consultant hoping to add value to a client's Internet business strategy look beyond the website and consider the customer relationship, marketing, process, logistical, and sourcing questions that contribute to a compelling business model. The ability to conceive an entire business system, rather than an isolated website or eCommerce storefront, differentiates the professional Internet consultant from the amateur.

Now that we've deconstructed and analyzed the concept of a business model, let's take a look at some of the common Internet business models in place today and see how they address the questions and issues we've raised here.

eRetail

It's not surprising that many early business entries into the Internet space were consumer-focused retail storefronts. They represent the most obvious Internet analog to the offline retail storefront that we're all familiar with and so required no leap of ingenuity to visualize, at least at first glance. It seemed pretty obvious that the competitive advantages of unlimited access, unlimited supply, and consumer convenience could provide significant impetus to online retail without a lot of business model re-engineering. Many companies, both existing enterprises and new Internet startups, made the migration from brochure-ware to online catalog shopping. The early success stories of the Net, such as Amazon.com, E*Trade, or CDNOW, were all pioneers of this eRetail business model. As the new economy has evolved, however, the quick success of some of these businesses has given way to extreme competitive pressure and to doubts about the viability of the business-to-consumer (B2C) "pure play" model.

On the positive side, innovative entrepreneurs such as Jeff Bezos of Amazon and Christos Cotsakos of E*Trade have built companies with extraordinary customer appeal and have personally defined new categories of business. Each of these pioneers has used creativity and customer focus to build an enterprise that is at the top of the food chain in his marketplace and that has shaken the foundations of his industry. To be "Amazon-ed" has become common slang for the process of being out-thought, out-innovated, and out-maneuvered by a creative Internet-based upstart in your industry. In 1997, a top executive of Merrill Lynch, in response to the success of E*Trade and other online brokerages, made headlines by decrying the danger and irresponsibility of online traders. Less than two years later, Merrill was changing its entire business structure to offer low-commission online trades to its customers. Many of the most inspired developments in Internet marketing were also created by these pioneers. From the use of community to foster site loyalty and consumer involvement to the use of transaction-based customer information to personalize the shopping experience, the early storefronts were innovators that have created many of the models that everyone selling on the Net now follows. While there are still, at this writing, questions about the ultimate profitability and viability of many of the B2C eRetail storefronts, there's no doubt that these entrepreneurs challenged some of the giant corporations of the day and "Amazon-ed" the sleeping giants into realizing that they'd better figure out how to compete in this new world.

The negatives of the pure B2C eStorefront are also well known. After five years in business, Amazon.com still cannot figure out how to make a profit on its millions of dollars in transaction volume. CDNOW, one of the poster boys of the early retail market, is in danger of going out of business, and some former glamour storefronts such as Boo.com and ToySmart have already succumbed. eRetailers from online drugstores to online pet shops are running out of cash and looking for buyers. The early conception of a warehouse-free retailer, who took orders through a website and then passed those orders to a fulfillment agent for shipping, has been abandoned as retailers realize they need to control the logistics of delivery and fulfillment in order to assure a positive customer experience. The cost of acquiring customers and rising above the din of dot.com marketing noise, including advertising, promotion, and the ubiquitous giveaways, has become one of the largest expenditures on every eRetailer's financial statement. The glut of low-value "ashtrays.com" entities that exploded in the gold rush atmosphere of the late 1990s made it that much harder for real value-creating retailers to find an audience. The "spray and pray" investing methodology of many venture capitalists (spraying money over many entrants in a market space and praying that one of them would find the management talent, technicians, marketing teams, customers, and business model required to create a profitable entity) has now turned into a financial drubbing that no amount of prayer will reconcile. Many Internet retail stocks have lost favor with investors to the tune of 80 percent or more of their value. Some analysts now question whether there will be *any* viable B2C businesses five years from now.

Is eRetail a fatally flawed business model, or will smart entrepreneurs learn the lessons of the pioneer days and create entities that will rival the Wal-Marts of the world? Or will it *be* the Wal-Marts of the world who bring their logistical and marketing expertise to the Web and finally make eRetail work? My take is not quite as negative as that of some analysts, but it's still all speculation—and time will tell. It seems clear that Amazon.com will in fact achieve profitability in the next few quarters and that some offline powerhouses will "get it" and go on to create online storefronts that duplicate their off-Net successes. For consultants, the questions we need to ask to be valuable advisors to our clients considering entry into the eRetail space are these:

- Does your proposed offering add any real value? Simply taking your offline store and popping it online is a weak excuse for an Internet business model. How are you using the Internet's unique capabilities to create a compelling value proposition for your customer?

- Does the organization and presentation of products on your site enhance the customer's control and experience? Does the customer have options that allow her to see the site organized in a way that fits her preferences and needs?

- Are you taking advantage of the Internet's inherent advantages of unlimited supply, unlimited time availability, and unlimited geographic reach? This can include issues such as globalization of currency and language and access to comprehensive virtual "shelves" of goods.

- Are you using the Internet's transaction and behavior-tracking capabilities to personalize the customer's experience? Are you enabling a community of interested individuals rather than a random assortment of shoppers?

- Have you looked at your business model holistically, taking into account the logistical, marketing, fulfillment, technical, financial, and design elements required to deliver a competitive customer experience?

Auctions

On May 29, 1995, Jerry Kaplan conducted a charity auction for the Boston Computer Museum entirely on the Internet. His small startup company, Onsale, had been unsuccessful at raising financing from the venture capitalists in Silicon Valley, but he believed so strongly in the concept of using the Internet as a forum for auctioning excess merchandise that he set up this event to prove his point. And prove it he did: From this symbolic start, Onsale had grown to a million registered users by 1998 and auctioned off over $200 million in merchandise that year. Kaplan had a brilliant insight that drove his consumer-based auction business: Auctions are more than just a way to exchange goods; they're a form of entertainment. Onsale's early advertising slogan urged Web shoppers to "get in on the action," then transformed "action" into "auction." Over 90 percent of Onsale's customers are male and, as Kaplan states, "We've figured out a magical way to sell to men. We've created a whole new way to sell goods that appeals to male hunting instincts, competition, and skill. Our customers . . . will eat just about anything that can be sold in the online auction."[15] This insight has driven some of the biggest success stories on the Net. Onsale, in its current incarnation after its merger with Egghead.com, is one of the three largest retailers on the Web in dollar volume, with 2000 revenues expected to exceed half a billion dollars. eBay, of course, is the leader in the online consumer auction space and, with Amazon and Yahoo, is one of the three most recognized Internet brands. eBay has taken Kaplan's concept of shopping as entertainment and created a legion of addicted fans. More importantly, eBay is one of the few Internet businesses that's actually profitable, to the tune of $2.4 million in profits on sales of $47.3 million in 1999. eBay is also wildly popular with investors; although subject to the wide swings in value that characterize Internet stocks, eBay's market capitalization at this writing is over $12 billion.

In their simplest form, Internet auctions simply translate the bid-and-ask mechanisms of traditional auctions to the Net, often adding the extra attraction of multimedia presentation of the goods on sale. The early auction sites quickly learned that, to offer a compelling shopping experience to their customers, they needed to add community aspects, such as places to chat about the Pez® dispensers or Beanie Babies® on display, and online reviews of products and sellers. They also quickly grasped the need to integrate payment and delivery processes into the site.

The auction paradigm has quickly gone far beyond the simple marketplace for Pez® dispensers, however. The auction model popularized by Onsale and eBay has mutated into exchanges for everything from telecommunications bandwidth to bulk chemicals, from energy to mortgage loans, and from used cars to office supplies. This list is far from exhaustive, as new corporate-sponsored and neutral vertical-market exchanges pop up every day. The pricing mechanisms of the exchanges are also diverse, with variations from the "bid and ask" model familiar to any stock market trader to the Dutch auction in which the seller progressively lowers the price until the first buyer "bites" to the reverse auction popularized by Priceline.com, in which demand, rather than supply, is auctioned off.

Many of the most successful software developers in the Internet marketplace have built their businesses around enabling these auctions and exchanges. Ariba, Commerce One, Freemarkets, and dozens of others have created Internet-based software platforms that can be deployed to offer customers any of these permutations of the auction business model. The auctions and exchanges available on the Net today transcend the categories of business-to-business and business-to-consumer; they enable anyone to sell anything to any individual or group of interested buyers.

For Internet consultants and business strategists alike, this proliferation of Internet auctions has a profound meaning. The auction model is an illustration of one of the methods by which the enabling technology of the Internet identifies and attacks inefficiencies in markets. The fragmentation and disorganization of most marketplaces pre-Net allowed intermediaries to build businesses and impose profits by offering purchasers the convenience of an aggregated, orderly shopping experience without the onerous transaction costs associated with searching out, researching, and negotiating with multiple sellers in multiple locations. This Net-based auction model is so attractive that, by 2002, 52 percent of online business is expected to be transacted via auctions, according to Forrester Research.[16]

The ability of the Net and the software offerings from Ariba and its brethren to create aggregated electronic marketplaces of products and purchasers from anywhere, anytime, threaten the business models of retailers and intermediaries everywhere. As an example of the topsy-turvy competitive environment that the Internet creates, eBay bought the venerable San Francisco auction house Butterfield & Butterfield, using its highly valued stock as currency to purchase the old-line veteran of the auction business. Not to be outdone, Amazon.com invested $45 million in the revered high-art auction house Sotheby's, with which it will develop a site for the exchange of collectibles such as coins, stamps, and memorabilia.

Exchanges do more than create a convenient marketplace that threatens to cut out the middleman; they also create a mechanism for exposing the true value, price, and cost of goods and services. When purchasers can see complete catalogs of products that fit their requirements, from suppliers around the world, at their convenience, from their desktop, how long can wholesale distributors retain their market positions? When prices rise or fall immediately based on the ebb and flow of supply and demand in real time, how long can manufacturers hope to sustain the "MSRP" (manufacturer's suggested retail price) fixed pricing mechanisms of the past?

The importance of the auction model on pricing can't be over-emphasized. It's critical to remember that fixed prices for goods, as obvious and permanent as they seem, are a relatively recent invention and a very vulnerable convention. Oil prices, for instance, once they were exposed to the dynamic auction model by becoming a tradable commodity on the open commodities exchange, quickly moved from a fixed price to a dynamic price set by traders. The economist Napier Collyns, a co-founder of the Global Business Network, a California economic consulting firm, is a strong proponent of what he calls the "barter economy." He thinks that people all over the world will one day buy the majority of their goods using online auctions. "For the first time, we'll really see supply and demand working," he says. The market, not corporations, will set prices. "It will be like the oil companies, which, for a hundred years, kept the price of oil in their own hands. Now the price of oil is decided on Wall Street."[17]

The new exchanges, from CheMatch in the bulk chemicals industry to Autobytel in the retail car industry, are disrupting the old marketplaces and squeezing enormous profits from their segments by finding and eliminating inefficiencies. As Autobytel CEO Mark Lorimer has said, even car dealers know that "sooner or later, the last stupid customer is going to walk through the door."[18] Altra Energy Technologies of Houston, one of the most successful of the new auction-based exchanges, has, in two short years of existence, captured more than 40 percent of all industrial buyers' propane trades and 10 percent of all their natural gas trades. Ingram Micro, a wholesale distributor of computer products to resellers, was stuck with more than $1 million worth of excess inventory each quarter. Then they created Auction Block. Rather than selling this excess off in bulk at fire-sale prices, Auction Block allows Ingram to auction it off, resulting in a doubling of revenues realized. "We always knew we were leaving money, a lot of money, on the table," says Ken Jenkins, a manager at Ingram. "We just couldn't figure out a way to get it."[19]

Not everything about the auction-based business model is rosy. Auctions can actually cause price distortions. People can get caught up in the competitive aspects of auctions and pay more than an item is worth and more than they would pay in the less competitive environment of a retail store. Economists, in fact, argue that auctions are inefficient for the buyer, since the price of the winning bid is often greater than the product's market value. Referred to in economic circles as the "winner's curse," this problem occurs widely in retail auctions, where individual buyers can react irrationally to the emotionally charged atmosphere of competitive bidding. Additionally, the financial aspects of the exchange business model are not yet clear. Will exchanges be able to collect revenue by charging participants a fee for joining, by taking a small cut of the action (commonly called the "transaction slice" model), or by actually taking ownership of the products, even momentarily, and then charging a margin for the convenience of handling and delivery?

Even the Securities and Exchange Commission has gotten involved in this debate, since some publicly traded exchanges report all revenue transacted through their sites as company revenues, even though their piece of the action may only be a tiny slice of that. Finally, after the dot.com crash of 2000, many analysts are changing their projections for the speed of acceptance of the exchange model. John Katsaros, a vice president at Internet market research firm Jupiter Communications, believes that it will be ten years or more before B2B eCommerce on the Web hits 80 percent of the total business-to-business transaction volume, and Yankee Group analyst Lisa Williams recently told *Business 2.0* that "Marketplaces won't take over the majority of B2B ecommerce."[20]

Internet consultants need to have an understanding of the various models of auctions that are in use in these exchanges. They fall into a few basic categories:

- The standard seller-controlled auction, in which sellers offer their products, collect bids, and determine who they wish to sell to. This is the typical "going once, going twice" auction that we're all familiar with from countless movies and TV shows, migrated to the Net, of which the eBay model is the prime example.

- The buyer-controlled or "reverse" auction, in which buyers advertise their desire to purchase a product or service at a certain price, and sellers decide whether they wish to complete the transaction. This is the Priceline "name your own price" model.

- The exchange, in which multiple buyers and sellers post their desire to buy and sell dynamically and matching offers are executed. Any stock trader will recognize this as the NASDAQ bid-and-ask model.

Apart from helping clients determine which auction model makes the most sense in their business context, Internet consultants must also advise clients about the following:

- *To have a clear strategy for revenue production from the auction model.* As we discussed before, there's real controversy over the long-term viability of the "transaction slice" model, as many analysts question whether exchange participants will accept paying a toll to perform their transactions. The fulfillment mode, in which exchanges actually take possession of the products, implies warehouse, shipping, and other logistical support. The method of collecting revenue and making a profit in the auction and exchange business is thorny and undefined, yet needs to be at the top of the list in the consultant-client conversation.

- *To remember that the information gathered from transactions has inherent value.* For instance, Egghead/Onsale will track the bids of losing bidders and inform them via e-mail when a similar item becomes available at their preferred price. Work with clients to ensure that they have a robust mechanism for capturing transaction data, tying it to specific customers, and analyzing it to deepen the customer relationship and to improve the site and the customer experience continuously.

- *To create systems that allow the site to regulate itself.* eBay has tackled the thorny issue of unscrupulous traders by creating a seller rating system that flushes thieves from the system. The ability to rate and rank sellers and products also creates the atmosphere of community.

- *To advise clients to focus on markets in which they have relationships and expertise.* One of the key determinants of success in B2B exchanges is domain expertise: Every marketplace, from chemicals to paper to sheetrock, has its own culture, its own measures of value, and its own relationships. The creators of exchanges must be familiar with these in order to set up an environment that is attractive to participants.

- *To look for ways to add value above the mere transaction.* Many exchange and auction sites are exploring add-ons such as specialized news content and community. For instance, Enron, the large natural gas supplier that has re-created itself as an Internet exchange giant, has created an energy news network that pipes the latest developments in the energy markets to the participants in its exchanges. Enron is also adding value for its exchange participants by offering such add-on features as insurance and weather futures contracts, which allow weather related businesses to hedge their economic bets against economic losses related to weather events!

Content Providers

I'm an active trader in the NASDAQ stock market, and one of my daily routines when I'm trading includes a visit to the Yahoo Finance site for the latest industry news; a check on Clearstation, a community of traders that offers recommendations and analysis; a look at CBS MarketWatch for the latest market action and analysis; and a review of Trading Markets, a website operated by a team of industry analysts that offers proprietary market commentary and recommendations. Most of these sites are free, supported by advertisers who wish to reach the audience of affluent, active market participants. I do pay a fee for access to Trading Markets because I've learned that the analysis is worth the cost.

The point of this glimpse into my private routines is to indicate that, contrary to much current popular analysis, the content model on the Internet is alive and well. There *are* many content sites, such as TheStreet.com, that soared in their stock market debuts and have since fallen to Earth. Many commentators in the early days of the Internet believed that the subscription model for access to content was going to be one of the most lucrative business models on the Net. Like everything in this environment, the pendulum has now swung in the opposite direction, and many commentators sound the death knell for the content model. As usual, the reality is a combination of both viewpoints. Some pay content sites will thrive; others will fade. Some sites will have value for some viewers, as Trading Markets does for me, and some sites will gain wide enough viewership to offer a compelling value to advertisers. Some, for reasons of competition, voice, value, experience, or inability to attract a viewership, will merge or expire.

I take a broad view of the concept of Internet content. Not only should proprietary intellectual property, such as the front page of *The New York Times,* be considered content, but also the search results of Yahoo or Alta Vista, the community information of iVillage.com and AOL, the news reported by ABCNews.com or CNN.com, and the entertainment content of MP3.com. Many commentators include portals as a separate Internet business model, but in my hierarchy they are simply another form of content. Just because in some cases the content is provided by a search engine, in some by professionals such as journalists and musicians, and in others by the community itself, as in chats and newsgroups, doesn't change the fact that it's the content that attracts the viewer.

In fact, the provision of content as part of the transaction is one of the main differentiators of Internet business. In the broadest sense, every viable Internet business is a content provider, as one of the key values of the Internet market space is the ability to take products and turn them from "stuff" into information-rich vessels. So Amazon takes each book and turns it into a website of its own, where authors can send personal messages to prospective buyers, readers can post reviews and comments, and communities can gather around and include the book in their "circle." Clearstation takes a simple security, such as a stock available on the NAS-DAQ exchange, and allows members to rate it, recommend or pan it, include it in model portfolios, and track its performance. CarSmart, rather than just posting a picture of a car and some advertising blurbage, provides detailed pricing, availability, and safety information, plus links to impartial rating sites such as Edmunds or Consumer Reports. Communities like AOL or iVillage combine content, commerce, and kinship to create a complete experience for like-minded Net citizens.

It's this ability to take an essentially neutral object of commerce, such as a shoe, car, or book, and turn it into an information-rich vessel of content that turns the Internet into the engine of added value that it is. As we discussed when we talked about basic business strategy, companies such as GE, before the Net, made tremendous efforts to migrate from product vendors to solution providers. This migration is, of necessity, focused around the information richness of the products that are sold so that a successful sale occurs, not when the customer buys the refrigerator, jet engine, or computer, but when the company and the client together implement that product in the way that provides the maximum value. Consultative, solution-oriented salespeople sell the information necessary to make the client successful, and the product is simply a vehicle to that success. The Internet, as we've repeated, is simply another step in that direction, allowing for cheap, convenient, and efficient transmission of the information content that clients need to make the right purchase decisions and to get value from the purchases they make. Consultants who look at content in this way will advise their clients wisely.

Collaboration Platforms

In the early days of the World Wide Web, when both the media and corporations were discovering the wide range of capabilities enabled by this new technology, the concept of intranets and extranets gained immediate popularity. The idea of using Internet standards, such as TCP/IP protocols and Web-based browsers, to create networks through which corporations could share forms, schematics, manufacturing information, product documentation, and other company information seemed to some the best use of these new tools. Firms rushed to migrate their networks to be compliant with Internet standards, then set up intranets to allow internal collaboration and sharing, and then, with the proper security in place, created extranets that allowed them to broaden the reach of collaboration to their trading partners, suppliers, and contractors.

In the few years since the first intranet was created, some companies have garnered a reputation for being leaders in the strategic use of Internet-based collaborative networks. Cisco, Hewlett-Packard, Mitsubishi Motors, and many others have used Internet standards to create networks that allow them to collaborate instantly with partners on designing, manufacturing, configuring, delivering, and supporting their products worldwide.

Cisco is the acknowledged master of this strategy. Through the use of three interconnected collaborative networks, Cisco has saved millions of dollars, built a motivated and informed team that leads the industry in results and retention, and assembled a worldwide empire of design and manufacturing partners that deliver the most competitive products in every market space in which it competes. The Cisco Connection Online (CCO) is the public face of this initiative, accessed through Cisco's main website at www.cisco.com. Through the use of this service, customers, resellers, and implementers of Cisco equipment can access detailed product specifications, personalized customer support, manuals and design documents, sales tools and presentations, as well as configuration and pricing information and can then actually purchase the gear they need. Cisco estimates that the use of this system, apart from the multi-billion dollars in purchases that it handles annually, has saved Cisco over $200 million a year in direct costs for customer support agents and technicians, while providing higher levels of customer service and satisfaction.[21] An added benefit of this site is the switching cost it imposes—once customers get used to the convenience and responsiveness of the site, they are reluctant to migrate to another supplier.

The Cisco Employee Connection (CEC), the second leg of this three-pronged collaborative network, is credited with saving Cisco operating costs of over $58 million annually by enabling benefit enrollment and status reporting, the network-based submission of expenses, employee communications, recruitment and retention, Web-based training, and online procurement, to name a few functions. More importantly, this system is credited as a key contributor to the loyalty and effectiveness of Cisco employees, whose revenue-per-employee achievement of $668,000 each is unmatched in its market space. I know from personal relationships with many Cisco employees that the availability of this superbly designed information resource is a key contributor to retention and team esprit de corps.[22]

As important as CCO and CEC are, however, the Cisco Manufacturing Connection is the cornerstone of Cisco's strategic Internet initiatives. Based on a strategic concept known internally as the "single enterprise system," Cisco has created a collaborative network that connects chip designers and manufacturers, component distributors, contract manufacturers, fulfillment companies, distributors, integrators, and resellers and allows them to function like one firm. Cisco owns just two of the thirty-eight manufacturing plants that build its products. Through acquisition, alliance, partnership, or business relationship, Cisco gains access to the technologies and competencies it needs to offer the most competitive product set. Through its investment in the infrastructure and applications that enable real-time collaboration, Cisco enables the designers, manufacturers, and implementers of its products to respond immediately to customer requirements, market conditions, and special circumstances.

Cisco is not, by any means, the only organization that has figured out how to use collaborative networks as a strategic advantage. On the contrary, examples abound of smart companies that are using this technology to revolutionize their value-delivery mechanisms. WebTV is a designer, manufacturer, and distributor of TV set-top boxes that enable customers to surf the Web using their televisions. But, unlike many other manufacturers whose name appears on their products, WebTV never touches the actual device. Through a complex chain of Internet-enabled relationships with component manufacturers such as Toshiba, built-to-order electronics manufacturers such as Flextronics, and licensees such as Sony, WebTV delivers value to clients by directing the efforts of a web of interconnected enterprises. Hewlett-Packard uses its extranet to coordinate manufacturing activities at its thirteen printer plants and eleven PC manufacturing plants worldwide. Mitsubishi Motors developed a dealer-connection network that allows it to collaborate immediately with five hundred dealers across the United States so Mitsubishi can select and manufacture those cars and trucks that are most likely to maximize its results. This system has cut vehicle lead times by 50 percent, with the corresponding savings in inventory carrying costs.[23]

Astute observers of this scenario should realize quickly that the effort to coordinate the activities of these suppliers is an effort in information sharing. From the design of the device to the materials list required to build it to the forecast for components to the tracking of deliveries for license management, each step of this collaborative manufacturing process is steeped in information. As organizations move toward the virtual, and as outsourced design and manufacturing becomes more the norm than the exception, product content information such as design drawings, CAD files, spreadsheets, text documents, bills of materials, engineering updates, bug reports, and the myriad other details that make up a finished product must be simultaneously available to all participants in the value chain. Some software firms, such as PTC and Agile Software, have jumped into this niche by developing Web-based product-collaboration software. This software allows designers to post specifications and engineering changes, route them through the appropriate levels of authorization, and make them available to the partners and contractors that need to see them, all through a secure intranet connection.

As in all the Internet business models we've reviewed, the information gathered from the transactions and interactions that take place in a collaboration network have intrinsic value. Through a thorough analysis of the data that is captured throughout the value chain, smart enterprises can make strategic decisions such as:

- What should the number, structure, and placement of my plants and warehouses be?

- Are all my plants, warehouses, and partners adding value? Should I close or disengage with any, or open more?

- How am I doing on inventory management? How can I optimize my use of inventory at the best cost?

- Are there any tasks that should be outsourced or insourced?

- Am I concentrating on my highest value products and services?

Consultants who are assisting clients in the design of collaborative networks need to be sure that the pertinent transaction data is being captured and that a strategic planning process is designed to analyze it and to continually improve the network and the firm based on that analysis.

Another point about collaborative networks: As with content, collaboration is a function that is bleeding into every Internet strategy. Most B2B exchanges, for instance, also have the capability for partners in their industry to step into a private "chat room" and develop one-on-one deals and alliances. Most exchanges also have the capability to create recurring transactions and to allow for the exchange of specifications and custom requirements. Collaboration in Internet strategies is not a single business model; it's a component of most complete Internet strategies.

Looking back at the Cisco example, it's clear that, as with all Internet strategies, consultants need to step back and take a critical look at the core functions and constituencies that the client firm is addressing. In Cisco's case, the functions of employee communication, customer and vendor relationships, and partner collaboration are the key areas that needed to be tackled in an Internet strategy. In different industries these key constituencies may differ, and it's the consultant's task to help the client think this through and build the collaborative network that most closely addresses those audiences.

Internet Business Service Providers

As we've discussed, disaggregation is a central outcome of the Internet business revolution, as enterprises look deeply into their business models and rethink their value propositions, core competencies, and supply chains. Just as "brick and mortar" companies need to make determinations as to whether they want to own or outsource their functions such as desktop PC support, shipping, or circuit board manufacture, so do Internet companies now have the opportunity to partner with companies that offer a wide range of outsourced services targeted at Internet business players.

From Internet infrastructure, through advertising management, to performance measurement, and to the complete hosting and management of websites, the Internet services business model has turned out to be one of the most lucrative and competitive marketplaces in this space. Companies such as Exodus Communications (providing secure and managed Web hosting services) through Inktomi and Akamai (providing technologies that optimize delivery of Internet content) to Doubleclick and AdAuction (which help Web entrepreneurs manage the selection and delivery of advertising to their sites) have sprung up and attracted the attention of both Wall Street and the Internet business community.

The Internet service provider space mirrors the Enterprise IT Model in that there are providers at all levels of the model. As we said in Chapter Two, the Enterprise IT Model divides IT functionality into the following layers:

- Infrastructure;
- Data;
- Application;
- Process; and
- Business.

If we analyze each of these layers in turn, we'll find that there is a robust market-place of businesses that are concentrating on providing services in each niche.

Infrastructure

Internet infrastructure providers range from companies such as Cisco (whose advertising boasts that "virtually all of the world's Internet traffic moves through Cisco equipment") to the traditional telephone companies that provide pure "bit mover" services, to the new-age data communications providers such as Qwest and Level 3, who are focused on building fiber optics based IP-protocol networks that deliver the high bandwidth that many Internet business models require.

Some very innovative and creative business and technical models have emerged in this space, such as that designed by Akamai, the current leader in Internet content delivery optimization. Through the use of proprietary technology and a distributed network of Web servers, Akamai offers services to Internet commerce companies and content providers that make serving information faster and more reliable. As the type of content changes from static text to dynamic media such as audio, video, and animation, many organizations are willing to pay service fees to providers such as Akamai to ensure that customers experience the best, fastest, and most reliable content delivery possible.

Another innovative player in this space is Inktomi, whose offerings actually bridge the layers of infrastructure, data, and application. Their infrastructure services include their proprietary Traffic Service, which boasts of its ability to "improve the quality of service for Internet users." Inktomi also offers streaming media services that fit into the data layer, as well as caching software, an application that Internet managers can use to speed up the performance of their sites.

Data

In Internet terms, data typically means content, and there are many entrepreneurs who have figured out that one billion websites gobble up a lot of content. From well-known providers such as CNN, ABCnews, and Reuters to newer entrants such as Real Networks, I-Syndicate, and Intervu, the list of content providers is enormous and growing. The New York Stock Exchange and the NASDAQ now get as much of their revenue from providing information on transactions as from the transactions themselves. Advertising content providers such as Doubleclick allow Internet entrepreneurs to outsource the entire advertising process, from attracting the right advertisers for their site based on interest and community, to designing the ads, to actually serving them up to Web surfers as they move from page to page on the Net. Even the pornography business, one of the most profitable Internet niches, has purveyors of content for those sites that appeal to those tastes.

Data on the performance and competitive positioning of Web businesses is also an exploding business. Organizations such as Media Metrix are totally focused on analyzing the speed, growth, revenue, profitability, and viewership of websites. eMarketer has created a stellar reputation as the premier analyst of Internet marketing activity. Even old-line businesses, such as the Neilsen ratings of TV measurement fame, have converted their business models to focus on measurement of Web traffic and results. Consultants should be familiar with these sources of Web statistics, as they provide eCommerce clients with valuable impartial information about the success (or failure) of their Web business models. Many of them also provide consulting services that advise clients on techniques for generating more page views, attracting more buyers, and optimizing shopping carts or search capabilities. As an example of how specialized this website measurement business has become, there exists a highly regarded firm that measures and consults on nothing but customer experience. Creative Good, a self-described site for "monitoring the customer experience" in eCommerce, publishes a weekly e-mail, Good Experience, that rates the best and worst of sites based on a simple theory: "The customer experience is the key driver of success online."[24] Creative Good publishes a customer experience "best practices" website, posts a "Hall of Fame" and a "Hall of Shame," and consults with clients to help create the most effective customer experience possible.

By investigating and exploring the trade magazines, and searching the Web itself, consultants can gain familiarity with these providers of data, measurement, and evaluation services and can help their clients select the ones that will add the most value for their customers.

Application

The Internet has enabled an entirely new business model—the application service provider (ASP). Due to a convergence of events, including the acceptance of outsourcing, the standardization of Internet network protocols, the ability of client-side browsers to run sophisticated Java-based applications, and the robustness and ubiquity of high-speed data bandwidth, it has become technically feasible for enterprises to have applications delivered on a per-use or transactional basis by service providers rather than having to own and support those applications internally. In the early years of computing, mainframe systems were too expensive for many enterprises, and so service bureaus were developed that allowed smaller companies to use applications and computers through timeshare arrangements. This ASP movement is a swing of the pendulum back in that direction, with the added benefit of rich, desktop-based distributed computing rather than the dumb green-screen CRTs of the mainframe era. We've previously reviewed *ad infinitum* the migration from product to service that has characterized the business environment in recent years, and this new business model is another example of that trend.

The standard ASP model is to deliver access to an application as a service over the Internet rather than as a licensed product with a one-time purchase fee. The ASP, in effect, rents the software to the client and takes responsibility for all the management, hosting, customization, maintenance, and support required to deliver the application's functionality. This model has expanded rapidly, however, to include other types of outsourced services delivered over the Net, such as outsourced infrastructure, outsourced process providers, communication service providers, and vertical-market service providers. Outsourcing of e-mail, as an example, has become a crowded competitive niche, with players such as Software.com, USA.net, Mail.com, Critical Path, and others attracting large venture capital investments and closing deals with the likes of American Airlines and Ford Motor. All of these providers have in common the fact that they are made possible by the standardization of the Internet as a delivery mechanism and the browser as an application platform.

Forrester Research estimates that Fortune 1000 companies spend an average of $8.9 million each for every large-scale business application they deploy. When maintenance, upgrades, and fixes are included, the per-seat total for a single new application comes to about $15,600. Another major IT analyst, The Meta Group, estimates that most of these organizations deploy and manage an average of fifty such applications.[25] When we do the math, it becomes clear that the cost associated with the old license-and-support model of software deployment is an expensive proposition. These expenditures have driven enterprises to consider alternatives to this old model and have created a business opportunity for astute entrepreneurs.

Other factors in the IT marketplace have also contributed to the growth of the ASP model. The shortage of application experts has driven many companies to explore external application deployment. The acquisition, training, salary, and retention of IT labor can make up more than 70 percent of the cost of application deployment,[26] and organizations typically can get little leverage from their investment, as dedicated expertise is needed in every vertical application in use within the enterprise. ASPs can leverage these experts across many enterprises that are using the same application and so obtain economies of scale that translate into lower application costs. The cost of running an internal data center is also enormous and subject to obsolescence (and reinvestment) at an increasingly rapid pace. When many applications for many enterprises can be hosted in one large data center owned by an outsourced service provider, further economies can be realized. Speed of deployment is critical in this "Internet-time" economy, in which access to a new application can drive real competitive advantage. ASPs with extensive facilities and staff—and with the application already running and ready—can deliver this speed. For all these reasons, the ASP model is gaining acceptance from both corporate strategists and from Wall Street analysts.

It's also important to note that the software giants, such as Microsoft and Oracle, are actively supporting this movement to rented software. Microsoft, for instance, has partnered with ASPs such as Digex, CenterBeam, and Concentric to offer usage-based access to its applications. Oracle has gone a step further by becoming its own ASP and offering clients direct access to its applications on a hosted basis. Other software developers, such as Ariba, CommerceOne, and Seibel, have also partnered with ASPs such as Corio and USInternetworking and have provided these partners with special versions of their software specifically engineered to enable usage-based deployments.

The ASP business model, however, has not been immune to the bursting of the Internet bubble. Pandesic, an early entry into the ASP market that was a joint venture of German software giant SAP and chipmaker Intel, abruptly closed its doors in late July 2000, sending out a bombshell e-mail note to its clients with the shocking message that "We are winding down our business because we do not see a timely road to profitability." Analysts blame Pandesic's business model for the surprise failure, noting that 80 percent of the company's client base was made up of small dot.coms with no revenues and unproven business models.[27] As an early entrant into the ASP market, Pandesic made the mistake of hitching its wagon to the star of the B2C marketplace, only to see that star fall as the problems inherent in consumer eCommerce became apparent. The revenue model was also an issue. Pandesic's transaction slice of 2 percent of all revenue generated by its clients' sites just wouldn't play in a market in which margins are slim and getting slimmer. As Randy Covill of IT analyst firm AMR Research noted, "Profit margins in retailing are just not that high. To say you're going to take that much away is a hard sell. Companies resist giving up a slice of their business in return for a service."[28]

Industry revenue figures are another indication that the ASP market, like many Internet markets, was over-hyped. The entire ASP industry generated a weak $300 million in revenue in 1999, and some of the largest, best-regarded players had huge losses. USInternetworking, for instance, lost $103 million on sales of $35 million, and Corio, Microsoft's main partner in the ASP space, lost $45 million on revenue of just $5.8 million.

Pandesic is not the only ASP that will bite the dust. According to The Gartner Group, 60 percent of the five hundred players in the ASP marketplace will be gone by the end of 2000, folded or consolidated. Many of the core value propositions that fueled the enthusiasm for the ASP model have been discredited. The idea that the same software can work as well for a paper manufacturer as for a computer wholesaler has been shot down by clients, who, in the flush times of the last few years, have decided to spend the extra money to build rather than buy, as that enables them to get the features and flexibility they want. Paula Stout, Pandesic spokesperson, in explaining the issues that forced them to shut their doors, emphasizes this point: "Our number one competitor was people who were building in-house rather than outsourcing."[29]

All is not gloom in the ASP space, however. Many sharp competitors in this market are learning the lessons of the crash and revamping their business models to address the failings. In response to the complaint that one size doesn't fit all in business applications, many ASPs are specializing in a particular industry. David Boulanger, a director at AMR Research, points out that smart ASPs will "get a reference customer in a particular industry and then try to resell that solution to other companies in that industry. You won't see ASPs going after twenty different companies in twenty different industries anymore."[30] The marketplace has also taught ASPs that customers won't change their businesses to fit a piece of software. ASPs are building consulting organizations that can help clients develop a complete solution, rather than just renting a canned piece of software. Trevor Gruen-Kennedy, chairman of the ASP Industry Consortium and an unofficial spokesman for the industry, still has high hopes for the ASP concept. He says, "In the fourth quarter of 2000 we're going to see a real end user community emerge, and we'll get past all the experimental pilots. They [the ASPs] are starting to make gains on wins and deployments."[31]

All of these factors complicate the role of an eConsultant in helping clients make the right decisions. Understanding the issues and keeping on top of dynamic developments is a must for advisors who hope to steer their clients to an appropriate decision in terms of outsourced services. As a consultant, you may be asked to advise both entrepreneurs thinking of becoming service providers, as well as enterprises considering the use of an external service provider to support their business applications. When advising clients considering an entry into the ASP market, consultants should counsel entrepreneurs on the following points:

- *Carefully consider your capabilities.* Where does your expertise lie? If you are a guru in telecommunications, explore the possibilities of providing hosted telecom services such as voice mail, Internet telephony, or unified messaging. If your expertise is focused on data center operations, consider an infrastructure hosting business model. Work from your strengths, as outstanding execution is required in this competitive marketplace.

- *Target your market.* Are you going after small/medium businesses? What applications or services do they require, versus the ones that the Fortune 500 enterprise would need? How will the support and maintenance requirements be specialized based on the segment of the market you are attacking? If you are targeting a vertical industry, is the market size large enough to support your model and is the value proposition compelling enough to allow you to exploit that market?

- *Decide how much customization and integration your offering requires.* Customization of applications to fit each client and the integration of applications with existing systems is a complex and expertise-intensive activity that requires professional services and project management capability. Consultants must help clients dig down into the realities of executing on the strategies they are considering.

- *Determine your marketing strategy.* Is the entrepreneur considering a broad strategy, which implies less customization and integration and more speed and ease of use, or a more vertical, customer-intimate strategy that will require the creation of a professional services organization, extensive relationship building, and heavy program management? Horizontally focused ASPs will assemble a suite of applications that will appeal to all companies, while vertical service providers will target a specific market such as government, healthcare, or education. The decision to go horizontal or vertical will drive the entire business strategy.

- *Understand that ASPs face the same build-or-buy decisions as their clients.* Because of the increasingly granular level of outsourced services available, service providers can assemble their data center, delivery infrastructure, support functions, and other processes from other providers. Corio, one of the biggest ASPs, for instance, actually uses Exodus Communications for its data center facilities! By helping entrepreneurs evaluate their market, positioning, technology, and service strategies, consultants can help clients decide how to assemble these components into the most profitable and competitive offering.

- *Know how customer service and support will be handled.* The decision whether to handle this in-house or to outsource it can have a significant impact on costs and profitability and on the level of customer satisfaction. Competent consultants must help clients walk through this important strategic decision and decide whether this is a core process they must control.

- *Focus on customer concerns.* Uptake of ASP services has been hampered by a few core concerns of prospects, namely control and security. Obviously, service providers wishing to succeed in this market must provide the most robust security feasible; and any breach of that security will be punished severely by the marketplace. Service providers must also address the control concerns of prospects. ASPs must make clients comfortable with their ability to keep up with growth. They must assure clients that they will be allowed to participate in upgrade decisions, to monitor their use of applications and facilities, and to apply the latest technology to their business needs. In short, they must be prepared to sell against the competition, which in this case is the internal deployment and control of the data center and application.

For enterprises that are considering the ASP model of application deployment, numerous issues must be considered, including the following:

- *Pricing model.* Since this deployment scenario is driven by the desire to gain economies and efficiencies, it naturally should follow that the enterprise gets a favorable deal. This business model is so new, however, that the pricing structures vary all over the map. Some ASPs look for a multi-year contract, typically from eighteen to thirty-six months. Others are developing software that allows monitoring of application use at a very granular level and so enables per-seat, per-use pricing. Consultants need to help clients perform a comprehensive comparison between their costs of internal deployment, support, and labor and the proposed external pricing structure and ensure that the deal makes sense.

- *Control and flexibility.* Information technology is a competitive weapon, and enterprises need to ensure that they aren't fighting new wars with old weapons. The traditional application outsourcers, such as IBM or EDS, manage individual data centers and applications on an enterprise-by-enterprise basis and can build flexibility into their contracts to ensure that customers stay up-to-date on software features. ASPs, with their shared-application model, have to satisfy a broad range of customers with any enhancements they make to their underlying software and so have offered clients less flexibility. Clients looking at an ASP arrangement must assess their own need to stay on top of the latest versions and features of the software they're using, and any contract must include provisions for upgrade of hardware and software and must allow the enterprise to participate in those decisions that affect their business.

- *Security.* Data stored by the ASP, whether on its system or on those of an external provider, must be secured, encrypted, and protected by robust security processes. Consultants can help clients ensure that the appropriate security technology, such as VPNs, firewalls, proxy servers, and encryption, are in place and used according to documented procedures. Enterprises should insist on some liability protection from the service provider so that inappropriate data access or data loss doesn't create undue liability.

- *Availability and performance standards.* The ability to process transactions according to defined performance guarantees must be part of the agreement, and enforcement methods must be documented. Average response times, measured by outside services such as Service-Metrics or Keynote, are recommended.

- *Redundancy and contingency standards.* These are necessary so that no single point of failure, either internal to the service provider or external, such as outsourced bandwidth, can impact overall system availability.

- *Scalability and growth capability.* These must be negotiated as part of the agreement. Consultants cannot let their enterprise clients get entangled in a multimonth agreement with a service provider that hinders their growth, strategic positioning, or competitiveness.

- *Continuity standards.* As many of Pandesic's customers found out to their dismay, ASPs can go out of business and take their clients' business-critical software with them. Most clients of ASPs decided on outsourcing precisely to avoid the expense of building an in-house IT department and so have no fallback capabilities if their provider shuts its doors. Ed Vincent, CEO of Citystuff.com, a Pandesic client who was left out in the cold when the provider went under, counsels others to build a clause into their contracts that grants them access to the ASP's software in case they cease operations. "It simply never occurred to me [to get that protection up-front]," he recently told *CIO* magazine, "but it will be in the next contract I sign!"[32]

Process

On July 26, 2000, the Federal Trade Commission charged seven Internet-based retailers with violations of the Mail and Telephone Order Rule and levied fines totaling $1.5 million. Among the offenses noted in the complaint were the failure to notify customers of delays in delivery of orders, failure to ship orders as promised, and the taking of orders that they couldn't reasonably expect to fulfill. Among those companies cited were large players such as Macy's, ToysRUs.com, CDNow, and KBKids.com, as well as Patriot Computer, HoneyBaked Ham, and Minidiscnow.com.[33]

For many of these organizations, this incident has been a catalyst to increased focus and spending on infrastructure and back-office functions. In fact, the FTC agreed to lower fines, originally as high as $1 million, for those companies that would agree to upgrade their capabilities. ToysRUs.com, for instance, has tripled the size of its fulfillment operation by adding new facilities in California and Pennsylvania. KBKids.com is spending $7 million to upgrade its fulfillment infrastructure.[34]

For many Internet businesses, however, the outsourcing of the fulfillment function is a better choice than massive expenditures on in-house capabilities. Take GroceryWorks.com, an entrant in the grocery home delivery space. "It would be crazy to think we could build an electronic logistics system on our own," says president and founder Kelby Hagar.[35] By partnering with fulfillment expert EXE Technologies, GroceryWorks has achieved on-time delivery for 97 percent of its nearly seven thousand daily orders.

Dominant players in the offline world of shipping and fulfillment are now introducing offerings focused on the dot.com world. Both Federal Express and United Parcel Service have announced eCommerce offerings that incorporate fulfillment services.

Shipping and fulfillment are not the only processes that Internet businesses can take advantage of. A review of a recent issue of *Business 2.0*, for instance, includes advertisements for outsourcers of human resource functions, customer returns, credit management, employee training, marketing, and even the complete IT function. Many of these providers blur the line between process outsourcers and ASPs we described above, but that line is not very meaningful anyway. The key point for consultants is that the explosion in interest and opportunity on the Net has also created an explosion in service providers willing to take over—and take responsibility for—key business processes. The concerns about security, performance, integration, pricing, and scalability are the same. And, as with the ASP issues discussed above, consultants must be prepared to help clients analyze their business strategies and make the right decisions about functions to outsource or keep inside.

Business

It's critical to note that this is just a representative sampling of some Internet business models that have garnered attention in this first inning of the Internet revolution. The strategies outlined here are by no means conclusive—and how could they be? If this is truly a transformation, as I believe it is, then the most innovative and surprising new concepts are yet to be born! The creation of Internet-enabled value chains explodes the model of the horizontal enterprise, doing everything from design to manufacture to marketing to fulfillment, and replaces it with a virtual model that assigns tasks to the partner or entity that has the greatest competency and efficiency. As the Internet business era unfolds, the different ideas that talented and creative entrepreneurs devise for disaggregating traditional businesses and creating new niches and capabilities is impossible to predict. What can be predicted, however, is that new models will advance that allow organizations to focus on their strengths, whether marketing, implementing, or inventing, and that depend on partners and allies—and even competitors—to provide key components of their offerings. Smart consultants who want to participate in this revolution must understand the issues we've outlined here, and must make it their business and devotion to invest the energy and curiosity required to keep up with the gyrations and mutations of this dynamic economy.

End Notes

1. Hammer, M., & Champy, J. *Reengineering the Corporation: A Manifesto for Business Revolution.* New York: HarperBusiness, 1993.

2. White, J. Reengineering Gurus Take Steps to Remodel. *Wall Street Journal,* Nov. 26, 1996, p. 1.

3. Sawhney, M. Going Global. *Business 2.0,* May 2000, p. 178.

4. Nickell, J. Auction This, eBay. *Business 2.0,* May 2000, p. 185.

5. Siegal, D. *Futurize Your Enterprise.* New York: John Wiley & Sons, 2000.

6. Negroponte, N. *Being Digital.* New York: Knopf, 1995.

7. Modall, M. *Now or Never.* New York: HarperBusiness, 2000, p. 84.

8. iVillage press release. iVillage Survey: What Turns Women On-Line. *www.ivillage.com,* Feb. 5, 1998.

9. Tchong, M. *www.iconocast.com.* July 1, 1999.

10.. Carpenter, P. *E-Brands.* Boston: Harvard Business School Press, 1999, p. 210.

11. Timmers, P. *Electronic Commerce: Strategies and Models for Business-to-Business Trading.* Chichester, England: John Wiley & Sons, 1999.

12. Slywotzky, A. *Value Migration.* Boston: Harvard Business School Press, 1996.

13. The Boston Consulting Group, San Jose, CA. *The State of Online Retailing 3.0,* April 17, 2000.

14. Lawrence, S. E-Commerce Spotlight: Hard Numbers on e-Christmas 1999. *The Industry Standard,* Jan. 24, 2000.

15. Littman, J. Gentlemen, Place Your Bids. *Upside Magazine,* June 1998, p. 64.

16. Daly, J. Let's Make a Deal. *Business 2.0,* June 1, 1999.

17. Cate, T. The Auction Economy. *RedHerring,* May 1, 2000.

18. Downes, L. Exchanges for Everything. *Business 2.0,* Jan. 17, 2000.

19. Daly, J. Let's Make a Deal. *Business 2.0,* June 1, 1999.

20. Donahue, S. B-to-B Better Be Patient. *Business 2.0,* Dec. 26, 2000.

21. Hartman, A., & Sifonis, J. *Net Ready.* New York: McGraw-Hill, 2000, pp. 254–257.

22. ibid.

23. Quinn, C. Intelligent Commerce and the E-Business Revolution: Achieving Supply-Chain Excellence Through Technology. San Francisco: Montgomery Research, 2000.

24. *www.goodexperience.com.*

25. Kula, J., & Weis, T. *Application Service Providers: End of the First Inning.* Boston: TeleChoice, Nov. 1999.

26. ibid.

27. Koch, C. Boy, That Was Fast! *CIO,* Nov. 15, 2000.

28. ibid.

29. ibid.

30. ibid.

31. ibid.

32. ibid.

33. Bacheldor, S., & Konicki, S. Long Arm of the Law. *Information Week,* Aug. 7, 2000.

34. ibid.

35. ibid.

chapter FIVE

Building the Architecture

THE DANGER OF DOWNTIME

On January 1st, 1996, America Online declared a change in its pricing policy: Rather than charging customers according to their usage of the service, AOL announced its intention to allow unlimited use for a flat monthly fee of $19.95. Over the next few months, the service was thrown into chaos as system usage spiked and the ability of AOL's telecommunications infrastructure to handle callers was overwhelmed. After being down for twenty-four hours in June 1996, AOL had to shell out $3 million in customer rebates.

On January 8th, 1999, the Charles Schwab & Company website crashed for an entire day, leaving customers unable to access their account records or perform trades. On April 26th, 1999, the site experienced a forty-five-minute outage in its trading systems that prevented customers from performing transactions in the middle of the trading day. Schwab eventually settled with over three hundred customers to the tune of over $1 million for problems accessing its online trading systems.[1]

During the week of June 7th, 1999, eBay, the popular consumer auction site, experienced numerous outages, including one twenty-two-hour outage that resulted in a 26 percent plunge in the company's stock price and a decline of 18 percent in items on auction at the site. eBay subsequently announced that its revenue for the quarter would drop from an expected $5 million to around $3 million due to the outage. According to audience measurement numbers from Nielsen NetRatings, Yahoo's auction site benefited significantly from eBay's outage. Yahoo hastily began a promotion of radio ads highlighting the fact that its auction site was available. The traffic at auctions.yahoo.com rose from about 62,000 unique visitors on Thursday to 105,000 on Friday and 135,000 on Saturday, according to Nielsen NetRatings. At Amazon.com's auction site, meanwhile, that number leaped from 86,000 Thursday to 132,000 Saturday.[2]

On February 1, 2000, E*Trade, the pioneer of online stock trading, installed a new software program on some of the servers in its Web data center. On February 2nd and 3rd, customers were unable to place buy-or-sell orders or access their account balances due to a glitch in the new trading software. E*Trade's stock price tumbled over 10 percent, from 62 to 55¼, customers defected in droves, and the New York State Attorney General initiated an investigation into the business practices of E*Trade and other online brokerages.[3]

On February 7, 2000, a coordinated "denial of service" attack by hackers overwhelmed the Yahoo site, causing the Web's second most popular destination (after AOL) to be unavailable for most of that day. In the following week, Buy.com, eBay, ZDNet, E*Trade, and CNN.com were targeted by the same type of attacks, and user access was disrupted at each site. Ironically, even the FBI, the federal agency with responsibility for policing these kinds of malicious activities on the Net, has been a victim. A distributed denial of service attack shut down the FBI's website for a week in May 1999. That attack was tracked back to a sixteen-year-old from Israel who also broke into the Senate and White House websites in retaliation for home raids of about forty members of his Global Hell hacking group.[4]

Fred Matteson, chief technologist for Schwab, commenting on the spate of system problems at the online brokerages, has remarked, "What's happened in online investing is that customer expectations have changed as the number of customers has increased. Now, the expectation is that there is no time that it is OK for the site to be down. As a result, the old notions of how we built computer systems are no longer valid because computer systems fail and our customers don't allow failure."[5] Maynard Webb, the president of eBay Technologies, agrees. Talking about his experience when he first took the president's job at the online auction house, he recalls, "I drove up to eBay and saw CNN and CNBC outside, and it gave me a sense of the kind of attention any blip might receive."[6]

These incidents highlight some important points about the growth of Internet business and the technical challenges associated with that growth:

- For consumers and businesses to migrate their critical activities to the Internet, they need assurance that the Net is robust, secure, and dependable. For everything from personal finance to corporate purchasing, downtime is unacceptable.

- Even for less critical activities like auction trading, the expectation level of users has risen dramatically.

- The cost of downtime, in terms of lost revenue opportunities, lost investor confidence (resulting in plummeting stock valuations), loss of customer trust, loss of competitive advantage, and actual monetary damages, can be staggering. Downtime of just one minute could cost sites as much as $10,000, according to the Standish Group, a research consultancy.[7] By that count, a two-hour blackout carries a price tag of $1.2 million.

- Security, performance, and redundancy issues take on a significantly elevated role on the public Internet, where, unlike the corporate data center, outages affect a whole world of users rather than just a department or a single organization.

Sites don't need to be down for customers to be driven to the competition. Studies show that slow download time is the prevailing reason for customers to leave a site and surf to a competitor's site.[8] While the "eight-second rule" (which states that customers will become impatient and abandon sites that take longer than that to load) is not corroborated by any research, many sites still use it as the standard. For instance, Jan Hier-King, senior vice president of electronic trading technology for Schwab, as part of her regular routine of keeping tabs on the performance of the company's site, uses a stopwatch to periodically sample the site and ensure that it meets the eight-second test. When interviewed recently by *The New York Times*, she tested the site with a stopwatch in hand and then noted with relief, "Everything looks good," when the site's Web pages loaded in less than eight seconds. "Hopefully, today will be uneventful."[9]

An Interview
with Chuck Krutsinger

In a recent interview I conducted with Chuck Krutsinger, COO for Interlink Group,[10] an eCommerce consultancy in Denver, Chuck gave me his opinion of the differences between client-server application development and Web development:

"I think that, with the Internet, IT is changing from what the game used to be. It's a completely new game that uses some of the same technologies and some of the same skills, but brings them to a whole new level. It's completely different to build a system that has a 99.9 percent uptime than one that has 98 percent uptime.

"It's like the difference between a 72 golfer and a 68 golfer. It's a few strokes, but it's a whole different level of play and competition. When you expose your company's brand through the Web, and when the customer's experience of doing business with you is through the Web, the demand is 99.9 percent uptime, immediate, intuitive usability, and flawless software. That's what our clients expect. IT departments never had to meet these standards before. When I developed claims systems in 1990, claims personnel went through several weeks of training on how to use that system and then went through several months of gaining proficiency. If I'm going online with an insurance company, I want to use the site right now with no training, no online help. So user interface design is at a completely different level. If the claims department system went down a few years ago, the claims department put up with that. If I'm a customer of an insurance company online, I'm not putting up with that.

"People in the IT field, whether consultants or IT professionals, need to really be clued in to what the new rules of the game are. How do you design systems for 99.9 percent uptime, for bug-free delivery, and for intuitive usability? I've never spoken to anyone at Amazon. My whole exposure to the brand is based on my experience at the site, how well they take my order, how well they ship it to me. Similarly with Schwab, a traditional brick-and-mortar company, I haven't spoken to anyone there in almost ten years. I do all my business with them online. I filled out the application online, sent them a check, do my trades. My whole perception of Schwab today is how easy is it to use their website. Schwab has back-office systems that their brokers use. If all they did was open those back-office systems to me, they wouldn't have addressed my real needs. I'm not a broker, and I'm not a captive audience. Those companies that simply extend their existing systems so that their customers and trading partners can get to them haven't filled the bill."

The architect of an eBusiness infrastructure needs to be concerned with all these elements. In organizations across the business spectrum, from those explicitly engaged in Internet-based consumer commerce to those integrating Net access into their IT infrastructures for research, development, customer service, or its myriad other potential uses, the transformation of the Web into a fundamental component of their enterprise infrastructure has resulted in fundamental changes in their approach to IT architecture and design. It's too early to predict completely how the Net will change the disciplines of IT architecture, design, and operations, but it clearly is driving systems designers to new levels of creativity in solving performance, availability, and contingency problems. The typical IT consultant, prior to the migration to the Internet, had a strong background in the disciplines of IT infrastructure or application design and could add value to clients in the creation of strategies for system robustness and performance. Internet architects must plan to incorporate new elements such as caching, IP traffic management, load balancing, and content replication and to provide a level of availability and disaster-resistance that was unheard of previously. Traditional methods of capacity planning no longer apply in this time of ubiquitous and constant connectivity, and old methods of growth projection, backup and contingency planning, and resource scheduling are no longer acceptable. The Internet consultant must turn the corner in her thought process and must recognize that the infrastructure that powers her client's Internet presence, in many cases, *is* the business. This realization creates a new benchmark of technical competency for Internet consultants and teams as they take responsibility for helping clients build IT architectures that deliver never-before-seen levels of value.

Before we look at the eBusiness technical design process I'll propose in this chapter, I want to insert a word of clarification. I won't try to lead readers to specific technical solutions in this section by talking about UNIX vs. NT or Oracle vs. SQL Server. I'm not going to delve into different caching solutions or the various vendors of Java-based shopping-cart applications. These offerings and technologies change so quickly, and the underlying technical requirements that drive these decisions are so complex, that this is not an appropriate forum for that type of discussion. I believe that, without quoting ancient Chinese parables about giving fish or teaching to fish, it's clearly of more benefit to have a discipline and a methodology that drive the decision process than it is to have a "canned" preference that is then force fit into all situations. Consultants who have a detailed and deliberate process to follow, whether selecting Web servers or database software, will always deliver better, more appropriate solutions than those who walk into client engagements with preconceived preferences based on yesterday's successes. In short, we'll develop a process for advising clients on infrastructure and stay away from specific product discussions.

eBUSINESS TECHNICAL DESIGN PROCESS

Many analysts, with the benefit of hindsight, have looked back on developments since the introduction of the World Wide Web and have created some categories for understanding the increasing sophistication of websites. The early commercial sites were typically static, one-way publishing vehicles, often used either by the marketing department to post the contents of the company brochure (thus coining the term "brochureware") or by the investor relations team to display the latest annual report or by human resources to offer a company list of e-mail addresses and telephone numbers. I'll call these Phase 1 sites.

On Phase 2 sites, businesses began to discover some of the interactive capabilities offered by development environments such as Java and CGI scripts and used these capabilities to begin a conversation with site visitors, allowing them to join a community of users, participate in rudimentary chat rooms, leave suggestions, and request information. This Phase 2 activity raised the bar on both sides of the interaction. These sites enabled customers to begin developing a relationship with both the business behind the site and with other site visitors. They forced the creators and managers of Phase 2 sites to add more sophisticated database and support capabilities, as someone needed to gather, analyze, and act on all the information generated by this interaction.

Phase 3 led to the explosion in eCommerce, as Web-enabled catalogs and shopping carts created a virtual retail environment and auction technology initiated the business-to-business exchange movement. The need for real-time inventory management, advanced transaction tracking and credit monitoring applications, and mechanisms for managing the complex back-office picking, packing, and shipping operations made Phase 3 another significant leap in complexity and brought to business sponsors additional requirements for financial commitments and additional management overhead.

Phase 4 websites incorporate all the elements described above, plus the added complications associated with the creation of virtual supply chains and value chains. The ability for partners across the value chain to share product forecasts, collaborate on requirement definitions and product designs, build products based on needs expressed by customers in real time, and grant visibility across the chain into the status of ongoing operations requires another level of commitment, as former competitors or suppliers become partners and are required to change their basic philosophies regarding the boundaries of the enterprise.

An important note in reviewing these phases of website development is that they represent an evolution over time. As strategists and their advisors grasped the implications of new technologies and applied them to their websites, they incrementally migrated toward greater and greater interactivity and functionality. The efforts of many individual enterprises mirror this evolution. A single company creating an Internet presence will often follow the same path toward increased complexity that the Internet community followed, starting as a brochure site and evolving toward a Web-enabled value chain. One of the most important lessons for eConsultants to remember is that this is not merely a technical exercise. Every elevation in the level of eBusiness sophistication requires not only advances in underlying technology, but new modes of corporate management, communication, leadership, collaboration, and cooperation.

This four-phase hierarchy of website sophistication is presented as a tool that consultants can use to help clients think about the results they're trying to achieve and about the commitments, both financial and in human resources, they're prepared to make. I recommend that consultants use this framework as a facilitation tool when discussing Web projects and help clients understand the fundamental theme: The operational, staffing, and support requirements increase exponentially as sites become more complex and take on more integration and business transformation components. This must be a central tenet of all our Internet technical activities. In all IT projects, the support and operational aspects of systems are as relevant in providing ongoing business benefit as the features and benefits designed into the system. In Internet projects, in which the technology is changing at an alarming rate, the systems we design are exposed to the whole world and not merely a department, and the competition for experienced staff is more ruthless than ever, competent Internet consultants must always remind clients of the importance of building a site that they have the staff, competence, budget, and consensus to maintain.

In their excellent book *Scaling for E-Business*,[11] Daniel Menasce and Virgilio Almeida introduce a structured approach to the design of e-business architectures that, I think, brings much-needed order and process to this previously ad hoc activity. I've built on some of the ideas presented by these authors and others to create an ordered design process that will help consultants think through the elements of Internet technical design and deliver a complete and robust solution for their clients. The eight-step "eBusiness Technical Design Process" I'll present here is based on my own experience in designing technical architectures, as well as the work of Menascé and Almeida and other mentors of Internet technical design such as Patrick Killelea and Linda Mui,[12] Simson Garfinkel and Gene Spafford,[13] and Lincoln Stein.[14] All Internet consultants, especially those with technical specializations, should review these works and understand each author's recommended approach before attempting to develop complex and business-critical infrastructures for clients.

Our eBusiness Technical Design Process, which is illustrated in Figure 5.1, is composed of the following activities:

1. Develop an Architecture Strategy. This is the overall "first take" infrastructure design, in which the technical designer begins to map, at an abstract level, the business models that emerge from the strategic analysis to a technical architecture. What are the database needs of the business model selected, the connectivity requirements, the Web servers that will be essential to delivering the business strategy? What software is being considered to run the required services? This is often called the "straw model," a rough prototype that everyone recognizes will change significantly, but it gives a starting point for discussion and design.

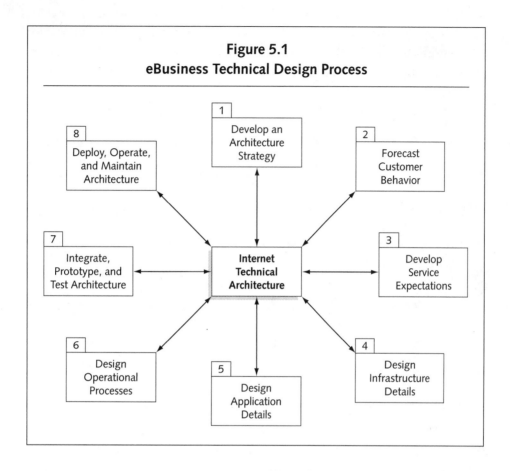

Figure 5.1
eBusiness Technical Design Process

1 — Develop an Architecture Strategy

8 — Deploy, Operate, and Maintain Architecture

2 — Forecast Customer Behavior

7 — Integrate, Prototype, and Test Architecture

Internet Technical Architecture

3 — Develop Service Expectations

6 — Design Operational Processes

5 — Design Application Details

4 — Design Infrastructure Details

2. Forecast Customer Behavior.   Customers obviously interact very differently with different sites, depending on both the site's business model and the customer's requirements. The customer's interaction with a consumer-oriented retail site, such as Amazon.com, will typically consist of a search or browse process, a selection process, and a checkout process. On an online trading site, customers may check their balances, look at stock quotes, access research, and make trades. Corporate purchasing managers using an industrial exchange may create an RFP, check on the status of existing RFPs or orders, enter a private "deal room" with a supplier, and negotiate a purchase. In each case, individual users may be "tire kickers," using the site to perform research before making an offline purchase, or they may be light purchasers or repeat customers. The exercise of modeling expected user behavior and building the site to best accommodate that behavior is a critical step in the architecture development process.

3. Develop Service Expectations. This is the process of deciding on the service levels that will be delivered to the users of the site. Based on the customer behavior forecasts in the previous step, the Internet architect must now analyze that behavior and start to forecast traffic loads, sessions, and service requests in an effort to quantify the scale, size, and characteristics of the technical elements. What are the expectations for download times, for site performance, for allowable downtime? How many customer visits are expected daily? What are the peaks of customer access that the site will be designed to accommodate? It's important to note that this is both a technical and a business measurement activity; for instance, it's critical for technical designers to understand the revenue expectations of the site. If the site is expected to deliver millions of dollars of revenue hourly, that will drive the technical design process in a specific direction. If, on the other hand, the site is primarily informational, such as a government site that offers access to the National Parks System, the service level requirements (and the money to be spent on supporting them) will obviously be different.

4. Design Infrastructure Details. In this step, the Internet technical architect begins to translate the conceptual models of the previous steps into explicit technical specifications. How big must the customer database be? How many items will be available on the virtual shelves? How many research reports, white papers, or customer reviews must the site hold, and how many simultaneous viewers must it be prepared to service? How many users will be trying to access the site at the same time, and what will this mean to the authentication, security, and customer activity tracking software? Which specific elements of hardware, software, network gear, and applications will be integrated to create this Internet business model? What will the architecture look like—where will traffic flow, which servers will be connected to which data stores, which routers will be attached to which network segments? This step is where the overall business strategy—and the expected customer behavior—begin to be turned into a granular and explicit technical specification that will in turn drive the selection and design of the final architecture.

5. Design Application Details. Every Internet business model, even those based on existing "canned" applications, needs to be designed and developed. The exact inputs, outputs, Web pages, forms, data elements, reports, and functions will be specified and documented here. This is not merely a technical exercise: In the highly graphical world of the Web, this is where the creative, customer experience, and branding experts will need to participate so that the "look and feel" of the site is in line with the business and marketing strategies of the client.

6. Design Operational Processes. The processes for the ongoing operation of the site, the continued modification and upkeep of the hardware and software, the monitoring and management of the network, and all other procedural and operation aspects of the client's Internet architecture must be developed here. This is where security, contingency plans, backup and restoration processes, software development, upgrade, and testing procedures, documentation standards, network management and troubleshooting, and emergency procedures will be developed and documented. It's important to note that, of the service interruptions I highlighted at the start of this chapter, many were based on process and procedural errors rather than on technical glitches. Most observers, for instance, believe that the E*Trade outage cited was based on faulty software upgrade procedures and that the famous "denial of service" attacks occurred because Web managers chose to ignore the advice of security consultants regarding their vulnerability to these types of assaults.

7. Integrate, Prototype, and Test Architecture. This is the step in which the infrastructure, application, and procedural elements specified in earlier steps are brought together into a working prototype and tested under the loads and scenarios forecast. In many cases, the vendors of hardware and software products will participate in these tests to ensure that their devices work as expected under the conditions predicted. Internet consultants must advise clients to construct rigorous and thorough testing procedures, as the possibility of damage to the business' competitive advantage from exposing an unprepared website can be catastrophic. Even now, many Web surfers are most familiar with Victoria's Secret and Encyclopedia Britannica as examples of sites that were unprepared for the traffic generated by their marketing campaigns.

8. Deploy, Operate, and Maintain Architecture. Clients expect their consultants to do more than simply advise; they expect them to take them all the way through successful operation of the systems they design. In this phase, Internet consultants work with their clients to take their Internet architecture out of the laboratory and migrate it into a production environment. This may mean involvement with the issues of facilities, such as the design of a data center for housing the infrastructure, and it may mean assistance with the design of procedures for managing staff or outsourcing vendors. Whatever the requirements, Internet consultants must take responsibility for the successful rollout of the architectures they design. Remember, this is not an academic exercise; it's the client's business, and—unlike the offline world—there is no business without the technology!

Now that we've looked at an overview of our eBusiness Technical Design Process, let's dig down into each of the steps a bit and discuss some of the issues and concerns that an Internet consultant must grapple with in order to deliver the best technology results for the client.

DEVELOP AN ARCHITECTURE STRATEGY

Debra Chrapaty, former president and chief operating officer of E*Trade, the online brokerage firm, said in an interview with *The New York Times* after her site was hit by software problems that made it unavailable for two days, "eCommerce really is like an iceberg. The website the customer sees is just the tip."[15] Internet consultants need to take Ms. Chrapaty's comments to heart, because they cut right to the core of the issue in building Internet business sites. Many clients, and even some consultants, are still focused on the graphics, presentation, and performance of the website that the ultimate customer sees when she clicks on an URL, but the actual architecture that delivers the competitive advantage for an Internet business is composed of many layers. It's our job to see, and to help our clients see, the iceberg that lies hidden beneath the surface and to be sure that we're diving as deeply as necessary to reveal all the technology required to deliver the business strategy.

One method of digging down into the hidden elements of the technical architecture is to begin visualizing the tasks and activities that customers will perform when they get to the proposed website. Will there be a registration process where new customers will enter some personal data that will be stored in a database? Will there be a login process for existing clients, where authentication will take place? What about a search-and-browse function for retail sites or a bid-and-ask function for auction sites? Will there be a shopping cart or an account balance or a download function? By reviewing the overall business model and decomposing it into these granular customer activities, we can, as designers, begin to get a clearer view of the technical components that will be required to enable these capabilities. We'll need to have thought through these possible customer interactions with the site in order to perform our next analysis phase, forecasting customer behavior.

At this early stage of the technical architecture design, it will be helpful to break down the total architecture into separate elements, to "divide and conquer," in an effort to take some of the complexity out of the process. From a basic architecture and infrastructure standpoint, many Web architects view the website as a four-tier architecture consisting of:

- The connectivity elements that link the site to the Internet;
- A Web-facing (or customer-facing) set of services;
- A middle tier of application logic; and
- A back-end tier of Web, application, and database servers.

The creation of some modular "black boxes" that can then be further divided into ever-smaller components is one of the central techniques of IT design. By taking a critical look at the functionality implied by the client's business model, dividing that into modular functions that are easier to visualize, and then mapping those business functions to a technology, we can divide and conquer even the most complex and overwhelming business strategy into a technology architecture that we can design and deliver. Starting with the four tiers described above and then further dividing each of those tiers into its modular component parts, we can come up with a "straw model" architecture that can then be the basis for our further discussion.

Remember, this is an exercise in modular function-point design, not a detailed technical specification. By this I mean that consultants must resist the inclination to begin designing the website or to start the argument over NT versus Unix before the basic functions that are required to deliver the business strategy are mapped out. We may know that we need a router to connect to the Internet backbone and a database server to store the customer records and inventory items. That's as far as we need to go in this phase. Not only is it counterproductive to begin the technical debate at this time, but it's also futile, as the subsequent phases will reveal the customer behavior, workloads, and performance standards that we'll need to support. So any technical decisions we would make here would likely be overruled by later discoveries anyway.

The deliverable from this exercise should be a functional map that broadly indicates the technology required to deliver the business functions designated by the strategy. For instance, wherever a data store will be required by the business, such as for customer records, inventory items, or billing records, a database should be indicated on the map. Wherever a Web server will be required to serve up Web pages designated in the business strategy, that should be documented. Applications necessary to deliver such functionality as auction capability or video streaming, for example, should be mapped out. The final document should give its audience an overall view of the number and purpose of technical elements required to deliver the business functions, but should leave the technical details to the later stages when the customer behavior and performance requirements have been defined in greater detail.

FORECAST CUSTOMER BEHAVIOR

As we've mentioned, different sites have different flows of activities and tasks for customers to perform. Some sites require registration and login; others don't. Other possible activities include simple and advanced search capabilities, browsing, review of account balances or shopping carts, downloading of content, access to customer service representatives or help screens, or payment and checkout.

As I mentioned previously, the best advice for this phase of the process is contained in *Scaling for E-Business* by Menascé and Almeida. They present a detailed process for modeling customer behavior, which results in a Customer Behavior Model Graph that can become part of the core documentation of the project. This graph can be used to predict customer activities and actions while visiting the site. By retaining and referring to this graph throughout the life of the site, designers and site operational staff can revisit the conceptual architecture of the site and can predict the impact of potential modifications to the site's layout. By comparing these initial forecasts to actual customer behavior, the designers can continuously improve the site to provide optimal service to visitors.

Although this forecasting process may seem complex, it's actually a simple method of walking through the possible site interactions in your mind (or on paper) and building a model of those behaviors. For instance, customers of an online stock brokerage, such as E*Trade, may perform the following activities:

- Connect to the site and view the market averages and news headlines posted on the main page;

- Select the "Login" button and enter personal authentication information;

- Get authenticated and then select the "Check Your Account Balance" button;

- Review the account balance and then select the "See Real Time Quotes" button;

- Check the quotations for the stocks of interest and then select the "Execute a Trade" button;

- Create and execute a transaction, then select the "Check Confirmation" button;

- Once the transaction is confirmed, the customer may decide to select the "View Research" button;

- From the Research page, the customer may decide to select the "Download" button for a particular article of interest and download that article to the local PC; and

- After receiving confirmation that the download was successful, the customer decides to "Log Off" the site.

Obviously, different business models will have different possible activities and different layouts. Even within the same business model, such as online retailing or brokering, different businesses will differentiate themselves by the layout and design of the site, and different entrepreneurs and their advisors will have very different ideas about design of the site and the desired customer experience. In many cases, the client will have a vague and conceptual idea of the site's design and will struggle with the requirement to articulate exactly how it will function. It is through this exercise of behavior forecasting that we begin to remove the fog from around the functioning of the Web presence for our consulting clients and start to drive down into the specifics of what the site will look like, how it will function, which choices customers will be able to perform from which areas and pages of the site, and all the other details of the real-world system that will deliver the business model.

This process of behavior forecasting requires us, once we've gone through the mental exercise of visualizing the possible interactions a customer might have with our site, to then lay out those actions and begin to think about transitions between the actions and how that will translate into page design. For instance, if a customer comes to the home page, what options will be presented there and how will a typical customer's session flow? What percentage of customers do we expect to access research and what percentage will want access to real-time quotes? Will customers want to navigate from the quotes page to the transactions page or from the research page to the quotes page? These mental visualizations bring us to the beginning of a site design as we start to think about the buttons, banners, instructions, and links that will need to be placed on each page to give our customers the functionality and experience they require.

Importantly, this exercise also drives the second activity of customer behavior forecasting, namely the analysis of that predicted behavior to arrive at a workload forecast. Once Internet consultants and architects have thought about the possibilities of visitor interaction with the site and have made some determinations as to the flow and frequency of those interactions, forecasts of the workload can be derived. For instance, new sites, in their early days, may have very intense activity in the new user registration process and so we would need to design heavy workload capability for that function. As the majority of potential customers have completed the registration process, the login activity will increase and the registration activity will decrease, so workload estimates will reflect that and resources may be redirected based on those forecasts.

DEVELOP SERVICE EXPECTATIONS

In any eBusiness model, whether profit or non-profit, consumer or business, retail or auction, there is an inherent tension between service expectations and costs. If money were no object, architectures could be built twice as large as they need to be to handle expected peak loads, twice as fast and twice as robust, or ten times, or twenty. But, since this is *eBusiness* we're talking about, and since profitability, or at least cost control, is the object of this exercise, the job of the Internet consultant and architect is to design an infrastructure that delivers the appropriate level of performance, scalability, and security at an appropriate price. Defining appropriateness is one of the first tasks of the consultant and client, as we discussed, because the retail site delivering millions of dollars of revenue will have a different service profile than the information site run by the government.

As with any IT architecture, Internet-based or not, the elements of service are the following:

- Performance or speed of response, that is, how long does it take for the system to deliver a screenful of data, process a transaction, or retrieve a set of records based on a database query;

- Stability, defined as the ability of the system to deliver consistent and reliable services over time;

- Security, the ability of the system to provide access to authorized users and to deny access to hackers, spies, curious or malicious employees, and other unauthorized users;

- Capacity or the ability of the system to provide the size and scale of resources necessary to deliver the expected functionality;

- Scalability, the system's ability to grow gracefully in response to additional needs for size, speed, or stability; and

- Serviceability or maintainability, the built-in design elements that allow the system to be maintained and serviced. These can include non-technical components such as documentation, procedures, and policies, as well as network and system management components.

Al Case, a vice president at The Gartner Group consultancy, has emphasized the importance of a robust infrastructure in the competitive Internet battle. "Two of the key factors that separate the successful dot.coms from the failures are an efficient infrastructure and the ability to integrate with the supply and distribution chains of suppliers on the back end," Case said. "The early entrants in the market, such as Yahoo, could afford to spend more on infrastructure than they spent on marketing because there wasn't much competition," Case went on.

"Other companies, like ValueAmerica, spent more to drive traffic to their site than they did on infrastructure, and they weren't prepared to scale. That's a prescription for failure. The company with a strong infrastructure and lousy marketing still has value. I'm not sure if the reverse is always true."[16]

To give you a window into some of the design decisions that are made in the real world, let's look at some of the decisions that practicing architects and managers have made when confronting the design process for service expectations of eBusiness sites. "We made a conscious decision to focus on speed as a key differentiator for us," said Jack McDonnell, president and CEO of Ameritrade. "We want to be the fastest, not just measured against other brokers but against all other sites on the Web. We think that's one of the keys to our success."[17] Ameritrade has spent more than $100 million to build out its IT infrastructure over the past three years. The company even suspended its advertising efforts in 1998 in order to focus on developing a robust, reliable, high-performing site.

Another profitable Internet company, CNet, a publisher of technology news and information, has a similar philosophy. "A lot of Internet-oriented corporations are willing to sacrifice performance for feature functionality, but we think that's a mistake," said Ted Cahall, CNet CIO. "If we think a new feature is going to degrade our performance, we'll stay away from it."[18]

Reliability also can cost a lot, according to Cahall. "At some point, you have to ask what an outage would cost you. You can make your site available down to the microsecond, but you might have trouble turning a profit because of what it will cost. So you have to make the trade-off between the cost of reliability and the cost of an outage. When we look at new initiatives," Cahall continued, "we do market sizing and forecasting to determine if it can achieve certain profit margins, not only from a market perspective, but from an IT perspective. Sometimes we have to take some very exciting opportunities and put them aside because we can't see them meeting those margins."[19]

Maynard Webb, the president of eBay Technology, agrees. "The more successful you get, the simpler you have to get," he says. "You have to make sure that anything that adds to complexity has a huge return."[20]

Jan Hier-King, the Schwab vice president we met at the beginning of this chapter, gives her analysis of the hierarchy of service expectations. "The number one success metric is availability, and number two is performance. They're more important than functionality. The wonder of the Web is that the customer knows about IT problems the same time you do. There's no camouflage," says Hier-King.[21]

Each of these Web executives, analysts, and architects understands the same lessons: Customer expectations for service are high; the old rules, while offering a foundation, don't address the new requirements; and interruptions in service are expensive, visible, and damaging to the brand.

eConsultants need to work closely with their clients to move past the vague rules of thumb and develop site-specific service expectations that address the unique needs of the particular business model. This exercise is similar to the exercise that technical consultants have gone through for decades, whether trying to arrive at service level agreements for an outsourced help desk or at "screen-snap" expectations for a client-server application, with the added complexity that downtime or unrealized expectations are much more widely visible and potentially have a make-or-break impact on the business.

The deliverable from this exercise should be a service level expectations document that defines the performance expectations across all the elements we enumerated earlier and that correlates those expectations with the realities of budget and schedule. As we said at the beginning of this section, if money were no object we'd make everything as robust as is technically possible. It's our job as advisors to help clarify in the client's mind the inevitable balance between resources and expectations.

DESIGN INFRASTRUCTURE DETAILS

In the early days of the Web, many enterprises, including large corporations, had websites composed of a single piece of software, such as Microsoft's Internet Information Services, running on a single server and connected to the Internet via a single router. Even the most rudimentary sites today are more likely to run a diverse collection of programs running on multiple machines in multiple locations, although typically looking like one site to the Internet end user. As we reviewed earlier, these complex infrastructures are typically composed of a four-tier architecture that includes the following elements:

- The connectivity elements that link the site to the Internet;
- A Web-facing (or customer-facing) set of services;
- A middle tier of application logic; and
- A back-end tier of Web, application, and database servers.

Once we've done the homework of understanding the basic business strategy, forecasting the type of customer behavior that strategy implies, and agreeing on the levels of performance and service the client expects to deliver to those customers, we can now begin to move beyond the "black box" functional diagram and begin to make decisions about the real-world technical elements, such as servers, routers, and databases, that will be required to deliver the enabling technology. This is the activity that IT consultants perform all their working lives, and the translation of theoretical capabilities into operational technology architectures is where many of us are most comfortable bringing our talents and experiences to bear for our clients.

In this phase, eConsultants open the "black box" of each functional element and name a specific piece of hardware or software that delivers that function. To design at this level of detail, eConsultants ask the following questions:

- How many redundant connections to the Internet will be required to deliver the guaranteed service level the client expects?

- What will the internal and external connectivity needs be? (These will obviously differ significantly for a local small commerce site versus a national commodity exchange, and from a supply chain network linking cooperative members of a manufacturing network versus former competitors trying to forge an industry exchange.)

- What will the customer-facing elements look like, and what functionality will they deliver? Will we be purchasing ready-made shopping-cart software, for instance, or building our own? Will we be using packaged personalization software from a vendor like Broadvision, or creating our own, as Amazon has done?

- Will our application tier require sophisticated legacy integration to give our customers access to data that resides on a mainframe system, or do we have the luxury of building a Web architecture completely from scratch? Will our database require advanced multimedia capabilities to display real-time video content?

- Will our hardware need to support millions of concurrent sessions, or just hundreds? Will we need to build complete redundant servers, or even redundant data centers?

This phase of the eBusiness Technical Design Process is actually a mini-framework of its own, and consultants attempting to develop a technology architecture will need to follow a structured process similar to the process I recommended in my previous book, *The IT Consultant*. Consultants must do a technology "as-is" assessment, must develop a "to-be" model based on the requirements uncovered in the initial phases of the engagement, and must perform a "gap analysis" that specifies all of the steps that must be taken to get the client from where they are currently to where they need to end up. I'll not attempt to include an architecture development process here, for a couple of reasons: First, I expect that my readership is mostly composed of IT consultants who have in place a structured set of techniques for developing IT systems, and second, because there are excellent references cited in the Bibliography that do a much better job of elucidating a design process than I could do in this space.

DESIGN APPLICATION DETAILS

Of course, the time comes in any engagement when we need to move beyond the analysis phase and actually design and code the applications themselves. Early websites were mostly brochures translated to the Net, and so were typically created by marketing or graphics departments. HTML was similar to other graphic markup languages that experienced designers had seen before, and the Web page as a design "space" was similar to the printed page. Even on those sites that offered some small amount of interactivity, such as the ability to register as a member or to request more information via e-mail, these capabilities were tacked on to the site by a webmaster and were typically not approached as structured software development projects. The teams that created these early sites were just as likely to be graphic artists as they were to be programmers, and so the structured methodologies that experienced programmers would bring to an application development project were often lacking. Many of these sites have needed extreme facelifts, as the competitive environment has mandated increasing website sophistication. This indicates clearly that many sites are being thrown out there as public beta tests, to quickly grab some land and have some Net presence rather than none. In a recent study, Jupiter Communications found that 46 percent of site designs are completed in under four weeks.[22] In an indication that the rush to market is a negative influence on site quality, the study found that 31 percent of new sites are redeveloped within the first six months. In the early Internet economy, where entrepreneurs had millions of venture capital dollars to design and then redesign their sites and speed to market was the driving force, this may have made sense. In today's more frugal and competitive marketplace, it certainly does not.

Websites now, of course, are likely to be a complex mix of applications, such as the following:

- Content management and publishing;
- Databases;
- E-mail and messaging systems;
- Advertising servers;
- Multimedia servers;
- Search engines;
- Shopping carts and other eCommerce applications;
- Personalization applications;
- Customer relationship management software;
- Web measurement and usage monitoring software; and
- Legacy integration applications.

This listing of elements that appear in many websites is not comprehensive, because many organizations have internally developed applications that may be hybrids of these functions or may serve industry-specific needs that aren't addressed here. The point is that the old days of static HTML Web pages are gone, and the competitive Internet business environment requires increasing sophistication in the applications that drive the Web business. These new applications need to be developed and delivered based on full-bodied development disciplines.

Although I won't attempt to go into depth on software development methodologies here, as there are many fine texts that do (I particularly recommend *A Methodology for Client Server and Web Application Development* by Roger Fournier [1998]), I will remind eConsultants to advise clients that modern Web development, unless it's for a rudimentary "place holder" site, is a complex discipline that requires a robust methodology and cannot be relegated to the marketing department nor to a lone webmaster. Just to reiterate some of the complexities of Web development, it's critical to remember that Web applications, because they are accessed over the public Internet rather than in a controlled corporate environment, are inherently less predictable and less controllable—and therefore need to be designed to a level of flexibility and fault tolerance unknown pre-Net. Because they are accessible to anyone with a browser and an Internet connection, they need to be self-explanatory and robust. Because they are the public face of the enterprise, they need to offer a superior customer experience, no matter what computing equipment the customer is using to access the site.

eConsultants, as they are guiding their clients in the creation of Web applications, must ensure that the client selects an application development methodology that enforces the appropriate amount of rigor in the software design, customer interface, logic, database, and legacy integration processes. The structured methodologies that lead software developers to understand their audience, to work incrementally by offering prototypes to the client and to representatives of the user community, to revise the design based on the input of those reviewers, and to build in a complete testing regimen have been proven over the last thirty years on many highly complex projects. Don't let the crush of "Internet time" pressure you into allowing clients to forsake those disciplines and risk their projects or their businesses.

DESIGN OPERATIONAL PROCESSES

The operational, support, and maintenance aspects of Internet technical design are as critical to success as the technical features and functions. One of the central lessons to be learned from the review of high-profile outages at the beginning of this chapter is that human and process errors were responsible for more of these glitches than were technology problems. The E*Trade site outages were attributed to an incorrect upgrade process, as were some of the Schwab problems. Superior Internet consultants work with their clients to develop robust, documented, and tested processes for everything from system changes to crisis management procedures.

As an example of how a procedural breakdown can impact an organization's e-business strategy and success, let's look at an incident experienced by Border's, the large offline book chain that's trying to make a dent in the tremendous lead gained by Amazon.com. Borders Online e-mailed tens of thousands of $5 gift certificates to customers on a Friday, just hours before Borders' website was scheduled to go down for maintenance. For those customers (about 5 percent of those who received the offer) who tried to take a look at the site so they could take advantage of the offer, instead of the pleasant experience of discovering a new, and perhaps better, alternative to Amazon, they received a "site busy" or "server unavailable" message. Not only did this create negative publicity for the fledgling site, but it highlighted the fact that all departments, not just IT, need to be communicating in order for eBusiness to work.[23]

Rick Vanzura, who resigned as president of Borders Online recently to head one of Dell Computer's websites, says, "That was a breakdown between marketing and IT. It doesn't sound like rocket science, but there's so much going on at a major website that it's pretty easy to have something fall through the cracks unless you're methodical." This is a perfect example of the need to integrate cross-functional procedures and communications into website operations. To make sure that the Border's debacle wasn't repeated, Vanzura started holding Monday morning meetings with the heads of marketing, content acquisition and management, customer service, production, and public relations.[24]

When websites first emerged as a critical component of competitive strategy for many companies, the entire operational responsibility was placed on a webmaster, a single "techie" with specialized technical skills and with little background in creating or managing ordered business processes. As sites grow in complexity and are partitioned into the four-tier architecture we've reviewed in this chapter, the requirement for a more professional and structured operational approach leads many organizations to create an eBusiness team or a Web operations group and to begin to codify the security, redundancy, backup, and change management processes, to name a few, that befit the management of a strategic corporate asset. Competent eConsultants must be prepared to assist their clients in the creation of these teams and in the development of robust operational procedures.

Let's do an overview of some of the areas that require robust operational processes in any Web-based business:

- *Antivirus protection management:* The activities required to prevent damage to software, loss of crucial data, or loss of brand image and customer loyalty due to virus attacks.

- *Backup and recovery management:* The planning and practice of backing up and recovering critical data to ensure the security and recoverability of information systems. In the online world, this practice also implies speed of backup and recovery and the ability to perform those actions without interrupting regular production use of the systems affected.

- *Capacity planning:* The activities that are used to predict the utilization of computing resources such as servers, operating systems, networks, and middleware;

- *Change management:* Activities related to the planning, coordination, and implementation of hardware, network, and software changes. This practice includes the evaluation of the impact of proposed changes and notification of all affected users of upcoming changes. It also requires the development of a contingency plan to restore the production environment to its previous state should changes not work properly.

- *Configuration management:* Activities that relate to documenting and monitoring the purpose of the hardware and software components of an IT system and their interdependencies. This practice is required in order to have records of the computing assets and the versions and revision levels of software running on those systems.

- *Database administration:* Includes the configuration and upgrading of production databases, the monitoring of database space utilization, and the running of database reorganization jobs to ensure optimal application performance.

- *Disaster planning and recovery management:* Activities required to ensure continuous business operations should a disaster occur.

- *Network management:* The monitoring of all IT assets that are connected to the enterprise network, including hardware, software, and connectivity resources, to ensure that all devices are operational and are delivering the expected levels of service and performance.

- *Security management:* Activities that monitor and protect IT assets from internal and external security threats by imposing restrictions on the use of these resources.

This is just a representative sample of the areas of IT management for which enterprises need to develop and document standard operational processes. In the world of internal IT, it is well-known that few organizations have robust, documented processes that are understood and followed by the IT staff. In the Internet world, where any operating glitch is instantly visible to the world (and will often end up on the front page of *The Wall Street Journal*), the development of processes, and the recruitment and training of an IT staff that will follow those processes, is a key element of success.

Competent eConsultants will help clients ensure that every Web application and site has a responsible party designated as the "owner" of the processes listed above, that that individual has the tools and escalation paths she needs to be effective, and that good standard operating procedures such as practice runs, drills, ongoing training, and documentation upkeep are being practiced.

INTEGRATE, PROTOTYPE, AND TEST ARCHITECTURE

The practice of testing and prototyping websites before they are released for public consumption has unfortunately been a victim of "Internet time." The perceived need for speed has driven many Web entrepreneurs to disregard this basic tenet of software development, thrusting onto their Internet sites applications that haven't attained the minimum level of reliability and robustness that a publicly accessible application must achieve. According to a survey done by Jupiter Communications, the Internet industry analysts, 6.7 percent of sites do not test Web applications at all, and 36.6 percent of sites perform only manual load testing of applications. Fewer than 57 percent of websites performed automated load testing.[25] This failure to test has real consequences: According to the same survey, 46 percent of users have on at least one occasion been driven to alternative sites because their preferred site failed. Eighty-four percent of users surveyed by Jupiter resent being asked to use features that have not been fully tested, even if the site warns that they may experience difficulties in the first few weeks after the release. Nearly 28 percent of users in such a situation indicated that they would leave the site. Twenty-one percent of consumers indicated that it was never acceptable for a site to fail.

With these survey figures in front of us, it seems obvious that it's our responsibility as eConsultants to advise our clients to perform thorough and complete testing of all applications that are part of an Internet strategy, whether they will be accessed by the public, by trading partners, or by employees on an internal intranet. Competent software developers always incorporate a testing and pilot phase into any application they create, and the software development methodologies developed over the past few decades present us with robust tools and techniques for that purpose. It's important to note, however, that Web applications present us with special circumstances we must address in our testing plans.

Web applications are accessible and visible to the entire world once they are released on the Internet. They represent the company and the brand. For these reasons they must present a level of stability and fault tolerance that surpasses the requirements put on an in-house system.

The very infrastructure of the Internet puts application testers in another difficult bind. How can you test the application from the end user's point of view and ensure that the user's experience represents the company and the brand, when you have no idea through what mechanism the user is accessing your application? Is the user in San Francisco, gaining access through a high-speed, dependable connection, on her Pentium 4.1-gigahertz processor, or is she in Calcutta dialing in through a 28K modem on a 486 PC? How do you test for the transmission vagaries that exist all through the Internet, which, after all, was designed as a "best effort" network with no guarantees that data would reach its audience at all?

With all these difficulties, how should eConsultants recommend that clients develop a testing program for their Web applications? Clients should use the testing and prototyping techniques from the well-known software development methodologies as a guide and ensure that every test program has a set of defined criteria for success or failure and a set of test cases and test data that is pertinent to the functionality at hand. Website testing needs to probe both the functionality of the application and its ability to handle the loads that were projected in the previous phases of the design process. There are automated load-testing applications available that can assist with the generation of traffic and sessions and that can be easily manipulated to generate loads that simulate the spikes in demand that may accompany a successful ad campaign, for example. Of course, test cases also need to be created to test the other elements that make up a successful website design, such as security, Java scripting, graphics placement and appearance, cookies, browser versions, and the myriad other details that make the development of Web applications so challenging. Finally, good testing procedure would lead us to test from the user end of the equation, perhaps by simulating a user environment, including perhaps the 28K modem and the obsolete PC, to assess the site's performance from that critical point of view.

DEPLOY, OPERATE, AND MAINTAIN ARCHITECTURE

Once eBusiness architectures are designed, developed, tested, and deployed, the team responsible for their ongoing maintenance and operations is on the hot seat. As we discovered at the beginning of this chapter, the inevitable glitches and outages that affect every system are magnified on the Net by the glare of publicity and the scrutiny of both customers and financial markets. It is also true that, in most cases, IT shoulders the burden, especially at the beginning. While some sites come out of the marketing or HR departments, many also are "skunk works" that come out of one department or other and are often led by the resident "techie" or webmaster. These sites, if they have value, are adopted by the organization and usually put under the direction of the IT team. In fact, a recent survey of the staffing and organization of websites showed that 27 percent of corporate websites are under the direction of the chief technology officer and his team.[26] Since these are corporate assets, it makes sense that they "come in out of the cold" and are managed as such.

Yet these assets are different from the IT assets of the past. While many of those assets and applications were tactical, Internet initiatives are often strategic—designed to counter serious threats or exploit major opportunities in an industry. As we have often noted, they are the public face of the company to the customer, the supplier network, and the financial markets. They are major investments, usually many times bigger than the typical "point solution" application that is installed to solve a particular tactical problem within the business. For all these reasons, eConsultants should be prepared to advise clients on matters that may seem a bit out of the realm of technical architecture, but are critical to the successful functioning of an eBusiness application.

There is a new type of IT organization emerging, called in some companies the "eBusiness Team," in others the "Internet Leadership Team," and in others the "WebHeads" (no joke!). This team can be a department, with the responsibility for the day-to-day operations of all production Internet applications, or it can be a steering committee, with advisory functions only. It can be directed by a chief Internet officer, whose only responsibility is leading and governing all eBusiness activities within the enterprise, or it can be led by someone who has another full-time job in the company and is acting as the chair of a steering committee that will set standards and apply procedures, but will leave the everyday operations to the departments or to IT.

The point is that, in most organizations, the size and scope of the threats and opportunities that eBusiness presents have been recognized and the need for appropriate leadership has been acknowledged. I use the word "appropriate" advisedly, as different forms of governance make sense for different projects and different companies. A traditional retailer moving into the eBusiness world may decide that a dedicated team with full operational responsibility is suitable, because the cultural and organizational consensus issues may be as critical to success as the technical ones. For instance, it's a well-known anecdote in the industry that barnesandnoble.com was the victim of internal sniping and resistance by the employees of the traditional stores. The creation of a chief web officer in that type of situation, with responsibility for a communication and persuasion program, is probably a good idea. In other organizations, where departments have created websites that are functioning well and have been recognized as corporate assets, a steering committee approach, to add some standardization and operational consistency, could be the right mix.

By keeping up with developments in this field, eConsultants can assist clients in selecting the right form of governance for their projects. The Internet trade press carries information every week about the projects underway in the Fortune 500 firms and the Internet pure plays alike, and this information is invaluable to the Internet advisor. We must help our clients understand that the form of leadership they select will have a huge impact on the success of their programs.

Although 66 percent of sites surveyed in a recent study indicated that they had dedicated teams focused on Internet initiatives, most also agreed that their organizational roles and responsibilities were poorly defined and understood.[27] eConsultants can assist clients by advising them to create documented staff positions and to assign responsibility and accountability in a manner that encourages ownership and performance. Many site operations will divide responsibilities by functions, so that, for instance, on a site that offers multimedia content, advertising, and community, there will be an individual responsible for each of those functions. This is just one approach, More important than the particular approach is the need for ownership and accountability.

Finally, eBusiness infrastructure, like a ship or a plane, needs to be managed objectively by metrics. There are many tools and services that assist the site manager in gauging and monitoring the performance of the site on a moment-by-moment basis. It is our responsibility as consultants to assist our clients in selecting the right tools, both internal and external, and in developing the metrics, warnings, and alarms that are most meaningful to the particular eBusiness at hand. From server performance to load balancing to number of page views to load times, there are tools that offer the operations team a dashboard for the performance of the site. External service providers, from Media Metrix to Neilsen to eMarketer, offer services that give a more global and contextual view to the site manager. eConsultants need to understand all of these options, and we must be prepared to help our clients select and deploy these measurement tools so that the eBusiness architectures we develop continue to provide the results we were contracted to deliver.

An Interview
with Larry Tanning[28]

I recently interviewed Larry Tanning, founder and CEO of Tanning Technology Corporation for TechRepublic, a Gartner Group website targeted at IT professionals. His comments are appropriate for this chapter because of Tanning's focus on back-end technology infrastructure and integration. Rather than pursuing a full-service consulting model that offers services from business strategy to design to build, Tanning has gone to market almost exclusively focused on the complex technical "heavy lifting" and integration requirements associated with eBusiness. This focus has worked out well, and the company has grown from its beginnings as a one-man firm operating out of the loft of Larry's Colorado mountain home to a global company with over $41 million in revenues for the first six months ending June 2000. Forrester Research, in its recent report entitled "eCommerce Integrators Exposed," awarded Tanning the top score in the technology category, which includes systems architecture and systems development. Tanning's client list includes such companies as United Airlines, Ameritech, The Hartford, Blockbuster, E*Trade, Federal Express, and Maersk Sealand.

Rick: First I'd like to congratulate you on your Forrester rating!

Larry: We're very pleased about it because it has us positioned and differentiated right where the industry is heading. We see the next phase of the Internet becoming much more complex and technology dependent.

Rick: I noticed in your comments about the press release that you mentioned three elements. You said that success in the new economy is based on speed, change, and collaboration. I'd like to drill into those elements with you a bit and understand your thoughts on each of them. Let's talk about speed, and this whole concept of "Internet time."

Larry: When I talk about speed I mean it two ways. First, in terms of quick time to market with new services and products, and second, in terms of much more demanding real-time processing. Speed is a double-edged challenge facing the next era of the Internet and will go far beyond the recent "cookie cutter" package approach and "Internet time" hype with many of the dot.coms that did not have sustainable business models. The next era will be dominated by more mature companies that must connect their infrastructure to the Internet and partners on a real-time basis. This will mean new interfaces and business processes to collect and transform transactions and content for customers, partners, and internally within their companies. I feel that we've just scratched the surface in the true meaning of Internet time.

Rick: I'm interpreting from your comments that you think there's been some hype around the migration to the Internet economy—and that you're expecting some of the more established enterprises to move in now and develop real competitive advantage on the Net.

Larry: I feel that we're in a nine-inning ballgame with the Internet economy and that we're only now in the fourth inning. While the first two innings were marketed as "Internet time," they were really often about getting something out fast to gain a stake on the Internet for equity purposes. As I said before, most did not have a proven or sustainable business model and will ultimately fail. We're now into the B2B exchange inning. There will surely be many exchanges that will be sustainable with a strong place in our economy. But many will fail. In the networked economy, real companies with proven business models will dominate. Their success, however, will depend on their ability to be flexible enough to deliver the right service or product offering. This requires a whole new level of integration within the enterprise and outside the enterprise with partners adding to the supply or value chain.

Rick: When you talk about collaboration, it brings to mind the Cisco "single enterprise" concept, where they use the Net to reach out to customers, to resellers, to other manufacturers, to other players in their value chain. It sounds like you believe that type of approach, the virtualization of the enterprise via the Net, is going to be a big part of the Internet economy's real value.

Larry: I agree. You're describing again the networked, eBiz, or grid economy that all the analysts are now predicting. Cisco is an early adapter of this highly collaborative approach. They've gotten out of non-core business functions to concentrate on what they do best. They've gone outside and found partners with whom they can work on a collaborative and flexible basis to deliver new products and services quickly. Companies need to focus on what they do best. Many business functions are becoming commoditized, so why be doing them when you can focus on what really differentiates you? I think that's what Cisco realized.

They made a rational decision to collaborate so they can move forward ahead of competition.

Rick: From my research into the Tanning Technologies business model and philosophy, I understand that you're not really competing directly with the full-service agency model, but you're very focused on the building of enabling technical architectures for Internet businesses.

Larry: We've been true to our deep technology roots and work with sophisticated users and buyers of IT. The bulk of money that most established businesses spend is in the technology area. We collaborate with strategy and design firms, but we also find that many businesses have a strong hold on their strategies, but difficulty in how they're going to make them happen. Tanning focuses on making strategies happen.

Rick: So in scenarios like the one we talked about with Cisco, where there are complex requirements to integrate with external suppliers, component manufacturers, resellers, et cetera, with different systems and networks, is that your sweet spot—the place where Tanning can really add significant value?

Larry: With the need for speed, change, and collaboration, we feel that we're well-positioned for the next phase of the Internet. We've been in IT consulting for a long time. The established Global 2000 are running on four generations of technology. While much of that technology was upgraded for Y2K, it was never designed for the 24 by 7 world of the Internet. These systems are doing a good job of running the business and there's no reason or cost justification to replace them. Gaining access to the critical data and content on these operational systems for new Internet offerings is what Tanning does well. Our deep technology experience and integration skills have led to integration frameworks and processes that allow us to build new offerings that leverage these core assets of companies in an unobtrusive way. This is what the next innings of the Internet will be focused on, and we're ready.

End Notes

1. Girishankar, S. E-Biz Sites Push for 100 Percent Uptime. *Internet Week,* April 9, 1999.
2. Janah, M. Embarrassing Sights for E-Commerce. *San Jose Mercury,* June 19, 1999.
3. ibid.
4. Abreu, E. Latest Attack Hits E-Trade, ZDNet Sites. *Industry Standard,* Feb. 9, 2000.

5. ibid.

6.. Kaneshige, T. Nobody Misses the Network Until It's Down. *CIO,* Feb. 15, 2000.

7. op cit, Girishankar.

8. Menasce, D., & Almeida, V. *Scaling for E-Business: Technologies, Models, Performance, and Capacity Planning.* Saddle River, NJ: Prentice Hall, 2000.

9. Richtel, M. As E-Commerce Surges, So Do Technical Problems. *New York Times,* June 21, 1999.

10. Interview with Chuck Krutsinger. © TechRepublic, Inc. *www.techrepublic.com.* Used by permission. All rights reserved.

11. Menasce, D., & Almeida, V. *Scaling for E-Business: Technologies, Models, Performance, and Capacity Planning.* Upper Saddle River, NJ: Prentice Hall, 2000.

12. Killelea, P., & Mui, L. *Web Performance Tuning: Speeding Up the Web.* Boston: O'Reilly & Associates, 1998.

13. Garfinkel, S., & Spafford, G. *Web Security & Commerce.* Boston: O'Reilly & Associates, 1997.

14. Stein, L. *How to Set Up and Maintain a Web Site.* Reading, MA: Addison-Wesley, 1998.

15. ibid.

16. Wilson, T. Profit Pressures: Tech As Dotcom Differentiator. Planet IT, *www.PlanetIT.com,* April 27, 2000.

17. ibid.

18. ibid.

19. ibid.

20. Dalton, G., Coping with an E-Business Emergency. *Information Week,* Sept. 19, 1999.

21. ibid.

22. Dodd, P. *User Interface Design.* New York: Jupiter Strategic Planning Service, Oct. 1998.

23. ibid.

24. ibid.

25. Foster, C. *How to Build a Failure-Proof Site.* New York: Jupiter Strategic Planning Services, 1999.

26. Dodd, P. Staffing and Organizational Structures. *Jupiter Communications,* Vol. 11, 1999.

27. ibid.

28. Interview with Larry Tanning. © TechRepublic, Inc. *www.techrepublic.com.* Used by permission. All rights reserved.

Web Marketing

EXPERIENCE MARKETING

I'm watching television with a notepad in my lap, tracking the commercials that pop up on the network program I've randomly tuned to. In the half-hour that I watch, I see commercials for new cars (my current car works just fine), feminine products (I'm a male), gasoline (I don't buy gasoline based on brand), cat food (I have dogs), cheese (I'm allergic to milk products), school supplies (I don't have kids), and a cholesterol-lowering prescription drug (I don't have high cholesterol). There's an old ad agency proverb that says half of all advertising dollars are squandered, we just don't know which half; but in my case 100 percent of the advertising I saw today was wasted. Even if the ads I saw were more on target than this random sampling indicates, I believe that most advertising is wasted on me because I consider myself highly resistant to mass market advertising. I'd venture to guess that, for many in my demographic cohort—people who grew up with TV and so are hardened to continual commercial interruption and who shop based on information rather than impulse—a high proportion of marketing effort is futile.

As we've discussed in previous chapters, the "four Ps" of traditional marketing–product, price, place, and promotion—have been overthrown by the Web. When the product can be tailored to fit each customer's requirements, the price is set dynamically in auction-driven marketplaces, the place is wherever a customer has Net access, and the promotion is based on Web-enabled interactivity and dialogue rather than scatter-shot broadcast messages, all bets are off for traditional marketers. The one-size-fits-all, interrupt-driven, broadcast nature of marketing as designed and practiced by the Madison Avenue ad agencies is becoming another casualty of the Internet earthquake, as prospects and customers become immune to the sound-alike, look-alike, bigger-better-safer-faster-healthier messages and seek out the rich information and real world experiences available in their trusted online communities.

One of the keys to understanding this migration is understanding that, in this Internet economy, products have mutated into services across the spectrum of businesses. In a bookstore, the book you hold in your hand is a product, and you, as a consumer, evaluate that product the way you would evaluate a bar of soap or a box of cereal. Does it fulfill the desire and satisfy the need that drove you to enter the bookstore in the first place? There are still some sites that present the book as a product with, perhaps, a picture of the front cover, a category, and a price. In fact, they provide less service to the potential customer than the offline bookstore, because the book can't even be opened and scanned. Then there are the booksellers, with Amazon in the lead, who have turned the sale of a book into a service—in which ratings, reviews, excerpts, categorization, recommendations, and communities of interest all converge into a personalized book evaluation service that customers can use to keep informed, learn about new developments or works in their field, and stay up-to-date in their business, personal development, and enjoyment of literature. This same phenomenon has occurred across industries, as the sporting-goods retailer and the car dealership go online and turn their warehouse of physical products into a repository of information and, ultimately, through the integration of community, information, and personalization, into a service. On the Web, we can very clearly see the difference between those who "get" these changes in marketing and those who don't.

This migration is important for consultants to understand if they hope to add value to the marketing efforts of their clients. In the world of products, the physical qualities of the truck, CD, book, or shoe speak for themselves. They are created and delivered and, except for after-the-fact services such as a lube job or brake alignment, the transaction is done. Services, on the other hand, are not created until we experience them. It's our experience with the service that defines it and our experience of it is personal and intimate. Product evaluation by the client is typically clear and simple: Does the truck, shoe, or book fulfill the need that drove me to purchase it? Service evaluation, on the other hand, is complex and personal. Do I like the tone and atmosphere of the interaction? Did it make me feel secure and comfortable? Was it easy and friendly? Was the entire experience, from my first encounter through the receipt of the product or service to the resolution of any problems and the logistics of payment, fair and convenient? The cup of coffee I buy in the corner doughnut shop may not be very different from the one I buy at Starbucks, but the total experience certainly is, as evidenced by the lines of customers willing to pay the upcharge for that Starbucks super latté.

As an example of the difference between product and service, let's look at the business model of the corner record store and the strategy of a website called Firefly. Firefly is a service of Agent's Inc., a startup that is experimenting with the concept of smart "agents" that help customers find the best prices and the most appropriate selections, or perform other searches, based on personal preferences. In the local CD store, customers can browse through racks of CDs, typically categorized by type of music. There may be a bestseller list tacked on the wall or a magazine handout that reviews some of the selections or—in the more advanced stores—a listening room or some samples of popular disks that can be heard through headphones. By contrast, Firefly is a service that allows fans to create a personal profile of likes and dislikes and then recommends likely picks. By allowing customers to listen to and then rate a long list of selections from various user-selected genres of music and by comparing each individual's ratings to the ratings in a wide database of ratings by other customers, Firefly creates a personal recommendation list using sophisticated group analysis and data mining techniques.

Firefly has since made the total circuit, as they've turned their process for delivering these recommendations into a software product that they sell to other sites for their use in creating personalized suggestions! I mention Firefly because it demonstrates many of the principles of Web marketing that we'll be discussing here.

First, Firefly uses the ability of the Web to deliver rich content, turning its product—CDs—into a service. By allowing the user to sample a long list of specific selections and then to rate them, Firefly uses the multimedia capabilities of the Web to create a total experience rather than a simple virtual record rack. Then, Firefly uses the immediacy of the Web to give recommendations in real time, when the customer is ready to purchase—unlike the bus billboard or TV ad that sends us a message when we're actually there to do something else. Firefly uses its wide reach to create a database of ratings and selections that can then be mined, essentially turning data into information that can be made useful to the retailer and the customer. Firefly also uses one of the central tenets of the new marketing theories—that marketers must figure out innovative ways to offer marketing messages that the customer will value, rather then messages that are focused on the product that the marketer is trying to hawk.

ADVERTISING IS DEAD!

Firefly illustrates some of the central possibilities enabled by the Internet. Before we drill down into the details of some of these Internet marketing strategies, let's briefly review the strategic underpinnings of this new marketing model.

As much as anything, the Internet is about power shifts. The power of the corporation to set prices is eroding as the power of the customer to name a price becomes more prevalent in both the consumer segment, due to entities like Priceline and eBay, and in the business segment, due to the ubiquitous auctions and exchanges. The power of the local retailer to get a premium price because he's the only local source is crumbling as the worldwide scope of the Net allows consumers to buy their umbrellas from a shop in London and their cigars from a tobacconist in Madrid. And the ability of marketers to jam repetitive and simplistic messages down the throats of passive listeners—or of publicists to transmit psuedo-news and have it blasted across the media as if it were real—is being displaced by communities of "publicists" who create their own version of the truth through their communities, reviews, and unofficial websites like StarBucked.com.

For those companies that are smart enough to dive into this new model of customer relationship, the benefits are staggering. Companies can create loyal, personalized associations with their customers on both an individual and a grand scale. The economies of scale enabled by the Net have taken the theories of one-to-one marketing and customer relationship management gurus like Don Peppers and Martha Rogers[1] or Arthur M. Hughes[2] and made them realizable. The brand, formerly an "image in the mind" set by repeated broadcasts of one-way messages from the company to the consumer, is now an aggregate of all the experiences the customer has—from the company name to the URL to the speed of loading the website to the selection and price all the way through to the community of people she "meets" on the site.

The word "relationship" is used advisedly, because the best sites know how to set up a mutually beneficial association with their clients, while the worst make the same old mistakes over again. For an example of a site that still doesn't get it, I'll relate an experience I had this week. I received a blind e-mail in my mailbox from an online home appraisal service that promised to tell me what my home was worth with no obligation. Because I'm in the market for a new house, I clicked through to check it out. The site first required me to register and enter a large volume of data about myself and then sent me to a second page to enter information about my home—its location, size, and condition—then, after about ten minutes of data entry, asked me for my zip code so it could give me my appraisal. After churning for a moment, it came back to tell me that "We can't offer appraisals in that zip code." After having been solicited via e-mail, and having entered my private and personal data under false pretenses, I now feel like my time and information were stolen and my trust violated. How hard would it have been to ask for my zip code first to see whether it could in fact offer me the service it had promised? How much money was wasted sending e-mails to prospects who couldn't be serviced and who are now unhappy and disappointed? Rather than building a customer base, this marketing campaign and site design has created an enemies list.

Contrast this with the approach taken by some of the acknowledged winners in the new economy. Dell Computer is famous for its "partner pages," designed to address the specific needs of individual customers. Tens of thousands of Dell customers have agreed to reveal their requirements and corporate purchasing forecasts because they get value in return—access to pages that are designed to make purchasing computers easier and cheaper, that enforce their corporate standards, grant them access to special prices and bundles, and allow them to order special services such as inventory tags or pre-configured PCs. Dell takes their Web-based customer relationships so seriously that they have established a customer experience council, reporting to the vice chairman and composed of senior executives from each of the company's lines of business. As senior vice president Paul Bell noted in a recent interview, "Every public company tells shareholders how it's doing [financially] every quarter, but few companies have a set of metrics that measure the customer experience from month to month, quarter to quarter [as we do]."[3] iVillage, the community destination site for women, is consistently rated in the top twenty sites in terms of viewership. As founder Candace Carpenter explains, "We get e-mail notes every day that say 'I have breast cancer and I came to your site and got help.' Or 'I'm trying to raise two little kids on my own and ten people came to my aid and gave me books to read, medical questions to ask my pediatrician, and ways to talk to my children—your site has changed my life.' The kind of loyalty that those experiences bring is unbelievable—it makes for a different order of relationships."[4] From the personalized recommendations at Amazon.com, to the reviews of outdoor gear at rei.com, to the personalized financial advice at Fidelity.com, winning Web strategists make a compact with their customers: Give me your personal information, tell me what services and features you value, and I'll use that information to serve you better.

eBRANDING

"If a product is something that is produced to function and exist in reality," says Phillip Durbrow of Frankfurt Balkind, a San Francisco-based international design boutique, "then a brand has meaning beyond functionality, and exists in people's minds."[5] The difference between sugar water and Coca-Cola, between sneakers and Nikes, between coffee and Starbucks, brand is a personal accumulation of experience, marketing, reputation, familiarity, image, and associations.

It's also a new economy cliché, as new-age marketers and teenage CEOs chatter on about "brand equity" and "brand recognition." Unfortunately, many of the references to brand are more focused on style than on substance. The comparison made by marketing guru Harry Beckwith in his book *The Invisible Touch*[6] is appropriate. Beckwith says branding experts try "to do what the Wizard of Oz did by projecting his outsize image on the drapes: persuade people he was something he was not." Beckwith goes on to make a point about branding that any Internet consultant (and her clients) must take to heart: "It is not slickness, polish, uniqueness, or cleverness that makes a brand a brand. It is its truth." Or, as Jason Olim, founder of CDNow, the online music retailer, has said, "Your brand isn't just what you say—it's what you do."[7] Point being, products or services become associated with brands in people's minds because they consistently deliver what is promised. All the advertising and slick presentation did Chevrolet no good when Honda built a better car cheaper, and all the Super Bowl ads in the world didn't help OurBeginning.com, Computers.com, or Pets.com turn a weak business model into an "image in the mind" of the consumer.

In fact, the January 2000 Super Bowl has become emblematic of the misunderstanding of brand that has overtaken the Internet economy. When Computers.com, a Web retailer of PCs and software, takes $3.2 million, over half of its first-round funding, and uses it to buy ninety seconds of Super Bowl ad time instead of using that money to build infrastructure or hire staff or build customer databases or perform market research, because, as their CEO Mike Zapolin asserts, "Our name is Computers.com. Once you hear it, we're very difficult to forget." It seems obvious that the concept of brand as an accumulation of consistent, positive experience has been lost. When Bill Croasdale, executive vice president of Western Initiative Media, a Los Angeles agency that buys advertising for clients, says "Advertising in the Super Bowl is a way of saying, 'Hey, look! I'm playing with the big boys.'" It seems clear that some dot.coms may not be getting the best advice from their agencies. When LastMinuteTravel.com, a site that competes with Priceline, Expedia, and Travelocity, some of the most successful sites on the Net, decides to drop $2.5 million on Super Bowl related promotions, including hosting an NFL breakfast for 1,500 and giving out 100,000 bags imprinted with its logo, it's not hard to come to the conclusion that some of the millions of dollars in venture capital money that swept over the Internet may not have been used to best effect.[8]

Michele Slack, an analyst with Jupiter Communications, the Internet consultancy in New York, gets right to the point when she comments, "A lot of these companies know what brand awareness is, but not what building a brand is all about. You can have all the awareness in the world, but if the customer doesn't understand what your brand is and how it's different, then you don't really have a brand."[9] For instance, Slack notes that when online pet stores "get e-mail from confused customers asking how they can buy a sock puppet [the ubiquitous mascot of the Pets.com online pet store], it's clear that the Pets.com brand is not as pronounced as it should be." And this after Pets.com's $2.3 million advertising blitz on the Super Bowl!

So after all this talk about what brand building is not, what is it? Who has done it successfully? and how does Internet branding differ from offline branding? How can an Internet consultant help guide his clients to successful branding efforts? What is the attraction of brand? Why is every business seeking it so actively? and how do you know when you've achieved it?

I want to again drop in a short disclaimer: Branding is an enormous topic, about which libraries full of books have been written, and we will not treat the topic fully here. Internet consultants without a background or an education in marketing basics should do some research on the topic, using some of the source and reference material cited here, in order to bring a more complete foundation to their client engagements. Here, I will attempt to review some of the efforts that successful (and not so successful) Internet enterprises have used to tackle the branding effort, and I'll cite some examples of branding programs that can be used as models, positive and negative, in advising clients.

Why Brand?

In a recent *Business Week*/Harris poll, 57 percent of Internet users stated that they return to the same sites again and again, rather than surfing around to find new sites that offer the services or products they seek.[10] Another *Business Week* article asserted that 75 percent of all Internet advertising revenues flow to the top ten sites.[11] When asked, in a recent survey by *Harvard Business Review*, what attribute was most important in determining where to shop on the Web, the number one answer was "A website I know and trust."[12] But customer loyalty is difficult to achieve and maintain. In a recent study by Digital Idea, an Internet marketing research firm, customer loyalty numbers are slipping, not improving. In the first quarter of 1999, 52 percent of shoppers had bought at least twice from the same Net retailer in the previous six months. But by the first quarter of 2000, only 35 percent of buyers had made a second purchase from the same Net retailer over the same time period.[13] The value of loyal customers—and the difficulty of creating and maintaining them—point toward the importance of branding.

These are the quantifiable elements that make brand building such a compelling exercise. The intangibles are just as important, if not more so. Brands create a positive bias in the mind of the consumer. They allow successfully branded enterprises to command premium prices, even for commodity goods like coffee. They carry what Harry Beckwith, author of *Selling the Invisible* and *The Invisible Touch,* calls "The Brand Placebo Effect."[14] As Beckwith describes it, due to The Brand Placebo Effect, "Our belief that something will do such-and-such leads us to believe that it actually did—even when it didn't. A brand does not merely attract clients, it convinces clients that they got just what the brand promised—even when they didn't!" Pretty powerful stuff! Many believe that it was Apple Computer's brand that allowed them to survive even when the product was no longer "insanely great," when, in fact, the product was far behind Windows and getting farther. Because the Apple brand was associated by fans with coolness, fun, creativity, and friendliness, it was able to be resuscitated when the human embodiment of the brand, Steve Jobs, came back to revive the company.

Now that we've reviewed the power of branding, let's look at some of the branding techniques that are being used on the Web.

How to Brand

In his incisive book, *eBrands: Building an Internet Business at Breakneck Speed*,[15] marketing veteran Phil Carpenter has taken a look at the branding efforts of some of the most recognizable sites—and at some more obscure sites as well—to deliver a lucid overview of Internet brand strategies that work. He has scrutinized the practices of sites such as Yahoo, Barnesandnoble.com, Fogdog, iVillage, and CDNow and has categorized their tactics under the following headings:

- Best Practices;
- Brand Awareness;
- Customer Commitment;
- Distribution and Content Alliances;
- First-Mover Advantage;
- Intimate Customer and Market Knowledge;
- Reputation for Excellence;
- Outstanding Value;
- Consistent Brand Image;
- Expand the Service to One-Up Offline Competitors; and
- Leverage Offline Assets.

With all due respect to Mr. Carpenter and the important research he's done, I'll reprise some of his findings here in a few of these categories to help Internet consultants understand the importance of each of these elements. I'm not going to review every category, but will hit the highlights that I think can be of value to consultants. Some of these categories, such as "first-mover advantage," will be a bit difficult to utilize now, as most obvious market spaces were filled in the Internet land grab of the 1990s, but other techniques, such as customer commitment and loyalty programs, should be part of every consultant's tool bag.

Best Practices

Many of the Internet brand practices we have already examined are described as "Best Practices" by Carpenter. For instance, in his look at CDNow, he cites the store's personalization of customer offerings, its communications with customers, and its broad product selection. CDNow follows the philosophy of "retail as service" as it emphasizes its ability to help customers discover the music that will enrich their lives. Its *Album Advisor* recommendation service stores music clips and reviews that can be easily accessed by customers as they search for the music they want.

Brand Awareness

Barnesandnoble.com had a unique problem: They had an existing brand that could be leveraged, but that brand also brought with it baggage of the offline image. As Ben Boyd, the company's director of communications, put it, "If Barnes & Noble is the Chair of the English Department, then we at barnesandnoble.com are the newest addition to the staff—very intelligent, very articulate, the hip new addition to the team. It's the same credibility, just a different presentation."[16] Like many companies making the leap from successful and well-known offline brands, barnesandnoble.com had to walk a bit of a tightrope as it tried to devise a brand strategy that was consistent with its offline brand—which had to be protected and not corrupted—and to develop a new brand that would be compelling and competitive in the new Internet market space. As Internet consultants, this is a scenario we'll encounter many times, and we must think carefully and creatively as we attempt to guide our clients to the best balance.

Customer Commitment

We've already discussed how the community at iVillage helps the site create loyal relationships with its customers. Customer loyalty and commitment are the key success factors in the Internet marketplace, as evidenced by the statistic we looked at earlier that states that 75 percent of ads are placed on the top ten sites. One of those sites, Yahoo, has recognized the need to develop committed customer relationships and has been a pioneer in the creative use of the Internet's unique capabilities to build that commitment.

In a recent study by NPD Group, an Internet market analysis firm, 92 percent of Yahoo users rate the service "excellent" or "very good," and 76 percent visit Yahoo first when searching the Web. Seventy-three percent bookmark Yahoo within their browsers.[17] This connection between the actual quality and utility of the site and customer loyalty again emphasizes the concepts I quoted from Harry Beckwith earlier: Brand must be based on truth, on real utility that the customer values. But the Yahoo team has also built some enhanced services that have since become standards of relationship building on the Net.

MyYahoo is a personalized home page that users can customize based on their particular needs and desires. A combination of a personal newspaper, stock ticker, mailbox, and portal, it offers all the searching capabilities of the Yahoo main page, plus the ability to see the news and events you favor in the format you prefer. The success of MyYahoo has spawned a host of imitators, including MySAP from SAP, the German business software giant, MyExcite for Yahoo competitor Excite@Home, and personal home pages from Lycos, Alta Vista, Amazon, and most other major sites.

By incorporating special services that encourage repeat visits, such as e-mail, customized stock portfolios, and chat rooms, Yahoo has achieved the coveted "stickiness"—that quality that causes users to return to the site and stay once they get there. Advertisers value stickiness because it gives them the opportunity to make repeated impressions and to target customers based on interests. These features have another distinct advantage: Due to the requirement for registration to access them, they force customers to reveal personal data, which can then be analyzed to improve the site and to target prospects.

This drive to build loyalty is a strategic effort made by the Yahoo team. Karen Edwards, Yahoo's vice president of brand marketing, explains, "We spend probably 90 percent of our time reaching current users and getting them to be more loyal."[18] Yet Yahoo's advertising budget has been smaller than that of many less established brands, and Yahoo has been one of the leaders in the "guerrilla marketing" movement, using such ploys as branded cars and neon signs to get the message out. Again, it's the quality of the service and its unique value to users that builds the brand.

As I hope these examples demonstrate, creative Net marketers can devise powerful marketing and branding tools that can significantly shape the success of the brand. Obviously, commitment to excellence and intimate knowledge of the marketplace are also critical success factors. Internet consultants who research the techniques that have made sites such as Amazon, Yahoo, and eBay successful, and who surf the Web with a critical eye thinking about the practices that are used by their favorite sites to draw them in and keep them loyal, will become valuable resources to their clients.

The Experience Is the Brand

According to Creative Good, a New York consulting firm that specializes in customer experience strategies on the Web (www.goodexperience.com), $19 billion in potential customer expenditures will be left unrealized in 2000 because of poor dot.com customer experience strategies.[19] Creative Good also estimates, based on their work with Internet businesses, that improvements in the customer experience can elevate the conversion rate—the number of visitors who actually make a purchase—by anywhere from 40 to over 140 percent. With industry conversion rates hovering around 2 percent,[20] just raising the conversion a single percentage point can have almost a $20 billion impact! These numbers, although based on some assumptions, should nonetheless indicate pretty clearly that better customer experiences can have a significant impact on Web-based business.

We've emphasized that, in the Internet economy, the branding methods of the past, in which a manufactured image is more important than the customer's actual experience of the product, are obsolete. No longer will a repeated one-way presentation be the central avenue to brand awareness in the customer's mind. The accumulation of experiences will build the brand. A positive brand experience causes the user to expect a superior product, and expectations color reality, as we learned in the Brand Placebo Effect concept explored earlier. Any negative experiences tend to be viewed as exceptions once a positive brand expectation is established.

Experience branding is not solely an Internet phenomenon. I've mentioned Starbucks multiple times in this chapter because I view them as an exceptional example of experience branding and marketing. Although the coffee aficionados I know insist that the coffee is superior, it's the entire experience, from the ambiance to the product presentation to the naming and selection, that makes Starbucks the popular destination that it is. The Hard Rock Cafe chain is another example of the experience brand. I doubt if many customers would argue that the food served at Hard Rock is superior in any way from the fare at the local diner, yet folks line up, buy merchandise, and look forward to visiting the Hard Rock outlet in every city they visit—because they have an expectation of an experience, including the memorabilia and the "vibes" that they'll find.

This is not to say that building an experience-based brand is easy—in fact it's a lot more complicated than building a marketing-driven brand. It's a lot easier to develop a series of beer commercials featuring sexy models in bikinis and handsome football players having fun than it is to get everyone in your organization, from the food servers to the kitchen staff to the coat checker to the telephone operator, to understand and exude a consistent and positive image. In the Internet world, business strategists, and the consultants who advise them, must build policies that create an online analogy to the offline concepts of consistency, friendliness, professionalism, and goodwill.

Obviously, for most customers the website is the company. The URL "domain brand name" that is selected, the speed of the site's load and response, the design—both technical and visual—the consistency and brand image, all of these elements make for a customer experience that is memorable and positive—or not. Yahoo, for instance, is easy and accessible to all, or, as Blaise Simpson, a director at Yahoo's public relations firm Niehaus Ryan Wong, has stated, "The Yahoo brand is associated with being very open. We want to keep the brand from being frightening in any way. It's not a luxury brand. It's a brand that can speak to just about everybody."[21] How this admirable goal is translated into a site design and a consistent brand image is the art of Web marketing. From the name, to the wacky advertising, to the guerrilla marketing efforts such as painted cars, Yahoo has succeeded in integrating its fun, informal, and approachable image into everything it does.

We mentioned before the challenge that Barnesandnoble.com had with the integration of its offline image with its new online entity. Many brick-and-mortar enterprises are facing the same challenges as they prepare to compete in the new world. How do offline retailers, whose stores can profitably carry only a few hundred items in stock, compete with their own online websites that can offer tens of thousands? How do conservative brick-and-mortar concerns that have built reputations based on their solid, dependable, and staid images project the modern image that the new economy requires without corrupting the brand? In some cases, separation from the existing brand may be the only viable alternative. In other cases, loose coupling with the existing brand, such as the BlueLight.com experiment under way at Kmart, in which the old brand name is used in promotion but the new entity also has its own identity, may be a smart tactic. There's no sure formula, but consistency and preservation of the brand must be balanced with the needs and competitive landscape of the new economy.

The experience must also include constant communication. Without the human interaction that characterizes business in the offline world, transacting business on the Web can seem cold and remote. Effective communication, from e-mails to live customer service on the site, can give the Web a human touch. Practical concerns also are important: When I order something from a live salesman, I can tell by our interaction whether or not he is understanding and receiving my order. On the Web, customers need confirmation that their orders, addresses, credit card verifications, and other practical aspects of the transaction are under control. Sites that communicate, both to develop relationship and comfort and to assure customers that their business is being taken care of effectively, deliver a superior experience.

WHO IS THE INTERNET CUSTOMER?

Now that we've elaborated on branding, let's talk about the target of all this marketing and branding activity, the Internet customer. In her excellent book on targeting Internet consumers, *Now or Never,*[22] Mary Modahl, vice president of research at Forrester Research Inc., shares some of Forrester's unique concepts of consumer categorization. In standard marketing, demographics are the central data points about individual consumers and groups of consumers. Demographics cover the basics: age, sex, salary, education, and so on. They are collected at an individual level and are then aggregated to give marketers insights into group dynamics. Some of this information can reveal a great deal. If marketers know how far your commute is, then they can guess how much you listen to the radio. If they know your zip code, then they can estimate the value of your home and then extrapolate from there your earnings. In standard broadcast marketing, demographics help marketers roughly target the appropriate demographic, so they can place beer commercials in the right places for beer drinkers and BMW ads in the right spots for likely luxury car customers.

In the Internet economy, however, demographics, although essential, are not sufficient. They can help us understand the factors that motivate and segment customers once they are online, but they do us no good in determining who will actually go online, in what numbers, from which groups. It may seem obvious that customers need to be affluent and technologically savvy enough to have and use a PC in order to be online prospects, but that does us no good in determining how many will go online in the next five or ten years or what they'll be interested in once they get there. As Modahl points out, "Nothing in the traditional arsenal of market research helps businesspeople predict how consumers will move to online shopping."[23]

To help business strategists (and their advisors) predict the potential behavior of online prospects, Modahl's firm, Forrester Research, has developed a new tool in the market research tool bag—technographics. Rather than simply looking at the demographic factors like address and income, technographics surveys attitudes—specifically attitudes toward technology—and uses that information to make predictions about the likelihood of a group going online and their behavior once they get there. By classifying individuals as technology optimists or pessimists and then matching that information with typical demographics, Forrester has developed a market research tool that is better suited to predicting Internet behavior.

For instance, according to Forrester's research, people over sixty-five are overwhelmingly pessimistic about technology, and those from Baby Boomer to age twenty are progressively more optimistic. This indicates that Internet businesses that are targeted or tailored to the youthful will garner more immediate interest than those that are senior-focused. Technology optimists are more likely to have been exposed to technology through their work, and so websites targeted at technology workers will probably be more immediately successful than those targeted at, for instance, blue-collar workers. Some of this may seem obvious, but by digging a bit deeper, the usefulness of this tool becomes clearer.

Many marketers will use the adoption bell curve to describe the "take rate" of a new product or technology. For instance, in Harry Beckwith's *The Invisible Touch*, Beckwith describes the "technology adoption curve," made up of the following:

- *Innovators,* who buy a new product or technology to be first on the block or for status reasons;

- *Early adoptors,* who will get on board quickly but tend to avoid immediate adoption;

- *Pragmatists,* who will buy a product once its utility to them is proven;

- *Late adoptors*; and

- *Laggards.*[24]

Modahl also uses a bell curve to describe her hierarchy of Internet customers, whom she categorizes as "early adopters, mainstream, and laggards." By matching the image and profile of the company to that of the target audience, marketers can use technographics as one more weapon in the arsenal. For instance, if your consulting client is one that would typically target the "technology optimist," that is, the young, technically savvy, professional with PC exposure at work, such as consulting clients in the financial services or specialized communications services industries, then that client can probably assume a quick uptake among early adopters, but would need to devise a strategy for attracting the mainstream audience and will need to decide whether the laggards are worth the time and money to attract. If your client's target is, for instance, the elderly population for a home health care product, using technographic analysis, you would assume that the "take rate" would be slower, with a much smaller population of early adopters, and you would advise that client to be sure that he's funded well enough to hold out until his target mainstream population comes online.

NEW ECONOMY MARKETING MODELS

We've looked at some sophisticated concepts in marketing as we've reviewed the fundamentals of brand building and marketing on the Internet. Let's now expand our exploration to look at some of the specific tactics that innovative eBusinesses are using to get their messages out to their target markets and to acquire and retain customers. The use of directories and search engines to attract browsers to your site, the use of e-mail, "opt in" lists, and viral marketing, and the use of other marketing methods such as the "guerrilla marketing" that Yahoo and other sites are famous for are all important topics in which any Internet consultant should be conversant.

Needle in a Pile of Needles: Search Engines and Link Exchanges

With the universal visibility of website addresses (URLs) on everything from cereal boxes to beer cans, many consumers will actually type in the address of the site they are looking for. This is a major departure from the early days of the Web, when dot.com names were still obscure except to early adopters of the Internet and surfers had little chance of finding anything without a directory or search engine. The early directories, such as Yahoo, were developed to solve this problem. Let's make a distinction between a directory such as Yahoo, which is hand indexed by Web librarians who look at every site submitted and make a judgment about where it should be categorized, and search engines such as Alta Vista or Northern Lights, which use software to read and store key words off actual sites on the Web and then store those key words in databases that are accessible to Web searchers. While Yahoo is the leader by far in the Web directory business—and a listing on its site has more likelihood of resulting in "click-throughs" to your client's site—the other search engines and portals are also important.

The importance of a prime listing on the directories and search engines is highlighted by the research done by Dan Sullivan, editor of *Search Engine Watch* (www.searchenginewatch.com), which shows that only 7 percent of searchers look beyond the third page of search results.[25] Some basic techniques that Web-page designers need to be aware of for getting noticed by search engines are as follows:

Page Title. The title of your home page is the place that a search engine will look at first and by which it will categorize your site. If you're selling bicycle tires and want to come up at the top of a search for bicycle tires, then having "bicycle tires" in your home page title is a good idea.

Meta Tags. HTML, the Web-page coding language, has the ability to include descriptive tags that are not visible to the Web browser but are used by search engines to categorize your site. Be sure that Web designers working on pages for your client take advantage of these tags to drive search engines to correctly categorize the site.

First Paragraph. Search engines will rate the language in your first paragraph more highly than other material on the site, under the assumption that you'll state the purpose of your site right up-front. It's also not bad advice from a purely human point of view: Tell browsers what your purpose is at the beginning.

The improvement of search engine placement has become an industry of its own, and the Yahoo category for "Search Engine Placement Improvement" has over one hundred entries. Some of the best of these services, such as NetPromote (www.cyberpromotion.com), will assist with the promotion of your site on outlets from search engines to directories through offline magazines and newspapers. It's important to remember that there are many other outlets besides the mainstream directories and search engines that can feature links to your site. Many Internet users are so focused on the Web that they forget that the Internet has other avenues, such as newsgroups and mailing lists, that could be appropriate promotion opportunities for your site. While it's bad "net-izenship" to dominate newsgroups and chat rooms with blatantly commercial messages, there's nothing wrong with taking a periodic look at newsgroups that are in your area of interest and responding or posting some subtle material that may point interested parties to your site. Key concepts here are *area of interest* and *subtle.* If you're a retailer of bicycle tires and you post barefaced ad copy to every newsgroup from comp.sci to alt.sex.fetish, you're setting yourself up for a blast of flame-mails.

Other channels for links include web-zines and trade publications in your field, print Web Yellow Pages, and context-specific sites. Another great conduit for generating click-throughs is the banner exchange, a reciprocal exchange program in which website managers and webmasters agree to post banners or links for each other. These programs have become very popular, with the Yahoo category for "Banner Exchanges" hosting over forty sites providing these services, some free and some for profit. The most well-known of these sites is Link Exchange, but there are many, some topic-specific and some geography-specific. These include everything from the Raleigh Banner Exchange focused on sites in the Raleigh, North Carolina, area to BannerWomen, focused on exchanges between sites with female-oriented content.

Of course there is always the standard banner advertisement, which is purchased from high-visibility sites such as Yahoo or AOL or from targeted sites such as golflink.com or Astronomy On-line. This type of advertising has become a billion dollar business, and the advertising revenue derived from banner placements drives the business models of sites from the search engines to many of the consumer-oriented sites, some of which earn more revenue from advertising than from product sales. Banner ads are a standard component of many commercial website promotional programs, and—for those sites with the budget to support them—can not only generate click-throughs but can also create brand awareness. Banner advertising is sold in three different models:

- *Impressions,* in which the advertiser pays a set fee per thousand viewers who see the site, regardless of whether or not they take any action or even notice the banner. As with billboards and television ads, you are paying for access to the viewer. General banner impressions like those that would be seen on a search engine front page are generally less expensive than tightly targeted impressions, such as on the golf or astronomy sites I mentioned earlier, or those targeted to specific demographics, such as financial or mortgage sites.

- *Click-throughs,* in which the marketing purchaser pays not simply for viewers who may or may not notice or act on the banner, but for the number of surfers who actually click on the banner to view the advertised site. This is the first step in developing a banner advertising model that pays for results rather than simple viewer access. Consultants should advise clients using click-throughs to be sure that they have negotiated the right to measure and audit the results to be sure that they are paying for actual site visits generated by that particular banner.

- *Surveys* are another type of results-oriented banner program. The advertiser pays only for surfers who not only go to the site, but fill out an information form that populates the advertiser's database. Obviously, this type of result has an even higher value than a click-through, as it allows businesses to create personalized marketing efforts based on the responses individual prospects give to the survey.

The banner advertising business is a large and complex topic and includes service providers such as DoubleClick—who outsource the entire Web advertising function, from banner design through placement, measurement, and payment, including the actual "serving" of ad content from their data centers and servers—and AdAuction—who works with advertisers to find unfilled space, both online and offline, for banners and other types of advertising content. Take a look at Yahoo's "Internet Promotion" category, where lots of service providers offer free consultations as well as white papers that serve as good reference material to the whole topic of Web advertising, search engine placement, and banner placement.

Viral Marketing

The classic example of viral marketing is the "Friends and Family" promotion created by long distance telephone company MCI, in which customers received a preferential rate if they could sign up their friends, family, and others whom they frequently called. By encouraging customers to, in effect, act as a sales arm of the company and by creating built-in "network effects" that increased the value of the offering by increasing the size of the network, MCI set off a new marketing practice that has come to its full fruition on the Internet.

The viral marketing concept was first brought to the Web by the founders and original investors of Hotmail, one of the pioneers of free Web-based e-mail services. With the simple placement of a line of text at the bottom of every customer's e-mail message encouraging the reader to "Get Your Private, Free Email at http://www.hotmail.com," Hotmail attracted, within eighteen months, twelve million registered subscribers. Hotmail, now a Microsoft property, currently has more than thirty-five million subscribers and still signs up more than 100,000 every day. Yet Hotmail has spent less than $500,000 on marketing, advertising, and promotion. Other free e-mail providers have spent millions in advertising and achieved a fraction of the user base.[26]

How did Hotmail pull off this tremendous growth, which eventually caught the attention of Microsoft, resulting in Hotmail's acquisition by the software giant to the tune of $700 million? By turning every user of the service into a salesperson, a technique known as viral marketing. Every outbound message conveys an advertisement and an implied endorsement from the sender. As an example of the power of this marketing concept, consider this: Hotmail is the largest e-mail provider in Sweden and India despite the fact that it has never advertised or done any marketing in those countries.

As another example of this technique, consider the viral promotion approach taken by Mirabilis, the Israeli inventor of the ICQ instant messaging technology that signed up twelve million users before America Online bought it for almost $300 million. To use ICQ, both sides of the online conversation need to download the client software. Each subscriber e-mails friends, encouraging them to participate in this new communication channel. The friends, if they enjoy the ability to find and chat with their comrades on the Internet instantly, repeat the pattern. One by one and two by two, this viral spiral creates a wave of interest and enthusiasm that money can't buy.

The typical viral strategy has a couple of critical objectives: (1) Speed the adoption of the new technology or service and (2) build in hooks to create barriers to switching. Both e-mail, which is a pain to change once you've informed all your contacts and printed your business cards, and instant messaging, in which both sides need the same client software, have these switching barriers built in.

Viral marketing has achieved such popularity conceptually that many investors and venture capitalists will look for a viral angle on deals they're considering. Internet consultants should guide their clients to seek some vehicle for generating this automatic word-of-mouth as part of their strategy. The Internet is a great medium for the replication of an innovative business model or a creative new technology. A great concept can spread more quickly over the Internet than has ever been possible in the physical world. Although it naturally lends itself to free communications or network applications, viral marketing is a marketing model that can work for almost any Internet application. The eCommerce and software distribution company Release Software, for instance, has developed an add-in viral marketing agent that works like this: Embed your software application in Release's eCommerce engine for electronic software distribution and encourage users to share the software with interested acquaintances. When a customer shares the application with a friend, it activates the embedded sales agent to offer a thirty-day trial period, after which the new user has to pay for the software. This ingenious tactic turns shareware into a sales opportunity.

Of course, as we've discovered time and time again, good marketing concepts can be corrupted and turned into annoying intrusions by overzealous marketers. For instance, Denver-based e-mail marketer Epidemic Marketing has developed a way to take viral marketing to a new level of intrusiveness and annoyance. Epidemic allows senders to embed graphic advertising links in their messages. Users download and install the epiNabler, which works with most e-mail programs. Why would people try to irritate their friends and correspondents this way? If the recipient clicks on the ad and buys, the sender receives a 5 percent commission on the sale, and the advertisers pay Epidemic five to fifty cents per click-through.

Permission Marketing

"Opt-in" or "permission marketing" has proved to be one of the most effective methods of reaching consumers yet devised on the Web. A recent survey of Internet users conducted by Internet marketing consultants FloNetwork and pollsters NFO Interactive found that 89 percent of those surveyed indicated that "opt-in" e-mail is their preferred means of receiving information about products of specific interest to them. The survey results underscore the overwhelming popularity of permission-based e-mail—69 percent of respondents believe it is the Internet's most powerful marketing tool, and 71 percent of permission-based e-mail recipients who took part in the survey said they usually click through to a company's website.[27]

Rather than interrupting thousands of undifferentiated e-mail recipients and hoping that some fraction will be interested enough to browse your site, marketers are discovering that it makes more sense—and is more cost-efficient—to target an audience of consumers interested enough in your offering to ask for more information or, better yet, to volunteer for an ongoing relationship. When customers agree to receive periodic newsletters or promotional e-mails because of genuine interest in the topic, whether it's golf or astronomy (typically by clicking on a "I'd like to be informed of offers about this topic" button when they visit or register on a site), the opportunity to develop a mutually beneficial relationship takes a quantum leap. Consultants should advise their clients to always give site visitors or customers a chance to "opt-in" to a club, newsletter, mailing list, or other permission-based relationship and to then use that permission effectively.

How do smart permission marketers deliver the best value to their customers? By following a few simple rules:

- *Teach!* Use the attention offered by the prospect to impart information of real value, not just marketing hype. People don't give permission to be marketed to; they give permission to receive valuable information. Permission can be taken away just as easily as it was granted, if all you do is use that consent to jam another series of undifferentiated broadcast messages down the prospect's throat. Teach the consumer about your product or service, especially how the customer can obtain the most value from your offerings. Always focus on the value to the consumer, not on your need to move more products.

- *Learn!* Turn the permission relationship into a dialogue. Give prospects an opportunity to speak back, and demonstrate that you've heard their feedback. As always, the marketplace, made up of individual customers, will tell you what they like and hate about the service, offering, newsletter, and e-mails. Listen and learn.

- *Earn!* Don't forget, however, that this is a business relationship. Don't let the flow of newsletters and e-mails go on automatic pilot. Develop some metrics for your consulting clients. Be sure that your permission campaign is helping them to identify profitable customers and giving those customers the information that they need to become more tied in to the company—and more profitable.

One-to-One Marketing

When I was a kid in Brooklyn, New York, the guy who owned the little candy store on the corner knew that my father smoked Winstons, that my mom smoked Tareytons, and that I liked butter pecan ice cream. He saved a copy of the Sunday *New York Times* for me, no matter what time in the day on Sunday I came down to get it, and he slipped a copy of the latest Batman comic behind the counter so I wouldn't miss it. He had the same knowledge of every customer in the neighborhood. It was unlikely that anyone who shopped at Phil's would go anywhere else. Why go through the hassle and inconvenience of developing a relationship with another store owner, having him ask what kind of cigarettes you need or what flavor ice cream you want and risk missing *The Times* or Batman?

With the demise of the corner shop, of course, and the dispersion of the old neighborhood, that level of personal service died away. The guy in the Walgreens sees customers from a five-mile radius, not a one-block radius, and it's a pretty rare occurrence for him to recognize you, much less know or care what brand you prefer. Obviously, the server on the other side of a Web connection cares a lot less. Yet people crave that personal attention. In a recent survey, customers rated "being recognized and made to feel important" as one of their most important factors in developing loyalty to a particular store. Yet only 33 percent said that their current stores or providers made them feel that way, even among the vendors like airlines and credit cards that spend millions in loyalty programs and reward giveaways.[28]

The one-to-one marketing philosophy is an attempt to re-create that personal attention and recognition in our impersonal mass market. This philosophy has gained a tremendous amount of momentum in the past few years, based on a confluence of events:

- The release and acceptance of the seminal work in this field, *The One to One Future,* by Peppers and Rogers[29];

- The development of sophisticated database technology that could capture and manipulate massive volumes of customer data; and

- The creation of customer relationship management software that could assist marketers in analyzing that data and creating targeted marketing programs based on the results.

The first event, the presentation of a new pattern of marketing by Peppers and Rogers, created a wave of interest in the possibilities of marketing to individuals rather than to groups. As we discussed, most marketing theory is based on demographics, under the assumption that folks who live in the same zip code, listen to the same music, and drive the same cars probably have a lot of other tastes in common and could be marketed to successfully by analyzing those similarities and appealing to them. Peppers and Rogers offered a different approach; as Martha Rogers explains it:

"The one to one enterprise would engage in a Learning Relationship with individual customers that worked like this: I know who you are. I remember you. I get you to talk to me. And then, because I know something about you that my competitors don't know, I can do something for you my competitors can't do—not for any price. This means the customer actually adds value to what you can do for her and will find it easier and less costly to do more business with you than to start over somewhere else."[30]

The one-to-one philosophy is based on a simple premise: Companies can gain better competitive advantage by winning a bigger share of each customer's business and by deepening customer loyalty through intimate knowledge of individual customer needs than by focusing on growing market share through new customers. Peppers and Rogers identified a four-step program that would help enterprises migrate to this one-to-one relationship with their clients:

1. *Identify.* Through the use of sophisticated sampling and database methodologies, each customer is tagged so that each can be identified throughout his interaction with the company. This was a reaction to the problem that many large enterprises had of keeping multiple records on customers, based on their interactions with different departments, so that, for instance, the bank where you have your mortgage, checking account, and credit card has three separate records and can't correlate them to categorize you, sell to you, or develop a relationship with you.

2. *Differentiate.* Once customers become visible across the entire enterprise, each customer needs to be differentiated to understand both the customer's value to the company and the company's value to the customer. Both of these elements are critical, as it's important for the company to know whether this customer is profitable, loyal, and long-term, and the company must know what it is that the customer values—price, convenience, completeness, or preferential treatment—in order to develop a strategy for developing a relationship that is both valuable to the client and profitable for the enterprise.

3. *Interact.* The best way to learn (and keep learning) about the customer's values and desires is to interact and record that interaction. Whether it's through the tracking of transactions or through offering periodic surveys and questionnaires

or through other feedback mechanisms, the one-to-one enterprise will offer a permanent dialogue with its customers.

4. *Customize.* Treat each customer differently, based on what is learned about the customer's needs, and about the customer's value to the enterprise.[31]

It's conventional wisdom that the Internet is a perfect forum for these concepts to take root. Because Internet businesses can be developed to track every transaction—in fact every page view and click—Internet marketers can obtain an extraordinarily complete picture of a customer's preferences and behaviors. Because the technology is now sophisticated enough to offer Web customers personalized pages based on their preferences and past transaction history, websites can offer the customization called for in this method. The personal recommendations offered by sites like Amazon are the classic example of this technique. The new Web-based marketplaces, servicing vertical markets like chemicals and raw materials, are also becoming adept at this technique by using a customer's history to offer personal categories of products and to seek out the deals and relationships that will be meaningful to that client and highlight them on the site. Dell's "Partner Pages," designed specifically for each major purchaser of Dell computers and offering only that gear that is officially sanctioned by that organization's "standards bodies," is another example.

Internet consultants should advise clients to develop their websites with these techniques in mind. From the capture of personal information at the beginning of the relationship to the tracking and analysis of transaction data generated by each and every customer transaction to the creation of personalized pages that highlight the needs, preferences, and requirements of each customer, these capabilities need to be "baked in" to the client's Internet strategy from the beginning. In cases in which the technology infrastructure already exists—and consists of legacy databases and multiple incompatible customer records—getting to this level of customer relationship is a daunting task. Listen to Patricia Seybold, industry analyst, from her book on Internet marketing, *Customers.com*: "You'll learn, to your dismay, that in order to really streamline tasks from the customer's point of view, you'll have to do major rework on your existing enterprise systems and business processes. Once customers start to do business with you via the Web, your company is left standing naked in front of its customers. Every wrinkle shows; every blemish spoils the customer's ability to help herself to information and transactions."[32] This is what Larry

Tanning meant by his phrase "the integration wall"—the difficulty of migrating and integrating data from legacy systems into a Web-enabled infrastructure that truly serves customers and that gives you the visibility and control you need to develop customer relationships.

Many of the large software vendors, such as Oracle and Seibel Systems, have mature offerings in the customer relationship management (CRM) field, which can add real value to this undertaking. Other "born on the Web" software development houses, such as Broadvision, Epiphany, and Art Technology Group, have developed software offerings that help with tasks like the capture and analysis of customer activities and the creation of personalized pages based on those "mouse tracks." Internet consultants should browse the Web pages of some of these companies and gain an understanding of the capabilities of these software offerings so that they can help customers select and implement them. They should also read the central works that put forward this marketing concept, such as the Peppers and Rogers and Pat Seybold books referred to above.

Community Marketing

We've talked about the success that businesses like iVillage have had with the community concept. Many of the most successful online businesses (iVillage and even AOL) were originally focused on the community aspect of the online experience. Even pre-Net, the dial-up online sites such as CompuServe and Prodigy built much of their momentum from allowing people with similar interests to get together and chat, share stories, give tips and pointers, and generally interact. Before the Web's graphical user interface came along, the Internet also had its built-in communities, such as newsgroups and Internet Relay Chat, where text-based "threads" allowed folks to form communities of interest.

There are many ways that community can be brought to a website. From the product reviews posted on Amazon.com's website, to the breast cancer support communities on WebMD, to the virtual conferencing enabled by sites such as Webex, the ability to communicate many-to-many enabled by the Internet opens new avenues of marketing interaction that explode the conventional broadcast model of marketing. Before the Net, broadcast advertising was the only way prospects could receive information about a company's offerings. Now, with the reach and interactive capabilities of the Net, one of the most effective ways to ensure that the information needs of prospects and customers will be met is to allow marketplace participants to answer each other's questions. No amount of vendor-supplied promotional brochureware can approach the credibility of contributions from other users.

Communities can be formed along two different lines:

- *Vertical communities* bring together Web surfers with a common interest—whether golf, astronomy, or day trading—or with common beliefs or values, such as Republicans or Zoroastrians. Professional societies, such as the Independent Computer Consultants Association, or clubs, such as the American Kennel Club, derive unique benefits from the ability to interact over the Web instantly and globally.

- *Horizontal communities* are composed of site viewers with a common attribute, such as teens, music lovers, or voracious readers. These types of affiliations are usually best served by informational communities such as peer product reviews or posted comments.

The vertical bond is much stronger than the horizontal one. Those who chose to be a member of the American Kennel Club are more likely to be interested in interacting with one another than are the overall horizontal group of all dog owners, for instance. Sites that can identify a strong vertical affiliation and add value for that group through a well-designed community on the site can develop a powerful loyalty engine.

Some examples of community programs include the following:

- Technical discussion forums;
- Interactive Webcasts;
- User-created product reviews;
- Virtual conferences and meetings;
- Expert seminars; and
- User-managed profile pages.

Internet consultants must help their clients understand that even mundane site features such as classified ads, job boards, and industry news can be turned into community elements by making them interactive. Classified ads seem static and dated in comparison with the interactive, user-created classifieds on marketplace auction sites such as PlasticsNet. Interactive community classifieds allow market participants to recommend products, vendors, and other listings to the author of the classified ad. PlasticsNet's 35,000 registered users generate thousands of classified advertisements every year. PlasticsNet also has searchable user profiles that allow users to submit contact information, Web links, and any personal or company information they choose. Other Web exchanges are also realizing the benefits of adding community elements to their sites. Altra Energy has discussion areas for members to discuss technical support issues and questions, as well as general discussion areas for each energy marketplace. HoustonStreet's live discussion forum, SquawkBox, allows energy traders to discuss industry topics and ask each other questions about the HoustonStreet marketplace.

The creation of communities is another Web marketing function that has spawned outsourced providers. Participate.com, as an example, has developed an integrated offering that incorporates strategic consulting, enabling software, metrics and measurement methodologies, and ongoing optimization to ensure that their customers, such as Hewlett-Packard, NBC, Ask Jeeves, and Ace Hardware, are obtaining the most benefit from the communities they've created. Working with an experienced community development expert can often add significant marketing muscle and customer loyalty to the commercial websites of our consulting clients.

Innovative Marketing

Yahoo has licensed its brand name to a snowboard manufacturer; visitors to the ski slopes will soon see boards with the familiar purple and yellow logo. They've plastered the Yahoo logo on the Zamboni ice-smoothing machine used at the San Jose Sharks hockey games. They've built a giant neon sign resembling a motel or restaurant billboard near San Francisco's major highways, where Silicon Valley commuters can't help but notice it. Yahoo has also issued a press release proclaiming the "udderly unique" pair of purple plastic cows the company has installed in lower "Moo York," wired to let people send "moo mail."

The auction site eBay has also done some innovative marketing by outfitting a couple of RVs and sending them around the country to swap meets, county fairs, and other venues where they can tell their story of interactive user auctions.

It's not just the major sites that engage in this form of marketing, often called "guerrilla marketing" after the book of that title by advertising guru Jay Conrad

Levinson. Outpost, the online computer and electronics retailer, shot gerbils out of a cannon at a recent event. BigWords, the textbook e-tailer, featured the character "Mini-Me" from the latest Austin Powers film dressed in a BigWords-branded orange jumpsuit and gave away twenty thousand mini-basketballs for their December 1999 marketing event. "Branded fruit" was invented by Ask Jeeves, the natural language search portal, which has placed promotional stickers on sixteen million apples, forty million oranges, and 100 million banana bunches. Di-Ann Eisnor, founder of Eisnor Interactive, one of the Internet's more creative guerrilla marketing firms, remarks, "There's so much damn noise it forces us to think through new and creative ways of talking to people." Eisnor works exclusively with Internet companies and boasts of the three "new media channels" Eisnor Interactive has conceived in recent months: The "branded parking space," the "branded hitchhiker," and the "branded chauffeur."[33] Halfway, Oregon, population 345, has agreed to change its name to Half.com in return for twenty-two new computers, a $5,000 donation to the local fair, and $75,000 to defray the cost of new road signs.

Internet companies desperate to capture the attention of consumers and journalists are enamored of these innovative marketing techniques, often called "extreme marketing" or "grassroots marketing." "There are so many startups out there with so [few] marketing dollars, but they need to be heard among all this noise, so guerrilla marketing becomes the holy grail," says Michael Diamant, CEO of New York-based iClips, a streaming-video message site. "Guerrilla tactics have become a hot topic for a lot more companies out there over the past few months."[34]

Some of these innovative marketing efforts, such as AOL's creative decision to send out mass quantities of diskettes and CDs introducing the service, have paid off big. Others have backfired. Guerrilla marketing, in the early days of the Internet, often took the form of newsgroup postings that interrupted the regular flow of online conversation and community to hawk a particular service, product, or website. These interruptions were not kindly taken to by the newsgroup regulars and often resulted in flame-mail campaigns in retaliation. Although guerrilla marketing has become a staple of brand awareness strategies, especially for startups and cash-strapped businesses, some of the tactics used by some companies have migrated from innovative to intrusive.

Evite is a website that allows users to organize events like picnics, family reunions, and birthday parties and then send electronic invitations (the "e-vites" of the title) to all the participants. It's also a company that's received a lot of press lately, not all flattering, about its aggressive use of guerrilla marketing. Their Valentine's Day blitz of San Francisco trade editors and media personalities by two "Cupids" dressed in diapers and angel wings was seen as creative and revolutionary by some. At the June 2000 public relations industry conference, Visibility 2000, Evite was cited as one of the best guerrilla marketers around. In terms of generating press notice by the Cupid stunt, however, the effort was a failure. The only major notice it generated was a negative article in *The Industry Standard*, citing Evite as the epitome of wasteful, intrusive, self-congratulatory "annoyance marketing."[35] Interviewed for that article, David Margulius, Evite COO, explained their marketing techniques this way: "Guerrilla marketing is at the core of everything we do; it's what gives us personality. The goal here is to turn Evite into a household name. Toward that end, we've assembled a team ready to do whatever it takes to attain that goal."

Now read the comments of *The Industry Standard's* Gary Rivlin, commenting on Evite's approach: "There's something slightly thuggish about Evite's methods, something inherently rude about a swarm of zealously peppy marketeers bullying you into listening."

I dwell on this not to berate Evite, but because Internet consultants must understand the options that they can employ when advising their clients on marketing techniques. As evidenced by the successful efforts of Yahoo, AOL, eBay, and others, out-of-the-box thinking in the marketing department works, especially with the edgy, avant-garde audience that makes up the Internet early adopters. And Evite CEO Josh Silverman has a valid point when he remarks, "I talk to my peers in the industry and they talk about the growing sense of disillusionment with traditional marketing mediums like radio and television and outdoor billboards, so what we've been seeing in the last few months is that people are paying much more attention to on-the-street guerrilla marketing. They've crunched the numbers and come to the point we've been all along, that guerrilla work is the way to go."[36]

The important thing for Internet consultants to remember is that, like all marketing efforts, guerrilla marketing must be pertinent to the audience, must not form a negative opinion in the prospect's mind, and above all, must be strictly measured by results, not by how much fun it is or how creative it makes us feel. As Di-Ann Eisnor of Eisnor Interactive says, "People think all you have to do is get out on the street and make some noise, but it's not that easy. It's sort of just Marketing 101. They forget that the idea of targeting is still important. They forget that you need to have a relevant message."[37]

THE MESSAGE FOR INTERNET CONSULTANTS

At this point in the book, it's probably becoming a cliché, but I'll say it again: The topic I cover in this chapter is huge and obviously cannot be given the depth and breadth of treatment it deserves in this forum. Internet consultants who are migrating to a full-service practice from a technically focused practice—and who don't have training and experience in the marketing and branding arena—can get an overview of these topics here. I hope those readers will have their interest and professional curiosity piqued enough by this treatment to seek out the original sources cited in the references and Bibliography and deepen their knowledge of this topic. As many of those quoted here have noted, the Internet space is so crowded and (in the land-grab environment) so undifferentiated, that marketing and gaining brand awareness have become both increasingly challenging and increasingly necessary. Internet consultants can add terrific value in this endeavor, but only if they come to the advisory table with the right tools, experience, and "hype detector" in place.

End Notes

1. Peppers, D., & Rogers, M. *Enterprise One to One: Tools for Competing in the Information Age.* New York: Currency/Doubleday, 1997.
2. Hughes, A.M. *Strategic Database Marketing.* New York: McGraw-Hill, 1994.
3. Reichheld, F., & Schefter, P. E-Loyalty: Your Secret Weapon on the Web. *Harvard Business Review,* July/August 2000.
4. Carpenter, P. *eBrands, Building an Internet Business at Breakneck Speed.* Boston: Harvard Business School Press, 2000.
5. Hawley, N. Brand Defined. *Business 2.0,* June 27, 2000.
6. Beckwith, H. *The Invisible Touch.* New York: Warner Books, 2000, p. 100.
7. Carpenter, P. *eBrands, Building an Internet Business at Breakneck Speed.* Boston: Harvard Business School Press, 2000, p. 89.
8. Anderson, D., & Hammer, B. Going for Broke on the Super Bowl. *The Industry Standard,* Jan. 21, 2000.
9. Hawley, N. Brand Defined. *Business 2.0,* June 27, 2000.
10. Hof, R., Browder, S., & Elstrom, P. Internet Communities—Forget Surfers. A New Class of Netizen Is Settling In. *Business Week,* May 5, 1997.
11. Green, H., & Hamelstein, L. To the Victors Belong the Ads. *Business Week Online* [*www.businessweek.com*], Oct. 4, 1999.
12. Reichheld, F., & Schefter, P. E-Loyalty: Your Secret Weapon on the Web. *Harvard Business Review,* July/August 2000.
13. Lake, D. WANTED: Loyal E-Shoppers. *The Industry Standard,* Sept. 2, 2000.

14. Beckwith, H. *The Invisible Touch.* New York: Warner Books, 2000, p. 100.

15. Carpenter, P. *eBrands: Building an Internet Business at Breakneck Speed.* Boston: Harvard Business School Press, 2000.

16. ibid.

17. ibid.

18. ibid.

19. Hurst, M. Dot Com Survival Guide. *www.creativegood.com,* June 12, 2000.

20. ibid.

21. op cit, Carpenter, p. 157.

22. Modahl, M. *Now or Never.* New York: HarperBusiness, 2000.

23. ibid, p. 4.

24. op cit, Beckwith, p. 58.

25. op cit, Carpenter, p. 24.

26. Jurvetson, S. Turning Customers into a Sales Force. *Business 2.0,* Nov. 19, 1999.

27. Based on a survey posted on the site of Internet marketing consultancy e-marketer *www.emarketer.com.*

28. The 1997 Retail Advertising and Marketing Association International Research Project on Loyalty Programs. Pittsburgh: Marshall Marketing and Communications, Inc.

29. Peppers, D., & Rogers, M. *The One to One Future.* New York: Currency/Doubleday, 1993.

30. Rogers, M. Foreword to *Loyalty.com* by Newell, F. New York: McGraw-Hill, 2000.

31. Newell, F. *Loyalty.com.* New York: McGraw-Hill, 2000.

32. Seybold, P. *Customers.com.* New York: Times Business/Random House, 1998.

33. The material on guerrilla marketing is based on reporting by Gary Rivlin, in his July 31, 2000, article, The Cult of the Marketeers, in *The Industry Standard.*

34. ibid.

35. ibid.

36. ibid.

37. ibid.

chapter SEVEN

The Virtual Meets the Physical

RESTRUCTURING THE CHAIN

There comes a point in every Internet business transaction at which the virtual meets the physical. As we've discussed in our review of Web marketing, the Web-based brand is an experience brand, creating an image of quality based on the business' ability to deliver a complete package of services that includes both the "customer-facing" elements like the site itself and the entire fulfillment chain that delivers the right item at the right time to the right address. At the instant that the customer clicks the "buy" button, whether it's a retail customer buying a blouse or a corporate purchasing agent bidding on a ton of steel, a chain of events must occur that will result in the delivery of the product in a way that enhances the customer's mental image of the brand. The fulfillment chain also includes all the internal processes within the business that accept returns, provide customer support, present requests for payment, credit those payments to the client account, manage inventory, forecast demand, and do it all at a profit.

In the early days of the Net, the theory was that companies could use the website as a collection point for customer orders and then aggregate those orders and send them to a fulfillment organization, thus becoming an "inventory-less" enterprise. The early Amazon model was based on this concept, with the assumption that distribution partners such as the Ingram Book Group would be glad to act as the company's fulfillment partner and would deliver the speed, accuracy, and quality that customers expect. But wholesale distributors are not in the retail delivery business, with its high fulfillment cost per order and its "one-sy, two-sy" model of delivering single titles to multiple customers. Amazon, and all its brethren in the first wave of online retailers, realized quickly that they'd need to develop a fulfillment function that they could manage and control if they wanted to attract and retain a customer base. Thus was one of the first of many myths about Internet commerce subsequently discredited. In a famous Gartner Group report published in March of 1999 entitled "The Fallacies of Web-Commerce Fulfillment,"[1] some of the early illusions of Internet fulfillment were exploded:

- Fallacy 1: We're selling over the Web, so we must be making money.
- Fallacy 2: Our differentiation on the Web will come from our front-end processes.
- Fallacy 3: We can always do back-end integration later.
- Fallacy 4: Our logistics operations can handle Web-commerce fulfillment.
- Fallacy 5: Our traditional supplier relations will support Web commerce.
- Fallacy 6: Our order management system can handle Web commerce.
- Fallacy 7: We can now sell effectively to anyone around the globe.

Although this report is now over a year old and its accuracy has been validated by events, there are still many entrepreneurs who build business models based on fallacious thinking. There are still those who think that posting a page on the World Wide Web makes you a worldwide company or that logistical processes can be wholly outsourced and that entrepreneurs can just assume that they will be handled efficiently. It's our central role as consultants to be aware of the guidelines for success outlined by analysts such as Gartner and to guide our clients past the failed myths of the past and towards business models that deliver the goods.

DELIVERING ON THE CLICK

Internet consumers, while privileged to have access to the great convenience, variety, and efficiency of this new medium, are denied the basic finality of completing the transaction and walking out of the store with the selected item in hand. Astute Internet retailers recognize this deficiency and construct their sites to set a clear expectation of when the item will arrive by posting shipping schedules and offering options for delivery dates. The best sites also keep the customer informed by notifying them via e-mail or by "where is my order" status reports on the site. In an environment in which customers are relying on a photograph in order to select their purchase and on an impersonal website to complete the transaction, the least the e-tailer can do is keep customers informed of their order's delivery status.

In a study performed for *Business 2.0* magazine by the fulfillment outsourcer Electron Economy,[2] a sizable portion of their test orders arrived late, anywhere from days to weeks after the specified delivery date. MarthaStewart.com, CVS.com, and LandsEnd.com, for instance, delivered nearly every order after the date promised. One of the test orders from MarthaStewart.com arrived a full month after placement. Eight of the test orders placed for the study never showed up at all! eToys.com, for example, failed to deliver one-third of the items purchased, and its customer service agents were unable to explain why those orders never were processed.

Another finding of the Electron Economy study was that some of the most fundamental functions of retail are ignored by many of the Internet e-tailers. What brick-and-mortar store would fail to brand the shopping bag you use to carry home your purchase? Even the local supermarket takes the trouble to print its name and logo on the paper bag you take home, yet the study found that many e-tailers either neglect to brand their shipping material at all, or, worse, ship their products in unreliable or unsafe packaging. WalMart.com, for instance, shipped a fifteen-pound ax in a box free of packing material and falling apart at every seam. According to the study, "The box was devoid of branding, a safety hazard, and a real danger to its recipient."

The study also cited instances in which a wire wastebasket arrived bent and twisted in a paper-thin plastic bag, and a shipment from Sears.com containing a broom was shipped in a black garbage bag, taped at one end to secure its protruding handle. In contrast to these breaches of basic retail etiquette, some companies differentiate themselves positively by their focus on the details of customer fulfillment. According to the study, PlanetRx.com delivered each item in a Ziploc-style bag, snugly secured with bubble wrap to ensure that products arrived in pristine condition. Similarly, Garden.com's packages, branded with fluorescent logos, contained biodegradable packing material and information regarding its disposal, plus a number of promotional items.

The value-adding eConsultant is constantly enhancing her understanding of the issues facing Internet enterprises by keeping up with the studies and analysis being done in the industry, she's scouring the trade press for the recommendations of the experts and the success stories that illustrate winning strategies, and she's looking at her engagements holistically, taking into account the back-end as well as the front-end issues, the fine details of packaging and shipping as well as the grand strategic themes, and providing her clients with the best advice across all the disciplines that together create competitive advantage in the Net marketplace.

Preparing for eFulfillment

The chain of customer service that sustains a real business model hasn't changed, even though much of the technology that supports that chain has evolved significantly. From the "silk routes" of the early traders in oriental fabrics and spices to the trading lanes of the sea that were dominated by the European naval powers, the rules of commerce remain simple and straightforward—sell it, then get it there. Now that the time and distance between the customer and her product selection have become abbreviated, the tolerance for logistical delay is also reduced. The requirement for quick, reliable, accurate fulfillment has become more central to a successful business strategy than ever.

Unfortunately, the fulfillment models that were implemented in the early days of the Internet were not up to the task, as demonstrated by the logistical failings of the 1999 Christmas season that we explored earlier. The instant turnaround expectations that the Net creates carry a hidden snag: Unlike the fulfillment models associated with mail, catalog, or telephone ordering, which allowed many companies to hide logistical problems because of long order cycle times, the customer's expectation of immediate fulfillment leaves no place to take cover. The Internet creates an environment that is extraordinarily demanding of a business' internal processes, as the website must have the ability to reflect current stock instantaneously, must offer guarantees of delivery time that are met without fail, and must reflect pricing information in real time. The story becomes more complex when we move from the world of consumer business on the Net to the B2B universe, where partners are not only buying and selling to each other, but are collaborating on manufacturing, design, and delivery and are creating customized versions of the value chain that include multiple outsourced functions scattered around the globe. How can we advise clients successfully in the face of these enormous logistical challenges? For those of us who are not business process experts, this element of Internet consulting is an even greater test of our advisory skills.

Just to give you a flavor of the complexity of the business process requirement, let's take a look at the list of business process elements published by the International Standards Organization in its ISO 9000 series of quality initiatives (see Figure 7.1).[3] For the uninitiated, ISO 9000 is an international set of quality standards created by this global consortium of standards bodies. The purpose of the ISO 9000 certification is to facilitate world trade by setting forth quality standards for virtually all the activities and processes involved in designing, producing, and distributing a product or service. The major American automakers, for example, have decided that all their suppliers must meet ISO 9000-related quality standards, a decision affecting at least fifteen thousand businesses. So have many electronic, medical device, chemical, and industrial equipment manufacturers, as well as more than thirteen thousand U.S. service firms involved in everything from IT consulting services to law and health care.

Figure 7.1
The International Standards Organization
(ISO) 9000 Quality Management Standards

The Twenty Areas of Business Activity Covered by ISO 9000

1. Management Responsibility
2. Quality Planning
3. Contract Review
4. Design Control
5. Document and Data Control
6. Purchasing
7. Control of Customer-Supplied Product
8. Product Identification and Traceability
9. Process Control
10. Inspecting and Testing
11. Control of Inspection and Test Equipment
12. Inspection and Test Status
13. Control of Non-Conforming Product
14. Corrective and Preventive Actions
15. Storage, Handling, Packaging, Preservation, and Delivery
16. Control of Quality Records
17. Internal Quality Audits
18. Training
19. Servicing
20. Statistical Techniques

As you can see, these standards cover the gamut of every conceivable internal process a business might need, from the management oversight required to give direction and vision to an enterprise, all the way through the internal chain of processes required to plan, design, track, and ship quality products or services. I'm not suggesting that Internet consultants or their clients need to plan for ISO 9000 certification any time soon, although the time will come when that will be an integral part of preparing for international Net commerce. I present this list here because I believe that Internet consultants will benefit from a review of these processes, since they are the central practices that every business enterprise must manage. This list also provides a framework for our ongoing discussion, in which we will look at some of these processes and try to understand the special requirements and constraints that the Internet economy imposes on these procedures.

It's clear that the speed requirements of operating in "Internet time" create the need for nimble, rapid fulfillment processes. In fact, IT industry analysts such as The Gartner Group count the ability to deploy these high-velocity, high-accuracy logistical systems as a key differentiator between winners and losers on the Net. Posting a dynamic catalog on the Web, with its requirement for constant updating of stock levels, pricing structures, and inventory items, is no trivial task. Creating a logistical organization that can consistently and quickly deliver the product or service is much more complex. Fulfillment, from the stocking activities that keep profitable items on the shelves, to the picking and packing that prepares them for shipment, to the shipping and tracking, to the resolution of issues and returns, is now event-driven and must react instantaneously to changes in customer preference, transaction volume, price, and quality.

What makes this so difficult? There are many structural impediments that consultants must learn to recognize. Many existing enterprises, built around a bricks-and-mortar business model, don't have the IT infrastructure to handle the real-time requirements of Web commerce. Interconnection along the links of the value chain is a requirement in this real-time economy, so that—from the customer back to the vendor and through the distributor, supplier, shipper, and support organization—data can flow as events occur. This not only strains the technology networks that have been developed between value chain partners, but it also strains cultures, as a new level of information sharing becomes necessary. Consultants must work with their clients to assess the linkages between themselves and their trading partners and must address the cultural issues that cause companies to keep information hidden that must be shared.

The use of EDI (electronic data interchange) and other hard-coded computer interfaces between partners was a tremendous step forward for many enterprises ten years ago. Now these legacy integration architectures and fulfillment systems can be a handicap. Enterprises that are exploring the possibilities of migrating their business models to the Web are discovering that the information required to manage high-speed fulfillment processes resides outside the enterprise—in the systems of their suppliers, distributors, and logistics partners. They are finding, when they begin to attempt integration with those external partners, that external data are often in proprietary home-grown applications and formats, are wrapped in processes and procedures that are difficult to understand and resist re-engineering, and are based on the principle that all meaningful data resides within the "four walls" of the enterprise. Thus, the challenge for organizations retooling for Internet commerce is often that they're not only retooling themselves, but their partners as well, to create a completely new value chain. As any consultant knows, re-engineering in one enterprise is challenging enough. Re-engineering across multiple independent entities reaches new heights of difficulty.

As consultants we must be prepared to advise our clients on the requirements for success, as difficult as that advice may be to swallow (or follow). It's incumbent on us as advisors to convince our clients that these fulfillment architectures are as critical to their success as the technology architectures that deliver their Web pages. These new high-speed eBusiness fulfillment architectures require new levels of collaboration between partners, as exemplified by the Cisco "single enterprise" model discussed earlier. Over 90 percent of the company's orders come in over the Internet, and of those, fewer than 50 percent ever touch the hands of a Cisco employee.[4] Cisco's contract manufacturers, some of whom make subassemblies like the router chassis and others who assemble the finished product, are always in the loop with Cisco's product forecasting because they are constantly connected to Cisco's extranet and manufacturing execution systems. Cisco's extranet has real-time connectivity to its partners' assembly lines, so Cisco product managers can make sure everything is on track with orders being routed through its contractors' facilities. Assemblers at the supplier's site affix a bar code on the router, scan it, and plug it into Cisco's automated testing software, which then looks up the bar code, matches it to a customer's order, and checks the router to ensure it is configured per the customer's order. If everything checks out, Cisco's software releases the customer name and shipping information so that the subcontractor can prepare the new router for delivery to Cisco's customer. Cisco claims that it has reduced the administrative overhead for processing and shipping a product from $100 per order to between $5 and $6. Cisco's revenue results illustrate the bottom-line impact supply chain efficiencies can have. According to AMR Research, Cisco brought in $713,000 per employee, compared with the Fortune 500 average of $192,000.[5] This kind of fulfillment network is an example of the efficiencies that can be implemented across the "ecosystem" by those companies that understand and embrace the possibilities and are prepared to make the financial and technological investment.

The integration of value chain planning into the IT design process is critical and requires executive-level consensus and participation. As a consultant, you need to ensure that this imperative is communicated and agreed to at the highest levels, as the company's IT professionals—no matter how experienced, professional, and competent—are not the right individuals to be driving the inter-company cooperation that a new value chain strategy requires. Where the IT organization can add tremendous value is in the creation of an internal IT architecture that is capable of reaching beyond the "four walls" and into the processes and data of trading partners. These architectures, some of which are available as packaged products from software developers such as Manugistics, Agile Software, and I2 Technologies, allow companies to collaborate with their partners to gain visibility into the status of supplies, products, and processes beyond the internal enterprise of the business, to reduce inventory cycle times through increased access to current stock and demand levels, and to better manage outsourced functions—in short, to better manage the performance of fulfillment processes within the business and throughout the network.

It's our job as consultants to help our clients perform an honest assessment of the readiness of their IT architectures to deliver the services required for eBusiness. Some of the components we need to look for to ensure that our clients are ready to participate in these new fulfillment value chains include the following:

Real-Time Data Capture.   One of the lessons of the Internet pioneers is that the creation of a virtual storefront requires sophisticated data captured in real time. In order to offer Web customers an up-to-the-minute view of the products offered, their prices, and their availability, the underlying technical architecture must be able to record and report on those things, and they must be continually updated so customers aren't selecting unavailable items. The consumer needs to know whether the item he sees in the catalog is out of stock or whether the item she purchased is lost in transit, and he wants to know immediately. The status of shipments must be recorded in real time and must be accessible via the site. These levels of immediate data capture and visibility are far beyond the capabilities of many existing IT infrastructures, and entrepreneurs or managers who wish to offer products via the Web, whether to consumers or to other businesses, need to take an honest look at their existing systems and assess their readiness for this type of data visibility. They also must have honest advice from their consultants regarding the complexity, both technical and organizational, of developing and deploying the systems that can deliver these capabilities.

Real-Time Reporting. Internet fulfillment systems need to alert managers when things are not going according to program, not afterwards. The old "management by exceptions" philosophy, structured around an after-the-fact analysis of results, won't cut it in this new environment. Systems need to be deployed that page, call wireless phones, send out e-mail alerts, or otherwise allow managers to respond in Internet time, so that customers are informed and satisfied now, not apologized to later.

Real-Time Planning. Systems need to allow managers to act on the reports they access, to change orders on the fly to respond to shifts in demand, to reroute shipments past weather emergencies or labor strikes, and to change forecasts based on customer preferences. These changes need to cascade throughout the entire chain so all partners can change their plans as well.

The challenge for Internet consultants and their clients is not only to understand and acknowledge the criticality of these changes, but to implement them not only technically but in human terms. The demands of this high-velocity environment on the humans who must deliver these services are enormous and must be factored into any plan for creating an extended value chain. Competent consultants must focus not only on the business and technical elements but on the communication, consensus, and change aspects of this revolution, and they must convince their clients to include the communications and training required to take their teams into the new world with grace, vision, and consensus.

We started this chapter by referring to the early Internet fallacy of the "warehouse-less" retail enterprise. To illustrate how the pendulum has swung in the past few years, one of the main topics of discussion in the Internet press this winter is the debate over the placement and size of warehouses required to fulfill the orders projected for the Christmas 2000 retail season. ToysRUs.com's widely reported failings of Christmas 1999, when it was so overwhelmed it had to stop taking orders two weeks before Christmas, were typical of that season's fulfillment disaster. The company had only one 500,000-square-foot warehouse, located in Memphis, Tennessee. It discovered the hard way that 500,000 square feet wasn't nearly enough space to handle the crush of orders received or to efficiently process the wide variety of items they needed to store, pack, and ship.

David Schatsky, senior analyst for Jupiter Communications, notes that even older brick-and-mortar retailers that began offering goods online last year experienced similar difficulties. "They may already have had warehouses, but warehouses that supply stores have different logistical requirements than ones that supply consumers," he says. Schatsky surveyed e-tailers after the last holiday season and found most have learned their lessons. "Forty percent said they planned to expand capacity of their warehouses," he said. "About 31 percent said they had it in mind to implement new order-management systems."[6]

ToysRUs.com has taken its 1999 problems to heart. It is making a significant investment in upgrading its Memphis warehouse and is building two more 700,000 square-foot-plus facilities, one in California and one in Pennsylvania. Competitor SmarterKids.com stopped using a third-party fulfillment partner, opened its own state-of-the-art warehouse in Mansfield, Massachusetts, and deployed new warehouse management software. eToys announced it has been reconfiguring its East Coast and West Coast distribution centers.[7] As these anecdotes should make clear, the eConsultant needs to stay informed on the latest trends on the business process front, as the developments in the back office and the warehouse are just as critical to the success of eBusinesses as the flashy graphics and quick load speeds of the website, if not more so.

SERVICING THE SURFER

At the beginning of this chapter we reviewed some of the fallacies of Internet commerce as offered by The Gartner Group. One fallacy that wasn't listed is the concept that, because the Web is a self-service environment, customers won't need help and support. Of course, customers—whether they're retail clients buying a pair of pants from Gap.com or a pharmaceutical company's purchasing agent buying a shipload of sulfur from ChemConnect.com—sometimes want to ask a question, seek advice, or make sure that their online transaction was recorded and processed properly. In short, they want to talk to someone.

"Last year, the Internet showed it could sell products and deliver them," says Kelly Mooney, managing director of intelligence with Resource Marketing. "This is the year the Internet is going to have to show it 'gets it' from a customer-service standpoint." Cristina Fernandez, vice president of customer service for eToys, agrees. "The difference with the Internet is the level of information customers expect to receive," she says. "They expect to know the status of the order, to track it, and to get a shipping confirmation–things that aren't available in the traditional catalog world." The Internet, Fernandez says, "has raised the bar of customer service for everyone."[8]

Most sites offer an e-mail address for questions and inquiries, and many now are utilizing services such as LipStream.com or LivePerson.com to allow users to chat with a support agent over the Internet. By providing customers with lots of choices for support, sites can project a warmer, more personal atmosphere and can convert browsers into shoppers. In a study conducted by Cyber Dialogue, a consulting group based in New York City, 57 percent of Internet customers polled said that they actively sought out the sites that provided them with the best customer service. Twenty-six percent of respondents requested some type of assistance online; that figure rose to 40 percent for the customers who purchased $500 or more per year from websites. In the same study, 55 percent of the customers interviewed agreed that calling a toll-free number was the best way to receive assistance. But 31 percent of them favored text chat, 23 percent relied on Web callback requests, and 23 percent consulted a Web page that listed answers to frequently asked questions (FAQs).[9]

The range of customer support options is similar from site to site. Customers typically can access a FAQ document to review the basics of interacting with a particular site and then have the option to send an e-mail, leave a voice-mail message for a callback, call a toll-free number to talk to a customer service representative, or "click-to-dial" on IP-telephony enabled sites. Consultants need to walk through these options with their clients and make sure that each is examined in terms of its applicability to the site's business and revenue model and that a comprehensive, integrated solution is devised. The processes that tie these together—such as trouble ticket systems like Remedy or Clarify, representative training so that responses are accurate, and resolution tracking so that FAQs and training can be updated based on problems solved—need to be included and integrated as well. Finally, the experiences of the customer service staff need to be analyzed by the site designers themselves, as the questions, problems, and concerns of the customer base will provide valuable information about what works—and what doesn't—on the site.

Consultants will add the most value to their clients' decision process on customer service by convincing clients that this is a strategic function that requires strategic planning. Apart from the core issue of "insource versus outsource," decisions must be made about the types of interaction that will be supported and the service level that is expected. In the early days, many sites simply posted a FAQ document and left customers to fend for themselves. This was often incrementally expanded into an e-mail box, then a voice-mail box, and finally a call center or "click-to-dial" capability. This is not a bad strategy for non-profits, for small, personal websites, or for "garage.com" sites on a low budget. For the serious commercial site, however, this strategy will not suffice, as customers will surf to another site that offers better customer service, as evidenced by our survey results above. Help clients set realistic goals for e-mail and call turnaround times, for hold queues, and customer abandon rates. If these concepts are new to you, then you may want to do a bit of research in the field by picking up magazines like *Call Center* or *Computer Telephony Integration*, both available at www.cmp.com.

Early in the Internet experiment, many sites built their own call centers and customer service organizations, but customer service costs can quickly add up. "Call centers are expensive to maintain," says Ford Cavallari, executive vice president for Renaissance Strategies, a Boston-based eBusiness consulting firm. "If you have all these call centers and integrated systems, it's not that much less costly than having all those retail stores in malls."[10] This is why many successful sites now utilize outsourcers and packaged solutions to handle their customer communications. This, of course, is one of those strategic questions that must be analyzed on a case-by-case basis, as many entrepreneurs consider their customer service operation to be a core differentiating factor and insist that it be built and managed inside the enterprise, while many others consider it a prime candidate for outsourcing to a specialist. For those who wish to retain control of this function internally, the use of software such as Kana or Brightworks to automate customer communications is a strong option. These tools use keyword search technology to parse incoming e-mails and route them to the best customer service agent or respond to them from an inventory of stock answers based on the analysis of the customer's query. Consultants can assist their clients with the needs evaluation, selection, and implementation of these tools, and clients can have the peace of mind of owning and controlling their customer interactions internally.

For those who decide to retain this function, another option is the networked call center. Call centers a few years ago were complex, expensive departments that were typically affordable and manageable only by the largest enterprises with the call volume to support the expenditure and management overhead required. In the past few years, however, the use of call centers has migrated to smaller businesses, as the technology of computer-telephone integration has become more affordable and the need for superior customer support has become a defining factor of modern business competition. Call centers are available now that integrate with existing local area network technology so that small enterprises that are using internal network environments such as Novell NetWare or Microsoft Windows NT can implement inexpensive servers and software that allow call center agents to access customer records and data automatically.

For those companies that are considering outsourcing, it's important to advise them that they can outsource the process, but that they will still need to manage that process through service level agreements and results reporting. Organizations can save money by not having to invest in technology or call-center staff. Some enterprises initially turn to an outsourcer to handle the overflow in their own call centers, but eventually decide to turn the entire operation over. Because they've done it before, outsourcers can quickly design and establish customer support programs, train agents, provide customer feedback, and adjust their technology and processes based on results and on customer demand. The major financial benefits come from economies of scale, because outsourcers can support many clients with their automated call distribution, interactive voice response, and customer relationship management technologies. Outsourcers have achieved cost reductions of 10 percent to 30 percent compared with the costs associated with internal department call centers.[11]

In this speed-to-market environment, one of the key advantages of partnering with an outsourcer is their ability to implement quickly. Startups or spin-ups that don't have operational experience in the call center world will benefit from the expertise and efficiency of an outsourcing partner who has "been there, done that," rather than struggling through the learning curve themselves. In fact, some enterprises outsource these functions at the beginning, both as a way of getting to market faster and as a way to learn the discipline, with the thought of taking it all back in house once they learn how to manage it.

Call center outsourcing agreements must be negotiated carefully, as calls handled by an outsourcer are often the initial interaction the enterprise has with its customers and so create that crucial first impression. Consultants who are advising clients on the outsourcing of this function need to help clients develop the most explicit, comprehensive, and cost-effective relationship possible. Clients should be advised to do the following:

- Visit the outsourcer's facility to check out the technology, the culture, and the people;

- Listen to some calls being handled and assure themselves that the image of professionalism and responsiveness they seek is being provided;

- Understand how the agents will be trained so they understand the client's business and can respond to customer inquiries quickly and accurately;

- Clearly agree on the scope of the outsourcer's involvement, for instance, whether the outsourcer will be responsible for every call through resolution or whether there will be some handoff;

- Understand how results and metrics will be transmitted to the client; and

- Determine their escalation options if problems arise, for example, are there termination options if the outsourcer consistently misses service level targets?

Many outsourcers are more than just call centers; they are customer service consultants. Companies such as trustedanswer.com or One-to-One Service Inc. work directly with you and your client to design a customized support and customer communication program. They help you plan modifications to the company's website and provide your customers with text chat and Web callback options in addition to answering e-mail messages. Some outsourcers also receive customers' voice-over-IP calls. By working with these outsourcers, you can create your own unique plan to determine how your customers receive online assistance.

The key point is that the "back-end" processes, including the fulfillment of orders, the management of inventory, relationships with key suppliers, and the support of customers, are just as critical to the success of the Internet venture as the "customer-facing" elements like the website and the brand's image and design. Internet consultants who want to deliver the whole package need to turn themselves into process consultants as well as technical consultants and business strategists.

End Notes

1. Younker, E., & Enslow, B. *The Fallacies of Web-Commerce Fulfillment.* Stamford, CT: The Gartner Group, March 17, 1999.
2. Electron Economy: The Web's Great Order Disorder. *Business 2.0,* Oct. 10, 2000.
3. *ISO 9000 Quality Management Standards and Vocabulary.* Geneva, Switzerland: International Standards Organization Publication, 2000.
4. Koch, C. The Big Payoff. *CIO Magazine,* Oct. 1, 2000.
5. ibid.
6. Haskins, D. Warehouses: When to Own, When to Rent. *Business 2.0,* Oct. 10, 2000.
7. ibid.
8. Gantenbeim, D. Customer Service: What to Do When They're Ringing Off the Hook. *Business 2.0,* Oct. 10, 2000.
9. Hollman, L. Internet Outsourcers Point Your Customers to the Web. *CallCenter Magazine,* Sept. 5, 2000.
10. op cit, Gantenbeim.
11. Allison, C., Kline, H., Stanco, B., & Smith, C. *The Corporate Call Center: Much More Than Call Handling.* Stamford, CT: The Gartner Group, May 16, 1996.

Change Hurts!

WHY MAKE A CHANGE?

One of my most instructive lessons in Internet strategy came from a fifteen-minute conversation I had with a well-known venture capitalist, a managing partner at one of Silicon Valley's premier VC firms. I was acting as a consultant to an Internet startup planning to offer Internet-based unified messaging, by which subscribers could receive all their e-mail, voice mail, faxes, and stock quotes delivered into one "rich mailbox," accessible by phone or Web. We were in the midst of a cross country "road show," presenting our concept and business plan to potential venture capitalists and other investors. We had done exhaustive research, and all the analysts and experts agreed that unified messaging would displace plain e-mail and take over the messaging world in the next five years. We gave the VC a polished and, we thought, persuasive presentation, and when we were done the VC asked us a very simple question:

"What's my compelling reason, as a consumer, to change to your product?"

Of course, we were prepared with industry charts and projections that showed that everyone would be using this service by 2003. The VC stopped us gently as we went back over those forecasts. "I'm getting e-mail, voice mail, and faxes now. Those methods work. I'm used to them. I know how to use them. Forget about what the experts predict. Why would *I* change?"

After a few more minutes of bobbing and weaving, my client and I grasped this experienced venture capitalist's essential point. Better technology doesn't guarantee a market or a business—nor does a better business model or better marketing—for one simple reason: *People resist change.* All of those things are necessary, but they are not sufficient. Change is a separate element that needs to be managed, and managing change is an exercise in understanding the psychology of your audience and those impulses that cause them to prefer the tried and familiar over the new, even when the new is better (which was far from a given in the Internet gold rush of the past few years).

Change is a factor to be reckoned with not only in the realm of the consumer. In the corporate realm as well, the evidence is clear: Change initiatives fail overwhelmingly. In studies by the consulting firms Arthur D. Little and McKinsey and Company,[1] the failure rate of total quality management (TQM) programs was found to be about 65 percent. In a separate study by James Champy, one of the original founders of the business process reengineering (BPR) movement,[2] the BPR failure rate was placed at around 70 percent. Writing for the *Harvard Business Review*,[3] John Kotter noted that more than half of the corporate transformation efforts he studied failed to get beyond even the initial stages.

These failed change efforts result in more than wasted time and lost productivity. They are one of the key drivers of cynicism and disillusionment in the corporate world, and they engender a vicious cycle of skepticism that makes each new program more of an uphill fight. Most corporate insiders have developed a finely honed capacity to cheer and wax enthusiastic about the latest corporate "flavor of the month" initiative when their manager is in the room, only to roll their eyes and invent witty disparaging catch phrases when they're back in the break room with their teammates.

These reflections on change have real significance for Internet consultants in a number of ways. For those consultants who are advising clients on the initial strategic development of their concept or business model, the lesson I learned from the Silicon Valley venture capitalist needs to be ingrained. Your client's business concept must answer in a compelling and undeniable way the VC's straightforward question: Why will the customer change to your offering? This is a real issue for most Internet entrepreneurs I meet in my practice. Financial projections and business plans that call for 10 to 30 percent of the target audience to migrate to a new product or service are common, yet experienced business analysts will agree that a reasonable expectation for market share penetration by a new product is closer to .01 percent. Just this week, I worked with a startup whose projections called for them to go from zero to seven million subscribers in eighteen months! In many cases, the very entrepreneurs who insist that every third person in the United States is anxiously waiting for their product to be released have made no plans to service those hordes adequately, no program to ramp up for the massive customer service, fulfillment, or logistics capabilities they'll need. Many entrepreneurs will cling doggedly to these projections, and it's an exercise in diplomacy for their advisors to help them understand that their numbers defy belief and will dilute their business case if presented to knowledgeable investors or prospects. Yet it is our duty as consultants to do exactly that—to bring over-enthusiastic entrepreneurs back into the realm of reality and to help them devise projections that are defensible.

For those consultants who are working within corporations to develop new eBusiness initiatives, whether they're carve-outs, spin-offs, or internal efforts, the management of change must be an integral part of your approach. As I hope I've made clear by now, Internet strategies involve deep, far-reaching, comprehensive, and potentially wrenching changes. The changes in the business environment that neutralize previously powerful competitive advantages like location, distribution, and brand; the differences in relationships with external entities like suppliers and competitors; the transformation in internal processes like inventory and logistics; the new messages that are required to appeal to the Internet-savvy consumer or business partner—all of these changes are far from trivial. Each one touches core constituencies, overturns existing internal and external power balances, and threatens conventional wisdom and familiar ways of doing things. Fundamentally, the act of conceiving an e-strategy redefines the boundaries of the enterprise, changing the playing field across the chain of values and relationships. Everyone knows just from seeing the daily stock market reports that the stakes are enormous. The combination of all these elements makes the job of the Internet strategist and her advisors critical, visible, and perilous.

CHANGE MANAGEMENT

All of the experts cited above, although each studied different types of change programs and came to some very different conclusions, agreed on one thing: Successful change requires leadership. Many enterprises have embraced this concept by grooming or importing leaders specifically for their Internet projects—leaders who, to use the current buzzword, "get it." eConsultants and the clients they advise must recognize that leadership with belief, with a sense of urgency, and with the ability to communicate the benefits and advantages of building the new world convincingly is a prerequisite to a successful change effort. In a recent interview I did with Charles "Tuck" Rickards, senior recruiting consultant and Internet practice manager for Russell Reynolds, the premier Internet recruiting firm, we discussed some of the characteristics that both startups and corporations look for when recruiting for leadership spots. I've included some of Tuck's remarks at the end of this chapter, as I believe that leadership is one of the key success factors for any Internet program. Russell Reynolds, in seeking those candidates who can display leadership in this environment, looks for a combination of characteristics that it has codified as "Web DNA."[4] These attributes include the ability to recognize new opportunities, the ability to "radiate vision," and the creativity to improvise successfully in an atmosphere of uncertainty and constant change.

It's important to state that this leadership cannot be outsourced to the consultant, an effort, unfortunately, I've seen too many times in my career. CEOs have come to me or my associates with the general message: "We know this Internet thing is a threat and we must react, but we don't know what to do next. Could you just come in and get it done?" Others make the critical mistake of viewing eBusiness as another IT project. Many have no idea what their competitors or partners are doing on the Net. It's the consultant's duty to help his client understand that, without the belief, vision, communication, and support of the leadership team, the Internet initiative will become like the travails of Sisyphus in the Greek myth, doomed to rolling the boulder up the hill just to see it roll back down as it reaches the crest.

In my previous book, *The IT Consultant,* I wrote at length about the issues of corporate inertia and about the techniques that successful consultants use to overcome corporate lethargy and to create the momentum that propels projects forward. I won't repeat all that material here, except to state some of that work's fundamental premises. I use the terms "inertia" and "momentum," from the realm of physics rather than psychology, advisedly. In the corporate world, the inertia of existing expectations, sunk investment in infrastructure and image, ingrained processes, and relationships is a physical force like gravity, binding people to traditional methods and making change difficult. In the pre-Net days, that was part of the point—to build a shared culture and a "way we do things around here" that was essentially conservative and stable. Long-term managers are afraid to "stick their necks out" for a change program that, experience tells them, has a less than 50 percent chance of success. IT organizations, which have typically been treated like back-office "cost centers"—enabling tactical functions but certainly not leading strategic change—often do not have the skills, desire, or mandate to be the leaders of company-moving initiatives. Corporate empires years in the making and self-defining for many long-time employees, defended with all the power that ego, self-interest, self-image, and emotion can muster, are not easily torn asunder even for the best of reasons.

Yet Internet initiatives, to be successful, require that all these elements be affected. The process and product knowledge, the practices, relationships, and other assets of the company that have been the very essence of sustainable competitive advantage now become the inertia that makes it vulnerable to the raids of the start-ups. The struggles of companies such as Borders bookstore to come up with strategies to compete against the incursions of Amazon is just one of hundreds of examples. It's not easy to walk away from the billions of dollars invested and millions of hours spent in building a brand and a business. Even those who do take the bold step of migrating from bricks to clicks, such as Egghead Software, are by no means guaranteed of success.

With all this said, however, it must also be recognized that companies *do* change. Even in the most pessimistic studies, there are those 30 to 50 percent of organizations that overcome all the inertia and gravity and do successfully implement those TQM, BPR, or customer relationship management programs. There are even those companies, such as Jack Welch's General Electric, that do it over and over again. Clearly, with all the studies and literature out there reviewing and analyzing the success and failures of change programs across the spectrum of companies and initiatives, we must be able to glean some useful principles and practices that we can use to help our clients face this potentially most difficult change they've ever tried to implement. In fact, there are, and we'll review some of those concepts next.

Helping Organizations Migrate

I referred to the article written by John Kotter for the *Harvard Business Review* a bit earlier, and I want to go back to it for a moment now. Although I just spent a few paragraphs describing how the changes inherent in eBusiness transformation are different from other change programs, it's also true that the fundamental elements of a successful change program have many similarities to the recommendations of

Kotter and other change experts. Kotter, Peter Senge,[5] Robert Schaffer,[6] and many other observers have come to some of the same conclusions about the techniques required to motivate, implement, and sustain change.

I've tried here to synthesize the characteristics, practices, and mindsets identified by change mentors such as Kotter and Schaffer to offer readers some guidance in the factors that enable organizations to change successfully in general—and to migrate to the new world of the Internet in particular. eConsultants add value to the organizational change process when they help their clients develop the following capabilities:

The Ability to Recognize the Internet Opportunity. Clearly, to provide direction in this new economy, leaders first must believe there are opportunities here, recognize them, understand them, and visualize how they may apply to the business. They must display a sense of urgency and boldness, moving forward with innovative strategies without succumbing to "analysis paralysis." Consultants can help in this effort by bringing their knowledge and research on how the best business minds, both inside and outside the client's industry, are applying these new business models to the opportunity the Internet offers. It's our baseline responsibility to educate our clients, to offer them the benefits of our experience, and to remain knowledgeable about the trends in the Internet economy so we can remain valuable advisors.

The Ability to Impart a Compelling Vision. The ability to develop a compelling vision, to personally evangelize that vision, and to persistently and consistently communicate it throughout the organization is a key skill identified by all of the change gurus. Again, consultants can play a constructive role here by helping clients to frame consistent and persuasive messages, to organize communication programs that target the right constituencies, and to gauge the effectiveness of those messages so they can be refined and redelivered to best effect.

The Ability to Build a Coalition. One of the factors we've discussed over and over in this book is the concept of Internet strategies as interdisciplinary. Leaders of these efforts must be skilled at evangelizing, involving, and gaining the insight, support, and participation of elements from throughout the organization. No corporate change project has a chance if the leader at the local level—whether it's a branch office, a department, or a functional area—is not seen by the rank and file as an advocate and supporter, or if constituencies feel that their voices are not being heard. This sometimes necessitates working around or across the typical lines of authority and command, a prospect that some organizations can find disorienting and counter-intuitive—yet it must be done. With the realm of change, ranging from the executive suite to marketing and through logistics, a coalition of leaders from across the board must be built and must be visible to the organization. By helping clients create messages that are consistent in tone and concept, yet tailored to appeal to the target constituencies with messages that resonate with them, consultants help clients build momentum.

The Iterative Mindset. Called "the 80/20 mindset" by Russell Reynolds,[7] this is the ability to put urgency and speed before perfection, to implement the good today rather than the perfect tomorrow. While the myth of invincibility around "first-mover advantage" has been shattered by the recent death of many first-mover Web players, it's nonetheless true that speed is a factor. It's also true, as we discussed earlier, that even the most established and successful players in the Web space continually innovate and experiment. So creating a product today, with the understanding that it will be refined and enhanced as the initiative moves along, is still important. The interviews with Skip McDonald of Luminant (Chapter One) and with Jim Highsmith of the Cutter Consortium (Chapter Two) indicate that the system development community has taken the iterative development process to heart. Clients, however, may not be so anxious to abandon their tried-and-true development methodologies or their conservative, change-averse strategic planning processes. It's the consultant's job to perform the risk assessments, allay the fears, and build in the assurance factors that will allow the client to move confidently into the new economic order.

The "Quick Hit" Mindset. One of the attributes that's mentioned consistently in the writings of the change mentors is the importance of setting some achievable short-term goals and hitting them aggressively. Change is a long-term undertaking and—even in "Internet time"—doesn't happen overnight. While the marketing campaign is being developed, the website is being designed, and the software is being coded and tested, it's not unusual for momentum and enthusiasm to flag. This is the time when a short-term win can make a tremendous difference. It can be as temporary as showing some examples of possible new logos, giving selected teams access to a prototype of the website, or communicating a new partner alliance based on the Net initiative. Any action that involves the organization, underscores the vision, indicates meaningful progress, and shows positive movement toward the objective can be framed as a win. It's important to emphasize that this is an active, not a passive, activity, in that we don't just pray that some element will work out with the right timing and visibility—we plan for it. Consultants add tremendous value when they purposefully include these "low hanging fruit" elements in their plans.

The Creation of an Innovation Factory. Every beginning project manager learns the difference between a project and ongoing operations very early in her career: *Projects* are short-term, have specific goals, and have a specific end point, whereas *operations* are repeating processes required to sustain the business over the long term. It should be the goal of every Internet leader to move her Internet change initiative from the project realm to the operational realm, by which I mean that the cross-culture, cross-disciplinary, process-busting, rule-breaking, innovative thinking that was painfully dredged out in support of the Internet project shouldn't be tossed away when the initial project is complete. It should be institutionalized—by keeping the cross-functional teams alive instead of disbanding them, by keeping the process of reviewing and rationalizing processes going, and by assigning someone the responsibility for keeping an eye on the changes in the Internet economy and bringing those new models and strategies back to the teams.

Sustaining Migration

One final note on the results of the academics and students of corporate change I referred to above: They all agree that sustaining change can be as much of a challenge as creating it in the first place. The emotions, empires, and anxieties that we cited earlier as obstacles to change don't magically go away. People may be convinced to sublimate them for a time or to transfer them to new areas and empires, but they can often come back to undermine the changes that seemed so successful and broadly supported in the early days. Sustaining change is an exercise that requires a unique combination of "hard" and "soft" skills. Objective measurements must be devised that clearly tell the story that the change has worked—that it is delivering the results that were envisioned and evangelized from the start. That's the "hard" part. The "soft" side is the organization's ability to deal with the human issues, the issues that revolve around vulnerability, such as "I just don't get this Internet stuff and never will!" or adequacy, such as "Our new partners understand so much more about supply-chain management." The organizations that have made their ability to change a key competitive advantage, such as General Electric, have acknowledged that change is not only a business discipline but also a human one and have built into their change programs methods for "taking the pulse" of the organization and the team members—to be sure that everyone is being included in the brave new world and that no one is being left behind or left out.

Consultants who do the necessary research to make themselves experts in these change disciplines and practices—and who analyze their engagements to gain insights into the successes and failures of each one so they can bring wisdom, judgment, and experience to their clients as they attempt to revolutionize their businesses—will be much more than simply consultants. They will be partners.

What do traditional companies such as Dow Jones, Aetna Insurance, Pennzoil, and Glaxo Wellcome have in common with well-known Internet ventures such as eToys, First Internet Bank, PlanetOut, and e-centives? Each of these companies has turned to Russell Reynolds Associates, one of the world's leading executive search firms, to fill key management roles. How does this leading search firm recruit the CEOs, CIOs, and directors who become the leaders of the new economy? What criteria do they use to select those individuals who "get it," who have that special combination of skill and experience that will enable them to thrive in the uncertain, experimental, and dynamic Internet environment? I chatted with Tuck Rickards, the leader of Russell Reynolds' Internet Practice,[8] to find out how one of the leading Internet recruiters seeks out and attracts these special talents. Tuck specializes in assignments relating to the Internet and convergent technologies, including eCommerce, content, software, and infrastructure. Tuck has personal experience in the startup world, as founder, chairman, and CEO of Virtual Emporium, an early entrant into the Web retail space. His experience as a vice president at Montgomery Securities and a financial analyst at Goldman Sachs prepared Tuck with unique credentials for his role as a top recruiter in the Internet marketplace.

Rick: Help us understand how the recruiting process works in the Internet space. Does a venture capital firm call you and say, "We've seen this great project, but they're missing these skills in their management team"?

Tuck: We are fortunate; we've had a global Internet practice, which was really the first integrated practice among the big search firms, for three years, so we've got very good relationships with most of the venture firms that are active in this space. It often comes from the venture side, or other clients we've done search work for. For the bigger companies, it's either new clients who've heard about our Internet practice or it's existing clients who are launching new businesses.

Rick: How do they frame their requirements?

Tuck: What most of them have is very good funding, a very good management team with some holes in it, and a business plan that holds water even in today's market. They have a "path to profitability," to use the buzzword. They come to us with a team with some holes in it. The first step of the process, before we even open a search, is to dig in and understand their business model. We're very consultative in our approach that way. We seek to understand the existing organization, what's there and what's not, and then typically it starts with one search, although it could be multiple positions for a B2B exchange, for example. We get into a very fine level of detail as far as what the job specifications are and what key competencies are required.

Rick: Obviously when you're filling a spot, candidates need to have the specific job expertise that the position requires, such as technical skills for a CTO or financial skills for a CFO. In the Internet space, cultural fit and the ability to thrive in an uncertain and changing environment is as important as those "hard" skills. How do you assess a candidate for cultural fit?

Tuck: I would slice it along different dimensions. For any dot.com or any emerging growth company that's under tremendous pressure, tremendous hours, tremendous change, the cultural fit is absolutely critical. I reduce cultural fit down to chemistry—can they work well together—and assessing that is very much an art, not a science. And it's very dependent on the mix of people around the table. If we step back and look at the business skills required, I'd put those into two buckets. Executive recruiters have always looked for a set of basic business skills for any particular search, a set of industry experiences that are relevant to that position. The second would be a set of functional experiences, whether it's technology or business development or general management—leadership experience. In the Internet space the missing piece, and the hard-to-figure-out piece, is what we've termed "Web DNA." The question is, what specific competencies, what specific skills are required to make sure that the person will be successful in an Internet environment? Let's pull that one question out and figure out how to interview for it. So that's what we've done with Web DNA.

Rick: Let's walk through the six "Web DNA" characteristics you've identified that help Russell Reynolds recognize good candidates for this new economy.

Tuck: The challenge is that in most cases—80 percent of our recruits for Internet companies did not come from Internet companies—they came from a range of other backgrounds, with general management experience, and they jumped into this Internet world. If you're not really careful with the matching and selection process there, you can end up with a square peg in a round hole. The six characteristics that we've defined seem to us to be the six recurring ones that are absolutely necessary for an Internet executive who "gets it." Number one, *they recognize opportunity,* and by that we mean not just that they recognize an opportunity, but understand the landscape in such a way that they recognize the big opportunities, the ones that their organizations should jump on. The second is that *they radiate vision,* and this is not just vision in the sense of being a compelling speaker. It's someone who has a view of where the world's going to be and will bend over backward in every medium possible to communicate that to his team and to clients and customers. Next is *the 80/20 mindset,* which I think is probably one of the most important ones. The key point there is that it's better to be 80 percent right today than 100 percent right tomorrow. One of the most difficult things for an Internet executive is forging a number of right decisions in a real-time environment with imperfect data. It's easy to get paralysis if you're not comfortable with that.

Rick: I'd guess that a lot of people with general management experience in a traditional company will really struggle with this concept that a good plan today is better than a perfect plan tomorrow.

Tuck: To put this into a technology context, if I'm a CIO who's used to bubbling up $15 million proposals to my CEO to sign off on in a ten-year technology plan, that's a very different environment, and guess what? The world is evolving around us and we don't know what the right platform is a year from now, but here are the four fundamental pieces we need today, so let's pick these pieces, maybe on an outsourced ASP basis, get some more data over the next month or two about what our customers want, and maybe replace those pieces or add three other modules next to them. To be able to develop and evolve those systems dynamically, that's a critical piece of being successful in this space. The fourth characteristic is *the ability to get the right stuff done,* and I'll summarize that by saying that if the average Internet executive has a fifty-item to-do list at any one time, a good Internet executive will not just focus on the two things that are important for today, but will figure out that if he does these three things, no matter where the business goes, they'll be important business building blocks that will lead to good things beyond that. It's not just prioritizing—it's understanding fundamentally what the right building blocks are and making sure you nail those.

Rick: The ones that are going to have synergy going forward and are going to have wide impact. . . .

Tuck: Exactly. The fifth characteristic is *being an organizational improviser*. In a nutshell, successful Internet executives are not empire builders; they're builders of networks of resources they can call out to get stuff done. And the final one is *being learning obsessed*. I don't care if it's a CEO or a CTO, it's a person who looks herself in the mirror and fundamentally questions everything that she does, looks for marketplace trends, watches what the competitors are doing, asks lots of questions. It's those types of people who will anticipate the challenges of to-morrow and turn them into opportunities.

Rick: Let's dig down into some of these attributes a bit more. For instance, when you talk about the ability to recognize opportunities, are we talking about do-main expertise or are we talking about a broader ability to look out over the horizon and see opportunities down the road?

Tuck: If you put a historical perspective on the ability to recognize opportuni-ties, within technology recruiting, a year or two ago clients were saying, "I know my business, but this Internet thing is revolutionizing the world. What is it, how is it going to impact my world, and what experience has this candidate had in making that happen?" Companies in any specific vertical were very interested in a Web-centric, cross-industries capability, even if it wasn't in their industry. The world we live in today is a clicks-and-bricks world, and people aren't look-ing for the CTO who's going to turn the world upside down and spend fifty mil-lion dollars doing it. They want the CTO who gets that world and gets the opportunities and can translate that into "What does it mean for me?" "What does it mean for my business?" "What are the opportunities to incrementally drive major change?" I think the world has evolved to where the challenge isn't necessarily in the opportunity to create whole new markets and new businesses, it's to creatively weave that into the fabric of existing businesses. It's a market that's evolved from one of ideas to one of implementation.

Rick: One of the attributes is "radiates vision." Is this an attribute that you look for in a candidate no matter where they're slotted in the organization or does a CEO need to be the center of vision in a Web company?

Tuck: In successful Internet companies, vision is not a staff function. It's a CEO's job. When we're talking to a CEO candidate and looking for vision, we're talking about somebody who can take an organization through tremendous opportu-nities, challenges, and conflicting priorities and keep them on course, and—even as the business model changes—keep the business compass on true north. If you don't have that in the CEO of an Internet company, I would rather be a seller than a buyer of that company's stock. For successful executives in other functions in Internet companies, I think vision is equally important, although it probably manifests itself differently. We've put a lot of thinking into this question of whether some of these competencies are more relevant for different functional people. The way I think about it is not, "Is vision more important in the CEO than in another function?" I think Web DNA is important in each of your functional building blocks; it may be 10 percent of one job spec and 90 percent of another. If you're going to screen to see whether somebody gets the Web or not, vision is an important part of that. If we're screening for a CFO, you obviously prefer someone who can count to someone who radiates vision, but for the CFO of an Internet company you still want to screen for the Web DNA components because you don't want him to blow up all the ideas that come to him because he doesn't get them.

Rick: So when you bring in a CEO to an entrepreneurial company, with a founder who has her own deeply held idea of what the business will be, how do you screen for the ability to internalize and disseminate that vision?

Tuck: Vision needn't be about having the idea that founds the company. Vision is the ability to comprehend and embrace a view of the world and then communicate it to everyone around you and rally the troops around it. If I'm the founder of a company, would I want to be the only one with vision and then force this series of robots to go out and execute my tasks? Or do I want to communicate a vision to the team at the Monday morning meeting and have them take that set of principles and core beliefs and communicate them to a hundred other people each, so that the hundredth person down that chain who has to make a decision that impacts the business has the right mindset?

Rick: When you talk about the attribute that you've titled "80/20 mindset," I assume you're talking about the ability to pick those things that have the most impact on the success of the venture.

Tuck: It's basically applying the software model to decision making, version 1.0, 2.0, 3.0 in rapid succession, and every one is better than the first because you've had a lot of customer input.

Rick: When you talk about "getting the right stuff done," that's also focused on doing those things that have an impact on the business, doing the right things rather than doing things right.

Tuck: Exaggerated to the nth degree, because the complexity of the decision-making process is such that you don't know what the end game is, so it's not only prioritizing when the end game is relatively clear and the impacts are obvious, but it's prioritizing when you're only 50 percent sure where you're going. And the litmus test is two years from now: "Did we have to throw away many things or were most of the things we did additive?"

Rick: "Organizational improvisation" is another attribute you've identified. The startups I've consulted with, folks are playing multiple roles, CEO today, PR person tomorrow, investment banker the next day, and maybe janitor the next. There's not a lot of clarity and definition around the job descriptions. Is this the capability you're identifying here?

Tuck: In the entrepreneurial stage, everyone is a player in a jazz band, and you're playing whatever role you're asked to play without a real script in front of you. When the company gets bigger and you add structure and an organization chart, with buckets that are divided up functionally, it's a mindset that says: "I don't care. I'll arrange this to get the job done, and the opportunity may change and the market may change, and I need to keep myself adaptable and flexible to meet whatever challenges come up." This is a common theme throughout any Internet company.

Rick: Is an underlying part of this concept that folks who need the big title, the corner office, and the team of coffee makers are not good fits for this new world?

Tuck: There's no problem with the corner office; you're just going to have to share it with ten people.

Rick: So I see this as a kind of a funnel process, where twenty-five possible candidates are identified at the top, and through the interviewing process the two or three likely candidates fall out.

Tuck: Can I add a level to this? Before the twenty-five candidates, there are two hundred companies that the person could come from in five different market segments. When we work with clients, because no one has done this before, we ask: "What's the job?" "What's the position?" "What kind of skill sets do you need?" and "Where could we go to find those?" The tough part is that we have to be very broad and yet prioritize those market segments. Then let's go find the individuals within those companies and get it down to a twenty-five person list, and then let's take it through this interviewing filter.

Rick: So how do you tell a compelling story that persuades talented people to participate in this process, to consider changing their lives to take on this new challenge?

Tuck: I don't think the executive recruiting industry as a whole does a very good job of managing one-on-one the candidate relationship. For instance, there are a lot of cold calls that don't make any sense. I hope we do a better job than the next firm, but I still think the paradigm works OK but not great. Two things are necessary. The best calls for the client and for the candidate are when the candidate knows you and your firm. You've got credibility in terms of knowing the industry and being able to add some value and some perspective, separate from the search assignment. It creates a desire on the part of the candidate to get to know the recruiter on the other side of the phone, because that recruiter is plugged in and knows everything that's going on. That's a different kind of relationship than "Are you interested in this job tomorrow?" If you're going to call somebody on a specific position, and you haven't gone through the process that we discussed before, and you haven't thought about the requirements and who are the right people, you have a lot of wasted calls. In today's market the one thing people don't have a lot of is time. To the extent you have a relationship before you get to "This is the ideal one for you," you're more likely to be successful. The good firms will focus on the relationship aspect.

End Notes

1. Why People Resist Change. *The Economist,* April 18, 1992.
2. Champy, J. Reengineering: A Light That Failed. *Across the Board Magazine, 32*(3), March 1995.
3. Kotter, J. Leading Change: Why Transformation Efforts Fail. *Harvard Business Review,* March 1995.
4. The Web Factor: Identifying the Potential for Internet Success. *www.russreyn.com.*
5. Senge, P. *The Dance of Change: The Challenges to Sustaining Momentum in Learning Organizations.* New York: Doubleday/Currency, 1999.
6. Schaffer, R.H. Successful Change Programs Begin with Results. *Harvard Business Review,* January 1992.
7. The Web Factor: Identifying the Potential for Internet Success. *www.russreyn.com.*
8. Interview with the author. © TechRepublic, Inc. *www.techrepublic.com.* Used with permission. All rights reserved.

chapter NINE

The eConsultant's Report Card

WHAT THEY'RE SAYING

The following press release was issued by Forrester Research, the respected independent IT analyst firm, on June 26, 2000

eCommerce Integrators Fail to Make the Grade, According to Forrester Research

U.S. firms will outsource close to $20 billion this year for the strategy, marketing, design, and technical services associated with building advanced eCommerce sites. The prime beneficiaries of this spending are the eCommerce integrators (eCIs)—professional services firms that design, build, and deploy these sites. Despite the demand for their services, the eCIs are characterized by widespread weakness. In a new report that grades the top forty eCIs in five categories, Forrester Research, Inc. (Nasdaq: FORR) concludes that none are capable of delivering excellence across all service areas and few can provide expertise in more than one.

For the Report "eCommerce Integrators Exposed," Forrester narrowed a list of 152 eCommerce integrators to forty leading eCIs. These firms were then graded on their strategy, marketing, design, technology, and business practices. Forrester used several research techniques to help assure accuracy—in-depth eCI interviews, extensive reviews of an eCI-provided reference site, and client interviews. After the initial findings were complete, Forrester allowed the participants to review the findings and correct any omissions or errors.

Forrester graded the forty leading eCIs on their strategy, marketing, design, technology, and business practices, examining several key factors within each category. Overall, the scores were unimpressive, with the highest rated eCI (Sapient) earning 35 out of 50 possible points and the average eCI scoring just 24 points. Equally important was the fact that no eCI proved capable of delivering a complete solution—each of the five categories was won by a different company, while none of the eCIs received seven or more points in all five categories.

"Despite the eCIs' claims to design and technology expertise, we found very little evidence of either in practice," said Paul Sonderegger, senior analyst at Forrester.

"Reviews of the eCI reference sites suggest that design fundamentals have yet to permeate these organizations. And few eCIs appear capable of delivering the features and functions that provide a real competitive advantage. But the eCIs aren't solely to blame for these results. With clients providing unclear or incomplete objectives and exerting tremendous pressure to deliver projects on time, many eCIs toss both site requirements and good processes overboard in order to get the job done."

Is it only the eConsultants cited in Forrester's study who are having trouble matching results to marketing promises? Is the Internet marketplace, prone to hype, exaggeration, and unfulfilled expectations, a breeding ground for discontent in the consulting business? In fact, the tide of popular opinion had begun turning against the consulting profession long before this study was issued. One of the top-selling titles in Amazon.com's consulting category is not the typical "How to Quit Your Job, Become a Consultant, and Make a Million Dollars," but instead is a harsh debunking of the profession entitled *Dangerous Company: The Consulting Powerhouses and the Companies They Save and Ruin* (1997). James O'Shea and Charles Madigan, two *Chicago Tribune* reporters, focused in this popular book on the dark side of the consulting profession, documenting the following tales of alleged consulting malpractice:

- A Fortune 500 company spent $75 million on consulting contracts, only to see sales plummet from $1.3 billion to $319 million;

- AT&T spent half a billion dollars in consulting fees with no sign of measurable results;

- A Bain and Company consultant provided government officials with information that helped send a former client to jail;

- Figgie International filed a lawsuit against such premier firms as Boston Consulting Group and Deloitte & Touche, charging these firms with fraud and incompetence after going through $75 million in fees without delivering the expected results;

- The British government took an $18-million action against Andersen Consulting based on the consulting firm's inability to deliver a new Social Security system as promised;

- And many others.

Other titles, such as *Consulting Demons: Inside the Unscrupulous World of Global Corporate Consulting* (Pinault, 2000) tell similar tales of unprincipled, arrogant, and unqualified advisors whose efforts leave the client with no tangible benefits and with inflated bills to pay. *The Value Creating Consultant* (Carucci & Tetenbaum, 1999), *High Impact Consulting* (Schaffer, 1997), and *The Consultant's Scorecard* (Phillips, 2000), although still critical of the lack of accountability or standards in the consulting industry, take a more positive tack by offering guidelines for consultants to follow in order to ensure that we in fact deliver value for money. These books all point out some important shortcomings of our profession: Consultants, unlike other professionals, have no standards body, no universal certification of competency, no obvious measure of success, and no general canon of ethics. Professions that have all these common standards, such as doctors and lawyers, are still subject to much criticism and ridicule. How much more susceptible to dissatisfaction and scorn are high-priced (and often arrogant) consultants, with none of these common principles to at least ensure that we're approaching our projects from a foundation of competency and ethical behavior?

In the Internet space, of course, where the very measurements that signify a successful business are in question and the debate over achieving profitability versus building market share is still raging, it's even more difficult to measure results. Is the creation of a website or a marketing campaign, as agreed in the consulting scope of work, sufficient for the consultant to declare success, or are there some more bottom-line-oriented results, such as revenues delivered or customers captured, for which we should be accountable? Is it the consultant's responsibility to point out to the client that his business model has holes or his market projections are hallucinatory? Is an eCommerce company's lack of success in a crowded market our fault, or is it the fault of the entrepreneurs and investors who failed to do their due diligence or allowed their visions of wealth to overcome their sense?

The obvious answer is, "It depends." If we've been engaged as simply a subject-matter expert, to write a Java module, or to create an electronic version of the client's logo, we may still have some responsibility to point out obvious flaws in our specific assignment, but our responsibility for overall business performance is limited. If, on the other hand, we've been engaged as a full-service strategic advisor, and we have neglected to ask the obvious questions about competition, financial expectations, business models, and customer experience, our level of responsibility has clearly risen. If we've taken on that strategic role without the experience, training, and competency necessary to discharge our commitments successfully, then we're in a whole other world of professional misconduct. There is clearly a broad spectrum of scenarios, with lots of nuance and room for interpretation, in the measurement of results from an eConsulting engagement.

WHY MEASURE eCONSULTING RESULTS?

One effect of studies like the Forrester eConsulting report is increased client skepticism and wariness. As clients and prospects read about the divergence between marketing and delivery for the major eConsultancies, they naturally approach every engagement with more caution and with more of a desire for measurable results. Consultants obviously need to be sensitive to these concerns and create an approach that assures clients of our commitment to results and our willingness to be held accountable. Those consultants and firms that don't address these client concerns will be at a clear competitive disadvantage.

I'm a strong believer in the concept of building market share by building depth within each client organization, rather than breadth across the marketplace. I'd rather have a few deep and sustained trust relationships with a handful of clients than many "quick-hit" projects that never result in a close partnership. Measurable results built in from the beginning of the relationship are one of the best tools for developing that trust and depth of alliance. By illustrating to the client from the beginning that I'm committed to their results, that I'm action oriented and bring a high level of urgency to my work, and that I'm prepared to take a financial stake in my success, I begin my engagements from a relationship, rather than a transactional, position. In the equity-driven world of the Net, this approach can lead to unique forms of partnership, since many Net-based ventures will offer options, warrants, or some other form of equity for consultants who help them attain their goals.

Another lesson I've learned from my experience building consulting practices is that a practice is like a ball rolling downhill in that it can really pick up speed with the right push, and that push is references. By creating a database of reference sites that can be called on to attest to your success, and by building those references around measurable results, consultants can give their careers that extra push that results in thriving practices.

When I ask consultants I'm mentoring why they've decided to enter the consulting profession rather than taking a corporate job, the most common response is "to keep learning" or "to be exposed to different situations and technologies." The best consultants are continual learners, taking something from each engagement and client encounter that makes them better and more valuable for the next assignment. Measurable results are a method for structuring this learning process, for asking ourselves specific questions about what went well and what went wrong, and for capturing the positive and negative lessons, so that we can continually improve our value and performance.

Finally, consulting can be quite ambiguous. Unlike the architect or the surgeon, we often have no clear deliverable or tangible achievement at the end of the engagement. Additionally, the Internet world adds another layer of haze to the mix, since every engagement is an experiment and the scorecard has not been written. Building in measurable results, to me, is a way to ensure that I can walk away from every engagement with a clear feeling of personal accomplishment.

CREATING MEASURABLE eCONSULTING ENGAGEMENTS

One of the books mentioned earlier, *The Consultant's Scorecard* by Jack Phillips, does an outstanding job of presenting a detailed and rigorous process for determining the return on investment (ROI) for consulting engagements. Through the use of a structured and meticulous evaluation process that includes the collection of financial data throughout the engagement and the conversion of that data to monetary values that can be objectively quantified, Phillips presents a methodology that consultants can use for those projects in which the presentation of a precise financial measurement for return on consulting investment is required. It's not my intention to try to replicate this important work here, but consultants should be aware that, in those cases where this kind of analysis is appropriate, a proven methodology exists.

My intent is instead to offer some fundamental guiding values that are pertinent to the eConsultant, with all the vagaries and special circumstances that the Net presents to us and our projects. My hope is that, by coming to our engagements with a results orientation and a high sense of urgency, and by bringing the willingness to be held to high standards of accountability, we can apply these basic principles to help clients feel they've gotten value from our relationship.

My principles for creating a measurable engagement are as follows.

Start with a Clear Engagement Definition. It's an axiom that if you don't know where you're going, one path is as good as another. In the Internet world, your client's business model and strategy are subject to constant change, even in the middle of an engagement. It's critical that a clear understanding be reached between consultant and client up-front. The scope, deliverables, schedule, budget, roles and responsibilities, and risks must be documented at the start of the engagement. This is obviously sound operating procedure for any professional, and in the eConsulting world it's even more essential. It should be a rule for every consultant that the more unpredictable the engagement, the firmer the underlying scope must be, so that when the inevitable changes occur there is a baseline of understanding between client and consultant that stands as the bedrock of the relationship.

Build in Measurement Up-Front. It's always good practice to define the criteria for success from the beginning of any engagement, because if you don't the client will define it for you, and it may have little relationship to the goals and success criteria you had in mind. This refers not just to the standard consultant's mantra of "setting expectations," but to taking that a step further and defining the quantitative measurements that will identify a successful engagement. Is the site designed for eight-second load with 20,000 sessions—or with 200,000? Is the catalog designed to search through 450 items in one second—or 45,000? Is the call center expected to support two hundred simultaneous calls—or two thousand? Whose market share numbers will we be using to measure site acceptance, Neilsen NetRatings, or Media Metrix? Clarity on measurable, quantifiable goals is one of the best methods for making the client feel like she's in the hands of a competent professional and for taking the emotion and subjectivity out of any disputes or misunderstandings.

Use Measures That Are Meaningful to the Engagement. It should be obvious that database projects need to be measured on database results and that revenue-generating projects need to be measured on revenue. The process of defining measurements with the client has another, more subtle advantage: It gives you insight into the client's priorities. If the client, when asked to participate in the process of defining success criteria, focuses exclusively on the technology aspects of the engagement and is more interested in counting the number of Flash screens than in the revenue model, that should tell you something about your need to counsel the client. If the words "customer experience" or "customer satisfaction" never are uttered, you have the opportunity to educate your client on these important aspects of successful eProjects. Helping the client define appropriate success measurements is one of the most important, and the most revealing, of project activities.

Measure Yourself Throughout the Engagement. Measurement is not just a post-implementation process. Earlier project methodologies called for a "project post-mortem," an unfortunate term that implies death rather than success. These post-implementation reviews were typically pat-on-the-back champagne celebrations for the successful projects and somber blame-fests for the less successful. My recommendation is that, especially in this fluid Internet space, touch points between the consultant and the client need to be much more frequent and, again, must be based on metrics. If we look back at the words of Skip McDonald from Luminant, we'll recall that the majority of eProjects are iterative. This means that each iteration must have its own set of metrics. Just because we know that the first site we build may be completely revamped in six months doesn't mean that we can neglect measuring that site to see whether it achieves its objectives.

Incorporate Objective, Outside Measurement Tools. There are a host of third-party rating and measurement services that specialize in both general and custom-designed measurement programs for Internet businesses. Services like Neilsen NetRatings, Media Metrix, NetValue, HeadCount, and many others offer statistics on page views, shopping patterns, and trends for your client's site. Other services, such as Vividence and Greenfield, provide more subjective data by recruiting Net users to rate and comment on your client's site. It makes it much easier to take any emotion or conflict out of your measurement efforts by incorporating objective outsiders into the process.

Incorporate Human Factors in Your Measurement Effort. Although I've stressed quantifiable metrics in this discussion, this doesn't mean that the human factors can be neglected. Customer satisfaction, training effectiveness, and process improvement are elements that often can only be measured subjectively, through interviews, surveys, or meetings. Build these elements into your plan alongside the harder metrics to obtain a complete picture of the success of your engagement.

Keep on Measuring—Look for Long-Term Results. Help the client gauge the long-term benefits of your engagement by helping to create a permanent measurement process. Through a combination of the third-party services we mentioned earlier, customer and team member surveying, and the typical revenue, customer acquisition and retention, and response time metrics, you can partner with the client to keep a close watch on the health and effectiveness of the solution you've created. This type of long-term outlook not only increases the comfort level of the client, but it moves the engagement from transactional to relational, giving you the opportunity to revisit the client periodically and make sure that the solutions still fit our ever-changing marketplace.

COMMUNICATING THE OUTCOME

Consulting is communication; that's one of the central tenets of the consulting profession. Clearly, dispassionately, and consistently communicating the results of your measurement process is the whole point of the exercise. Planning for the communication of the outcome is as important as the actual measurement, as it sets the project up for adjustment and course correction along the route, keeps the enthusiasm and consensus strong, and reassures the stakeholders that progress is being made. It keeps the consultant's role in the project's success visible, while allowing the observant consultant to gauge the reaction of the client and ensure that they are also perceiving the consultant's role in a positive light.

There are a few principles that consultants should keep in mind when preparing to present results:

- *Understand the audience.* The measurements of various consulting projects, the activities within those projects, and the metrics associated with those activities should be targeted to different audiences. Clearly, board members and senior executives are interested in overall project results and strategic implications, while IT managers and users may be interested in much more tactical and granular measurements. The chairman of the board likely has little interest in the minute-by-minute page load statistics, which the data center manager absolutely needs to know. The department manager may have little interest in the competitive advantage as measured by Neilsen, but will certainly want to understand user satisfaction with the training program. Analyze and understand the motivations and interests of your audiences and present outcome reports that are meaningful to them.

- *Take the emotion and ego out of reporting.* Reporting should be a dispassionate and quantitative exercise, so review your presentations and be sure that any hyperbole and opinion are carefully weeded out. The whole purpose of objective measurement is to get past the distrust and jargon that surrounds our profession, so beware of "revolutions" and "paradigm shifts" in your discussions and focus instead on facts and figures.

- *Deliver good and bad news.* This process can be easily tainted and corrupted by the natural inclinations to "spin" the news, to deliver only the positive results, and to try to manipulate the perception of the negative. Don't succumb to the temptation to hide or color the bad news. Deliver it as forthrightly and clearly as you deliver the good news; this is the only way to retain your credibility and to impact the outcome of the project for the better.

Communication is a process that must be planned and managed. The best and most successful consultants follow a structured communication planning and delivery methodology to ensure that clients are getting the information they need to evaluate the project's progress, to make adjustments, and to understand the consultant's contribution to the result. I won't try to offer a communication process here; I've presented a detailed one in my previous book, and there are many excellent references on this topic in the Bibliography. The important point is that consultants have a reputation, fair or unfair, of lacking accountability and of delivering poor results, and therefore the burden of proof is on us in each engagement. The only way to develop a reputation within the client organization and the business community is to manage your reputation yourself by setting clear and measurable objectives and by communicating your results to the client in a persuasive and fair way.

chapter TEN

Surfing the Wave: Keeping Ahead of the Changes

AGE OF RAPID CHANGE

In the information technology environment in which most IT consultants grew up, technology changed quickly, but we typically had a few years to gain proficiency in a new operating system or application before the next one came along. Many consultants I know got their start doing simple PC installations or elementary network implementations in the early days of networked computing. In those days, an understanding of Novell NetWare or Ethernet was enough to earn you the title of consultant. As clients became more comfortable with the technology and as IT teams caught up with our level of technical expertise, the bar was raised, and consultants, to remain competitive, needed to bring more technology depth, business savvy, and advisory skill to the table.

In this global experiment called the Internet, the strategies, business models, and technologies that define the new economy are in constant flux, as new ideas are tried and adopted or discarded. At the same time, pressures to use Internet technology for competitive advantage are more intense than ever. As eConsultants, we are subject to competitive pressure as well, as our crowded business segment experiences some of the same market realities that are driving many dot.coms to merge, reorganize, or fail. The combination of all these factors makes it incumbent on us as professionals to focus on developing our skills so we can add maximum value for our clients, partner with them to create lasting business models, and maintain our own competitive advantage in a congested eServices marketplace.

In my previous book, *The IT Consultant*, I outlined a development program for IT consultants that included not only the technical elements, but also the project management, business context, communications, and negotiation skills that make for a rounded consulting professional. Rather than attempt to reiterate those principles, I'll refer you to that work and to the other works I've listed in the Bibliography. I'll instead focus on adding to those ideas by reviewing here some of the resources that are specifically pertinent to the eConsultant, those websites, magazines, and tools that can help us to stay on top of this rapidly mutating landscape and to remain trusted and valuable advisors to our clients.

DEVELOPING YOUR STRATEGIC SKILLS

In the chapters of this book that covered basic business strategies and their application to the new economy, we looked at some case studies of companies that have done it right, as well as some examples of companies that have made some errors along the way. For IT consultants aiming to become Internet strategists, I believe that there is no better teacher than the experiences of those who are boldly experimenting in this new marketplace. For this reason I've included a chapter later in this book entitled "Tales from the Fall," which gives readers a snapshot of some of the obstacles that pioneers in the Internet marketplace have run into. eConsultants have a wealth of resources for keeping up with the ongoing evolution in this new economy, and I've listed a few here, with many more in the Bibliography.

The General Business Press. The Internet economy is an area of prime interest to all businesspeople, and the general business press has jumped into this space with both feet. *Fortune* magazine has become one of the most forward-looking and influential publications covering developments in the Internet economy and has recently spun off some of its coverage into a new magazine entitled *eCompany Now.* Both are worth reading, as are *Forbes, The Wall Street Journal, Barron's,* and *Business Week.* For deeper strategic analysis, *The Harvard Business Review* is the grand old man of business journalism, with contributions from the leading academic thinkers in business strategy and a surprising concentration on new economy issues. All consultants, and especially eConsultants, need to make the investment in their professional education and keep up with basic business developments through these resources.

The New Economy Business Press. This new business market has spawned a plethora of magazines specifically focused on happenings in the Internet world.

I especially recommend *Business 2.0, Red Herring,* and *The Industry Standard,* the "big three" in this sector. *The Standard,* a weekly publication, is a great tool for keeping up with the short-term activity in this segment, and its sections on deal activity, metrics, and global events make it indispensable to the Internet advisor. *Business 2.0* and *Red Herring* are excellent strategic references, offering in-depth studies of specific Internet business models and strategies and presenting detailed analysis of the strengths and weaknesses of these approaches that can be very instructive to the Internet consultant about to engage with a client. Other important new economy business publications include *Internet World* and *Fast Company.*

The Technical Press. Consultants can get some great information on technical issues from publications like *Internet Week* and *eWeek.* These weekly "trade rags" offer detailed reviews of specific hardware and software solutions, as well as opinions from veteran reporters on the directions in the eBusiness marketplace. Publications like *Network Magazine* and *Network World* are the best resources for tutorials on the latest technical developments and their real-world applications. *CIO* and *Information Week* deserve special mention for their in-depth coverage of the management and strategic issues that our clients struggle with every day. These are the magazines that your clients in IT management are most likely to review, so it's important that you read them and keep up with the currents that are sweeping through the executive suite or boardroom.

The IT Analysts. Throughout this book I've quoted from IT analysts such as The Gartner Group, Forrester Research, Jupiter Communications, and DataQuest. There are many other consulting and analysis firms that provide expert opinions, market forecasts, and metrics on topics ranging from consumer behavior to B2B revenue projections. Some other important analyst organizations include The Meta Group, The Yankee Group, Giga Information Group, and Info Resources. Although many of these are fee-based services, the reports and analysis they produce are often available from other sources. For instance, The Gartner Group owns a website called TechRepublic (for which, in the interest of full disclosure, I'm a columnist), which publishes abstracts of Gartner's reports for the IT community to access without fee. Many of the other sites also publish abstracts or summaries of their research, which, although abbreviated, can still be valuable.

The Web. The Web is the greatest repository of business information ever devised. In all of my writing and consulting activities, I use the Web as a gigantic library and typically find more information than I could ever use on any topic. Using the Web effectively, however, is an acquired skill. Some of my favorite tools follow:

- The websites of the magazines and analysts I mentioned above. Each of them has a complete archive of articles and commentary on any Internet-related subject and is easily searchable, so eConsultants can find and review a wealth of information about the strategies and technologies that are significant.

- Other websites that are valuable for eConsultants, such as industry associations and databases. There are many academic sites that are designed for researchers, and some of them are specifically focused at consolidating IT research resources. One of my favorites is the ITMweb (www.itmweb.com), which provides links to sites that cover the IT gamut, from ASPs to Knowledge Management to website design tips, and everything in between. Techguide (www.techguide.com) is a complete collection of technical tutorials that I've accessed hundreds of times to make myself an "instant expert" in technologies that I needed for a specific engagement. IT Toolbox (www.ittoolbox.com) is another tutorial site with excellent training material and comprehensive links to other sites where eConsultants can find information pertinent to any engagement. I also use the Venture Capital Resource Library (www.vfinance.com) to find VCs that are a good fit for my clients. There are databases of angel investors, incubators, and consulting companies, just to name a few.

- One of the most valuable resources for business strategists and researchers is the collection of library servers available on the Web. The Library Web (www.kb.nl/infolev/libweb), a site offered as a public service by Thomas Dowling and maintained at the University of California at Berkeley, is a researcher's dream, offering access to both academic and public libraries across the country and the world. Many of these libraries offer online access to their stacks of periodicals, opening the world of specialized trade publications and general business magazines to the Web researcher.

- Specialized Web resources, from the ASP Industry Organization (www.aspindustry.org) to the XML Cover Pages (www.oasis-open.org/cover/xml.html), are specialized sites for every technology and industry that would be of interest to Internet advisors. I spend some time every month checking out the websites of organizations like the World Wide Web Consortium. Using the search engines (I get the best results with Northern Lights), search for the technology area you need and be prepared to spend some time sifting through the results.

Take a look through the Bibliography for a more comprehensive listing of resources and websites that consultants can use to stay on top of the developments in this field.

AN APPROACH TO CONSTANT DEVELOPMENT

Now that we've taken a look at the multitude of resources available for eConsultants and researchers, let's talk a bit about a process for approaching an engagement. In my consulting practice I work with IT consultants and sales teams every day, and one of the clearest indicators of success or failure is their attitude toward preparation and research. Those teams and individuals who have developed a process for performing research on the industry, competitive landscape, culture, and history of clients and prospects do well, win bids, and develop deep relationships. Those teams that are resistant to doing the homework and don't have a technique for uncovering the issues before they walk in the door are forced to sell based on price and often lose the bid anyway, as they have a hard time understanding the client's issues and articulating their added value. Research and preparation are potent competitive weapons for individual consultants against the larger shops: Most big firms sell on the fact that they have experience across a broad range of industries and situations, and one-person consulting shops often don't have that broad base to sell from. Consultants who do their homework and walk in the door with a deep understanding of the client's organization, industry, and competitive situation, and who can talk knowledgeably about the challenges facing that client, can often persuade the client that they can bring value to the engagement.

That said, how do consultants go about preparing for a sales call or an engagement? I personally follow, and teach to my consultant-students, a research process that follows these steps.

Research the Company First

Understand the company with whom you're about to engage. If the company is publicly traded, use the investor resources that are available on the Web or in the library. On the Web, Yahoo Finance is a great place to start. This site provides a wide range of tools for understanding a company, from company profiles to research abstracts, and also offers rankings of companies within their industry segments. Do a search on the company name, check the movement and direction of their stock, see how analysts are rating them in their industry group, understand from their industry group listing who their competition is, and go to their website to see how they portray themselves. Yahoo Finance also offers a listing of current and past news stories about each listed company. This is a service of extraordinary value to the researcher, as it allows you to make yourself an expert in the history and challenges of any publicly listed company.

Other investing sites, such as Multex and Hoover's, provide different views of this fundamental information. Publicly traded companies are required by the Securities and Exchange Commission to file informational reports, called S-1's, 10-K's, and 10-Q's, to inform the investment community of their risks and challenges. These reports are quite revealing, as they often give a very different picture than the public relations spin that is visible on the website. These publications can be found on the investing sites I mentioned.

For companies that are not listed on the stock exchanges, this research can be a bit more difficult, but it is still possible. Use the search engines, such as Yahoo and Northern Lights, to search for the company name and see whether you can ferret out any news or analysis on the company. Visit their website. Check their industry associations or publications (most industries have both trade organizations and specialized publications, which can be found on Yahoo). Often the company you are researching will be mentioned or will advertise, or you can find industry-wide issues that will be pertinent to the client.

Research the Industry

Understand the industry in which the client competes. Use the investing resources we reviewed above to get a complete picture of the industry and its challenges. Hoover's offers industry profiles that place every company in its industry and describe the financial results and expectations for each industry. These listings are a great source of information, as they allow you to link through to each company's website, then jump back to the industry listing; so, in an hour or so, you can get a complete picture of the competitive landscape and the unique market niche and strategy of every player. Make it your business to understand not only the specific company with which you are about to engage, but also their competitors.

The industry publications and associations are also an important resource for this type of research. Competitors in an industry, such as the pharmaceutical industry or the construction industry, often talk very candidly in their industry associations and magazines about the problems and issues they face, as they assume that this information will be of little interest to outsiders. Astute researchers have access to the knowledge that only industry veterans would typically own by reviewing the discussions and articles posted on "insider" websites.

Look for impartial analysis on the industry. Using the analysts, business magazines, and search engines mentioned above, look for articles and analyses on the specific industry in question. If I'm about to engage with a bank, for instance, I'll search through the archives of *Business Week, CIO, Business 2.0,* and *The Industry Standard* and read every article I can find about the eBusiness efforts and initiatives in that industry. Clients will take notice if you can cogently discuss the endeavors of their competitors in the Internet space.

Research the Technology

If the client firm is in the telecommunications industry, it's not enough to understand the business environment and the competitive positioning. It's also critical to build up some fundamental understanding of the underlying technology that drives the industry—and also wireless, or streaming content, or electronic publishing. If the client is investigating CRM, or Web-page personalization software, or data mining, use the tutorial websites and technical magazines listed above to gain some depth in the technology and the options available. Visit vendor websites so you can talk knowledgeably about the similarities and differences between offerings. Not only is this a chance to demonstrate to the client your depth of technical knowledge, but it's also an opportunity to expand your own technical horizons. One of the best parts of the consulting profession is that, due to the serendipity of client engagements, I get the chance to make myself a technical expert in a wide variety of fields while expanding my ability to add value for my clients.

Research Your Own Competitive Position

Understand your experience with the client's business. What relevant experience do you have with the client or the industry? If you are a single practitioner, do you have any experience in your portfolio that is pertinent to the problem at hand? If you are a member of a firm, reach out firm-wide and investigate the engagements and relationships that are in the firm's portfolio so you can bring the right experience and expertise to the project.

Understand your client relationship. Do you have any relationship with the client, or is this a new prospect? It's critical that you engage at the right level. Strategic Internet projects are rarely successful when they're driven from the IT or departmental level, although tactical "spot solutions" can be. If there is an existing client relationship, be sure that you understand how that helps (or hinders) you. If you (or your firm) have done a great job for the client in the past, make sure that this experience is referenced. If there are any negative remnants from a previous engagement, deal with those as well—fix them or be prepared to help the client understand why circumstances are different this time. Some systematized selling programs counsel sales teams to rate everyone in the organization as a friend or foe, advisor or resister. In complex selling engagements, this is a good idea, as it makes you think through your individual relationship with each decision maker and enforces the development of a selling strategy for each situation.

Understand your competitors. Know who else the client may be negotiating with and understand their strengths and weaknesses and how you can compete against them successfully. Does your competition have an existing relationship that may be giving them an "inside track" to success? Do they have a particular expertise or industry experience that gives them a competitive advantage? Knowing the answer to these questions helps you develop a winning competitive strategy.

Consultants who utilize the tools at their disposal to keep improving their strategic and technical knowledge—and who follow the research process outlined in this chapter—will experience the continual learning that makes our profession such an intellectual joy and will win in the competitive eConsulting marketplace, earning the opportunity to participate in the most challenging and rewarding projects.

Tales from the Fall

A YEAR OF CHANGE

In the year that I've spent working on this book, the Internet business environment has changed significantly. The bursting of the Internet "bubble" predicted by stock market analysts and journalists alike has come to pass, and stalwarts of the glory days are now shadows of their former selves. In every sector of the Internet economy, former high-fliers have crashed to earth as unsustainable valuations have come back to reality. The AMEX Internet Index, a basket of Internet stocks, has fallen from its high of 701 to its current 462, a punishing 35 percent; but this number alone doesn't tell the whole story. In the Internet consulting sector, for instance, two of the hottest names in 1999 were Scient and Razorfish, and their stock prices reflected the glamour of this segment of the IT consulting business. In the IPO frenzy and the "eBuilder" boom that followed, Scient reached a high of 133 and Razorfish hit 57. Today Scient is at 3 and Razorfish is at 2. The descent in this sector is not limited to these two players; MarchFirst, the combination of the USWeb/Whitmann-Hart consulting powerhouses, went up to 81 before plummeting to today's 5. iXL, whose CEO, Bill Nussey was named "Consultant of the Year" by an industry association in 1999 and who used its high-priced stock as currency to purchase thirty-eight IT services firms between 1997 and 1999, saw its stock tumble from 59 to its current 2 after announcing disappointing earnings and the departure of its famous top consultant.

It's not just the eConsulting sector that has fallen from grace, however. Just a year ago *Fortune* magazine called Yahoo "the new blue chip,"[1] describing how mutual fund managers were piling into the stock to avoid being left behind by its constant ascent. In the year since that article was published, this "blue chip" has gone from 250 to 30. Likewise that other symbol of the new economy, Amazon.com, has fallen from 113 to 22. Across the spectrum of Net based businesses, from the online brokerages to the B2B exchanges, the environment, both on Wall Street and in the competitive marketplace, has gotten much tougher. The catch phrase of the day has gone from "capturing eyeballs" to "path to profitability," as in, you'd better have that path clearly laid out if you expect to get funded or sustain your stock valuation.

I dwell on this because it's critical for eConsultants to know what works and what doesn't. In the interest of presenting a snapshot of the current state of the Internet economy, I've compiled some material about some of the sectors of this market space, the high hopes that they had for world domination when they came out of the garage or the VC's (venture capitalist's) office, and where they are now. The stories I've selected are not all negative. I've included a couple of accounts of Internet sectors that have fallen from grace to illustrate some of the excesses and errors of strategy that eConsultants must understand in order to counsel clients well. There are success stories too, and I've told a few of those anecdotes here. Even in the tough environment of late 2000, some entrepreneurs have built strong businesses based on innovative concepts, strong fundamental business strategies, and great execution. As Seth Neiman, managing partner at Crosspoint Venture Partners, notes in our interview (Chapter Twelve), the failure of many Internet ventures in this early period of experimentation doesn't indicate that the revolution was a mirage. We're still in the early days of this transformation, and the shakeout of weak ideas, weak strategies, and weak managers is a healthy and necessary episode in the development of a sustainable renovation of business practices. If I believed that today's downturn was a repudiation of the Internet experiment, I wouldn't be focusing my career on working with clients in this marketplace, and I wouldn't have spent this year writing this book. These narratives, good and bad, are designed to help eConsultants learn the hard lessons that only the marketplace can teach.

TOYS ONLINE—NO GAME

The online toy segment seemed like a no brainer–looking through an online catalog of toys and games at your own pace, at your own convenience, with the kids snug in bed, versus trying to tow your kids through the aisles at a swarming toy store, as they grasp at every item and inevitably start to cry when they can't have everything they see. And, in fact, the online toy segment has had success in building a critical mass of customers and revenue, projected to reach $610 million this year and to top $3.6 billion, or 10 percent of all U.S. spending on toys, by 2004, according to Forrester Research.[2] So why has the sector become the poster child of failed dot.coms, second only to the pet segment in the amount of ridicule heaped on it by journalists and market analysts? Why have highly visible and well-funded ventures such as the Disney-backed Toysmart.com and Viacom's RedRocket.com decided to step away from this bonanza? What made KBKids.com drop its plans for an IPO, and why did eToys' stock drop from $86 a share to its current $2?

As with many of the other consumer segments, one of the problems was the sheer number of competitors. Drawn more by the IPO payoff potential than by market economics, the number of competitors exploded between 1998 and 1999. With ten major players and scores of minor local toy shops in the market space, the cost of getting the message out to the potential customer overshadowed the revenue that the segment could generate. Disney's Toysmart, for instance, spent $25 million in advertising to generate a measly $6 million in revenue.[3] Many of the online toy stores fell victim to the two big lies of the Internet's B2C explosion, namely the invincibility of first mover advantage and the need to capture market share before worrying about profitability.

There were also some built-in disadvantages that were not apparent except to those who know the vagaries of the retail toy business. Unlike books, for example, toys are not easily returnable to the manufacturer, so predictions of the hot products and the right quantities had better be accurate or toy retailers are in for a nasty write-down of inventory, as Amazon.com learned last year when it was forced to write off over $30 million in excess inventory in its toy division. The yearly frenzy over the hot toy of the season, whether it's a Cabbage Patch Kid, a Beanie Baby, or a talking Elmo, is in fact an effect of the toy industry's long lead times, requiring retailers to order products up to eight months in advance. Due to the low average cost and large bulk of many toy items, the relative picking, packing, and shipping costs are quite high compared to other online retail items such as books or CDs. For all these sector-specific reasons, the online toy business is a clear example of the difficulties of moving an offline business to the Net, especially for those who have no operating experience in their chosen sector.

How have the strategies in the online toy market changed based on the lessons of the last few years? Some players, like Kbkids.com, have changed their models completely, looking at the site as a convenience channel for their customers rather than as a blockbuster stand-alone business. The company's lowered expectations are clear in the comments of Michael Glazer, KB Toys CEO. "By next year," he told *The Wall Street Journal*,[4] "it [the website] will no longer be a drain on KB Toys." Others are going for the niche market, for example, SmarterKids.com with its focus on the educational toy market. Finally, some are going for market heft through alliances, as evidenced by the joint venture between Toys R'Us and Amazon.com. Whatever the strategy, the investment markets have clearly lost patience with the experimentation and are looking at Christmas 2000 as the make-or-break event for the toy e-tailers.

B2B—2B OR NOT 2B?

At the end of 1999, as the Internet-based e-tail hype gave way to the reality that selling dog food on the Internet was probably not the stuff of which revolutions are made, the attention shifted to the B2B marketplace. Many analysts predicted that by 2001 there would be more than ten thousand B2B sites[5] in industries spread across the business spectrum. In a typical forecast, DataQuest predicted that B2B eCommerce would reach $7.3 trillion worldwide by 2004, or 7 percent of the total global economy![6] Forrester Research, in its February 2000 report "eMarketplaces Boost B2B Trade," predicted that B2B eCommerce will hit $2.7 trillion in 2004, reaching 53 percent of all online transactions.

How times have changed. Deloitte Consulting, in a recent study,[7] counts 1,488 B2B sites—far from the ten thousand once forecast—and dropping fast. According to John Ferreira, head of B2B services at Deloitte, "This is an unsustainable competitive environment. There can't be this many players."[8] In fact, Forrester Research, in an August 2000 report entitled "The eMarketplace Shakeout," reversed some of its earlier predictions, forecasting that over the next three years eMarketplaces will go through a massive consolidation, leaving fewer than two hundred survivors. How did this B2B marketplace go from ten thousand potential players to fewer than two hundred? What are the market dynamics that caused this total rethinking of the B2B opportunity?

The first answer is the most obvious: Habit. Many potential customers of the B2B exchanges have deeply ingrained relationships and practices that drive their procurement processes, and these habits are hard to break. The Internet, to many, is still an alien environment, unproven in the core business functions that are touched by B2B commerce. As we discussed earlier, Internet supply chain projects require companies to open up formerly hidden and confidential procedures, and many potential beneficiaries of the Internet's supply chain efficiencies are hesitant to reveal those secrets.

It's not just habit, however. Many potential participants in Net marketplaces question the underlying business model itself. Why would a supplier or buyer pay the transaction fees that are at the core of many exchanges' revenue models, simply for the right to post an RFP (request for proposal) or an offer to sell—activities that they can do now through the U.S. mail or via e-mail? The broader exposure that was considered a key advantage of the Internet-based B2B model has also had the effect of driving prices to their lowest denominator, an effect we discussed at length earlier. While this may be great for the purchaser, it certainly takes some of the incentive away from the supplier, without whom there is no exchange.

Most analysts agree that the future of the B2B market will be less friendly to the neutral exchanges that provide a simple venue for transactions and will instead favor those exchanges that can bring unique value to the participants. The pioneering B2B site FreeMarkets.com, for instance, employs industry experts as consultants to help participants in its various markets participate successfully. Glen Meakem, Freemarkets' founder and CEO, has said, "This is a place where professional buyers come and work with our professionals to get things done."[9] The sites that have done well so far in this space fall into two categories: The brick-and-mortar players, who can leverage their domain expertise and existing infrastructure, and the industry consortium.

W.W. Grainger, the 75-year-old industrial parts supplier, is a perfect example of the former, with a Web presence that generates over $100 million annually and expected to grow to $400 million by 2001. More importantly, Grainger's sites are profitable. Richard Keyser, Grainger's CEO, says, "We think it will be difficult for the smaller players to keep up, especially when larger customers are demanding so much. You can't just be an Internet company. You have to understand the business to do well."[10] The much-touted auto industry consortium, Covisint, and its other consortia brethren such as the food industry's Transora and the computer industry's HighTechMatrix may succeed or they may not, but one thing is certain: They have had a chilling effect on the growth of B2B pure plays in their markets. What entrepreneur or VC is prepared to invest time and money into developing a marketplace to compete with the clout, relationships, and deep pockets of a consortium of the leading players in an existing market?

FALLING UP

So in this perilous market, where the conventional wisdom is often wrong and the herd mentality ran many businesses off the cliff, who were the smart entrepreneurs and managers who were able to swim against the tide and create growing businesses and rising company valuations, even as many of the dot.com darlings of Wall Street and Super Bowl ads were packing their bags and going back to their corporate jobs? Let's look at a few creative business models that may have staying power even after the hype is gone.

Delivering Efficiency

Nistevo is not a well-known name in the Internet trade press or on the stock screens of Internet day-traders, yet it has succeeded in the crowded B2B marketplace with a simple yet elegant strategy—they've combined innovative software with a real-time exchange that uses the Internet to help companies save millions in freight costs. Using Nistevo's software and members-only network, companies such as Monsanto, General Mills, Land O'Lakes, and Pillsbury post information about trucks that will return empty after a delivery. Other companies can book those trucks, creating efficiencies for both sides. By combining elements of a software business, a professional services business, and an Internet exchange, Nistevo has created a unique, hybrid service offering that provides many of the supply chain efficiencies that prognosticators have been predicting for the Internet. Nistevo's Contract Management service allows buyers and sellers of shipping services to build an electronic catalog of transportation rates and preferred carriers. Buyers and sellers can then collaborate online to agree on a set of established prices on a portfolio of services, thus creating a virtual contract that eliminates the need to continually renegotiate on shipping charges. Their Collaborative Logistics service creates a "spot market" for unused shipping capacity, similar to the Internet marketplace for unused bandwidth created by companies like Rate-X and Band-X. No longer do trucks have to travel across the country empty, wasting space and fuel, due to the inability to line up shipping contracts in time to meet the truckers' schedules. All this is wrapped in a sophisticated tracking system that gives manufacturers unprecedented visibility into the whereabouts of their products in transit.

The CEO of Nistevo may never join Amazon's Jeff Bezos on the cover of *Time* magazine, but by strategically recognizing an opportunity for introducing efficiency into an inefficient market, and then creating a complete offering that includes all the elements the customer would need to take advantage of those efficiencies, Nistevo has created a business that has drawn the attention of some of the premier investors, partners, and clients in the world.

Meeting Needs

From the beginning, the Internet has been a communications medium, a place where individuals across the world could correspond and collaborate to interact about their areas of interest, from the serious to the frivolous. As the Internet medium has migrated from the simple text-based interface of the early "chat rooms" to the rich multimedia presentation available via the World Wide Web, the possibilities for enhanced levels of communications have expanded as well. This was the opportunity that the founders of Webex, Subrah Iyar, chairman and CEO, and Min Zhu, chief technical officer, recognized in 1996 when they collaborated to form an Internet-based conferencing venture. Based on four years of development by Zhu, the team believed they had a unique technology that could transform Web-based conferencing from the klutzy text-based chats common in the Net's early days into a smooth mix of real-time voice and video. The partners believed that, as the standards for Internet bandwidth grew and more businesses invested in the technology required to deliver multimedia connectivity to the desktop, there would be a market for rich collaborative conferencing tools on the Net. They used the early version of Zhu's software to slowly build a base of satisfied customers, including Oracle, Lawson Software, Adobe, Yahoo, PeopleSoft, and Ricoh.

What were the strategies that Zhu and Iyar followed to ensure that they were not just another dot.com casualty? They made it a point to avoid anything that could jeopardize the company's core vision of superior customer service, so they ruled out potentially costly distractions such as operating their own data center, choosing instead to outsource their Web servers to a hosting service. In contrast with many of their contemporaries who were solely focused on cashing in with a "quick flip" IPO, Iyar and Zhu avoided venture capitalists in the beginning, fearing they would rush the startup to launch prematurely and cause them to lose focus on their long-term objectives. The first round of VC financing, a comparatively modest $25 million, did not come until December 1999. Their marketing campaign, featuring RuPaul, the drag comedienne, with the tag line "Meetings Are a Drag," garnered them some quick brand recognition, but they avoided indulging in the excesses of multi-million dollar Super Bowl advertising campaigns.

Have Webex's strategies paid off? Webex's IPO, offered in late July of 2000 at $17 a share, closed that day at $33 and powered to $56 in September. Although not immune to the downward trend in Internet stocks, Webex stock has held above its offering price, making Iyar a very wealthy entrepreneur, to the tune of about $130 million. More important, according to Iyar, is the fact that he's created a business that will last. "We are not just another fad," Iyar says. "Our technology works better and does more, and consumers like it."[11]

LESSONS FROM THE FALL

So what do consultants need to take away from the experiences of the last few years in the Internet marketplace? The most important lesson is not to believe the hype. Everyone, from entrepreneurs to VCs to analysts and journalists, has an interest in inflating the size and potential of Internet marketplaces, and there's no real risk for them, as predictions are forgotten quickly in this experimental environment. Consultants and clients must make their own conclusions about the real potential for their concepts, and they must be backed up by both specific research and common sense. Individual customers make individual decisions to migrate to or ignore a new market offering—and don't much care what the pundits say.

These lessons also indicate the death of "Internet time." The vaunted first-mover advantage may have some value, as it seems to have had in the cases of Yahoo, Amazon, and eBay. It has failed far more often than it has succeeded, however, as the hundreds of retail sites that blew through millions of dollars trying to build traffic and brands based on nothing but speed-to-market have learned. A more careful analysis will tell us that, for those businesses that have built-in stickiness and network effects, that gain value based on their growing number of participants, such as eBay, or for those who bring real innovation to a marketplace, such as Amazon, speed may be an advantage, but for many it turned out to be their downfall. As Steve Mott, president of Priceline's doomed "name your own price for groceries" business, Webhouse, recently told *Business 2.0,* "Webhouse consciously wasted money building components of our business model two or three times. We crossed our fingers and prayed that a doomed technical architecture would see us through. We pursued customer growth at all costs. We accelerated our rollout from twelve months to four, at great risk to our operational integrity. The final lesson we can take from the Webhouse experience: Speed can kill."[12]

Another key lesson to learn from the contrast between the winners and losers is that the winners focused on the fundamentals of business strategy and ignored the "this time is different" mantra. As any stock market trader knows, "this time is different" is the kiss of death, both in markets and in business. The fundamentals do indeed apply. In the Internet economy as in the traditional economy, competitive advantage is based on a unique concept, knowledge of the industry in which you compete, a strong management team, a robust technological underpinning, a brand that has a positive connotation in the consumer's mind, wise allocation of resources, and great execution. Inexperienced managers with copycat ideas, indistinguishable brands, me-too technology, wasteful spending, lack of domain expertise in the industries they attack, and sloppy execution will not prevail. "Replicating a brick-and-mortar business assuming that brick-and-mortar people were slow and didn't get it was never a good idea," says Robert Higgins, managing general partner of VC firm Highland Capital Partners. "You are not going to steal someone else's business, but if you create something unique, you can be successful."[13]

From the online toy market we explored in this chapter to the online pet supplies and furniture markets, entrepreneurs learned the truth of Higgins' words. These simple truths may have gotten lost in the euphoria of the Internet moment, but in hindsight it's clear that they still rule the day in the business world. eConsultants, out of all the players in any Internet project, need to be the voices of reason, the ones who can see through the fog of hype and bring the conversation back to the fundamentals every time.

End Notes
 1. Nocera, J. How Yahoo! Became a Blue Chip. *Fortune,* June 7, 1999.
 2. Bannon, L. Rough Play. *The Wall Street Journal,* Oct. 23, 2000.
 3. ibid.
 4. ibid.
 5. Anders, J. B2B: Yesterday's Darling. *The Wall Street Journal,* Oct. 23, 2000.

6. Knight, L. Triggering the B2B Electronic Commerce Explosion. *DataQuest,* April 3, 2000.
7. Anders, J. B2B: Yesterday's Darling. *The Wall Street Journal,* Oct. 23, 2000.
8. ibid.
9. ibid.
10. ibid.
11. Schoenberger, K. Bad Karma, Good IPO. *The Industry Standard,* Dec. 18, 2000.
12. Mott, S. Trial by Fire. *Business 2.0,* Dec. 26, 2000.
13. Helft, M. Reports of the Death of the Dot-Com Have Been Greatly Exaggerated. *The Industry Standard,* Oct. 30, 2000.

Where the Internet Is Going

chapter TWELVE

LIFE-CHANGING EVENTS

The new economy is real, and the changes that will flow from this explosion of innovation will indeed change all of our lives. Now that we've moved past the euphoria and unreality that accompanied the first wave of Internet businesses, we can settle back, learn the lessons that economic experimentation teaches us, and move on to the real revolution. The transformation will be created by those companies that follow a few simple rules of successful entrepreneurship: (1) Find unproductive markets and figure out how to introduce new efficiencies; (2) use technology in creative and innovative ways; (3) create unique intellectual property; or (4) invent an entirely new business segment.

A look back at another instrument of business revolution, the automobile, offers some instructive lessons. "Everyone recognizes the effect that the car has had on productivity and life," says Joseph Stiglitz, an economics professor at Stanford University. "The fact that there was an enormous amount of consolidation, from several dozen companies down to three car companies, doesn't mean it wasn't real."[1] And as Hal Varian, author of *Information Rules* (1999) and dean of the School of Information Management at UC Berkeley, has said, "From 1904 to 1908, 240 companies entered the automotive business, the Internet of that time. In 1910 the industry went through a consolidation, and many companies went out of business or were absorbed into other firms. As the industry matured, those 240 companies had to be winnowed down to a dozen or so. Initially Ford priced his product low—just like Amazon selling books at a 40 percent discount. This built the market."[2] Revolutions in business come and go, but the fundamental laws of competition and economics remain in force.

The ability to innovate that has made Silicon Valley the engine of our economic boom will not go away. In fact, many analysts believe that the real innovation is the fact that creativity and breakthrough thinking have been institutionalized in our high-tech firms, as new forums for advancing collaboration and ingenuity, such as internal incubators and "skunk works," have become central to the business models of firms such as Intel and Cisco. And the Silicon Valley behemoths have no monopoly on inventiveness. "Suppose that Napster [the music-sharing technology invented by 19-year-old Shawn Fanning in his dorm room] is launched with the cooperation of a record label for a $20 a month fee," premier venture capitalist John Doerr recently told *The Industry Standard*. "That's a huge business."[3]

The horizon also looks bright, as broadband technology and wireless communications become mainstream technologies, bringing unlimited bandwidth and untethered access to every Internet user. The ability to be constantly connected to the Net, either with a multimedia-capable connection at home that offers the ability to deliver film, sports, music, news, and information on demand, or with a portable device that offers access to all the data (and all the users) on the Net in a convenient format, will take this revolution to new heights we cannot yet imagine.

The venture capital community has been one of the engines of this innovation, as the availability of capital for experimentation and development has proven to be one of America's unique competitive advantages, one that the rest of the world is now emulating. This method of funding business innovation was successful long before the Internet transformation, and it will continue to fuel the growth of this economy. Indeed, the amount of money raised and invested so far in 2000 is an all-time record. VCs have invested $60 billion through the third quarter of 2000, up from $33.2 billion in the same period last year, according to figures from Venture Economics. "The smart VCs will see that this is really stage zero or stage one and that the big transformations have yet to take place," says Andrew Whinston, director of the Center for Research in Electronic Commerce at the University of Texas.[4] Because of the central role that venture capital has played in this transformation, I thought it fitting to end this book with an extended conversation with one of the most astute and forward-thinking of the VCs in Silicon Valley.[5]

In a recent cover story, respected business technology magazine *Red Herring* asked the question: "Who Wants to Be a Venture Capitalist?"[6] Silicon Valley venture capitalists have moved into the popular culture, glamorized as modern day swashbucklers, taking multi-million-dollar risks based on business concepts scrawled on the back of a napkin. For those who follow the VC industry, of course, the reality is quite different. For every deal that rips through the IPO market and achieves spectacular returns, there are projects that never achieve their potential due to faulty business models, weak management teams, unexpected leapfrogs in technology, feuding founders, or a myriad of other startup perils. Successful VC firms must have the *ability* to foresee the direction of the marketplace, the *restraint* to resist the herd mentality that often overcomes the investment community, and the *discipline* to sift through the hundreds of business plans that come their way to select only those that display the concept, technology, business advantage, and management team that can execute and sustain the business over the long haul.

Consultants and IT professionals interested in the future of the Internet and information technology business can learn a lot from the insights of successful venture capitalists. I recently chatted with a VC whose firm was named by *Forbes* as the most financially successful venture capital firm in the world, based on public market returns over the last three years. Seth Neiman, managing partner at Crosspoint Venture Partners of Woodside, California, is a member of the team that developed and incubated Ariba way back in 1996, before the potential of the Internet B2B exchange model was apparent; pioneered the high-performance network infrastructure market through its investment in companies like Efficient Networks, Foundry Networks, and Juniper Networks; and invested in Brocade before the storage area network marketplace took off. Crosspoint's investments in Brocade Communications, Juniper Networks, and Foundry Networks alone have resulted in over $40 billion in market capitalization. Brocade was one of 1999's three best performing NASDAQ IPOs.

An Interview
with Seth Neiman

Rick: Let's start with an overview of Crosspoint, and then let's talk about your particular interests and specialties.

Seth: The short form on Crosspoint is that the firm is thirty years old, we have six investing partners, we have a little over $2 billion under active management, we are well known for very early stage incubation, seed, and first-round investing, in particular in the communication space. We were named by *Forbes* earlier this year as the number one venture capital firm worldwide, based on actual returns.

Rick: Congratulations!

Seth: Thank you. We're proud of that, and proud, of course, to be associated with the companies that actually made that happen. For CIO groups, who are most of our customers actually, that list of companies is probably valuable. We're involved as the lead investor in Brocade, Foundry, Ariba, Covad. Those are the front-page *Wall Street Journal* ones.

Rick: Not a bad portfolio!

Seth: Thank you. So that should give you a flavor of us. I think one of the interesting things about us is that we're all people with very long operating backgrounds, fifteen years or more; we've all started companies and run them, so we're really industry people from a very early age. I think an interesting place to start is, if you look at what we've done and how we do it, a few things stand out. The first is that what we try to do is build dominant new companies in brand new markets. We're not interested in the quick-flip IPO candy, or as John Mumford [Crosspoint Founding Partner] likes to call them, "frou-frou.com." In particular, we're not interested in anything that can't be a very large business that produces substantial value for its customers. The tendency is to focus on deep technology businesses, businesses that sell to other businesses. That shows up in a lot of ways. In that long list of our companies that made up the bulk of the top ten IPOs in the last year, there are a large number of incubations. Brocade was incubated in this office. So was Ariba. That really gives you a flavor for how we think about this. We look at it from a very deep operational point of view. Where are the important long-term, high-margin, high-growth markets going? Where is there a deep intersection between technology and technology directions, and what is the entry point into a brand new, extremely large market? From a strategic point of view, what the firm is always focused on is the disruptive nature of communications technology. So if you were to step back and look at the theme of Crosspoint's investing from a marketplace point of view, what we have tried to do is identify where changes in communications, particularly in communications technology, have created these changes in big new landscapes; and that's followed a pretty natural evolution. Not that we predicted the evolution, but once you put it all together you can see that we were following this trail. This first led us to enterprise data, then to wide area networking, to broadband, then to optical networking—these service providers that run on top of these deployed networks.

Rick: That's where an Ariba might fit in.

Seth: That's right—an Ariba or a Covad. Or an awful lot of what we're interested in in communications. Of course, along the way you run into some wonderful serendipity like Brocade, where we saw the opportunity for a storage area networking technology to emerge, and through a lot of hard work and a lot of good luck and just unbelievable execution by the company, it ended up presiding over the founding of a whole industry. That's really what we like to do. We don't look for the crevices in the current landscape.

Rick: You're not looking for the little niche that somebody can come in and grab and make a quick hit?

Seth: We're not interested in that. You know, there's a lot going on. We're sort of in a completely anomalous time of life, in public markets, in venture investing, and in business creation. We call that the "New Economy," and of course there are a lot of opinions about all of this. I think it's important to divide it up. There's investing and the financial piece of this, then there's new business creation and the trends in the market. A lot of people try to play it safe with a straight-line trend, and that just doesn't work from our point of view. We've seen the period where the Internet was painted with one brush—one day it's great, the next day it's terrible. We're at the point where we ask, "Is it time to be doubters?" I don't think any deep-thinking person would accept that. What we've gone through is a really interesting period where the Internet is completely changing significant parts of both the economic and the technological landscape. If you're a historian, you'd have to go back to the rise of Venice, where the whole world is getting reinvented because the nature of trade, business-to-business activity, is being altered.

Rick: So you think that the common analogy to the telegraph or the railroad is shallow, you think it's much deeper.

Seth: Absolutely! When you look at something like the railroad or the telegraph, those are both really important, but there are ways in which their impacts are limited and they're fairly obvious. With the Internet, the impact is much broader—and for that reason deeper. I think we've entered a period where everything will be tried. It's not well-known that Alexander Graham Bell couldn't get funding. When you have these big enabling technologies it's hard to point at the killer app.

Rick: It's hard to visualize what we're really talking about.

Seth: Right, the Internet is like that. It was pretty obvious what the railroad would do. It wasn't obvious what the telephone would do. We're in a period where, because data communications has become fundamental to business, making it ubiquitous and wide-area is changing all of business, including the marketing side, which is the part that has gotten a lot of the attention. But it's also changed all the underlying enterprise-oriented compute technology. What isn't true is that everything goes on the Internet. We have been in a period where the theory is that everything will go there. I don't think so. I think everything will be tried.

Rick: Everything is being tried.

Seth: And some things will work. One of the most interesting parts is that that experimentation has transformed new business creation, the stock market, and the role that private equity or venture capital really plays.

Rick: I was just about to go there. Your conversation leads to the question. Is it the role of venture capital to participate in that try-anything process to see what really shakes out and what ultimately brings value?

Seth: Absolutely, and I would take it a step further. There is no other institution that can do it. What's happened is that the fact that we've had this wide reinvention requires that new business creation become a dominant force in the economy. With that, the process of new business creation has matured and changed. One interesting thing that a lot of people have focused on recently is the rise and fall of the "dot.bombs," as they have been affectionately labeled.

This is very instructive but can be misleading. This is a very appropriate thing. One of the natural things is that, as consumers got attached to the Internet, marketing and selling to consumers would get attached to the Internet, and so every basic version of that has been tried. A lot of things were tried that, to be frank, with our point of view on strategy, we scratched our heads and said, "That's not going to fly in the long term." E-tailing was never going to be a high-margin, high-growth business. Retail is a low-margin, difficult business, and it doesn't turn into a high-margin business because you go to the Internet. That doesn't mean that great new businesses can't be created. Amazon is a terrific company, obviously. But it doesn't become any different than bookselling. It's just next-generation bookselling, with greater reach and greater opportunity to extend its brand than a brick-and-mortar company.

Rick: And it has the opportunity to do some unique things that a brick-and-mortar company can't do, like turning a product into a service.

Seth: Exactly. There are all kinds of tricks, and some of them add value; but at root the business, although different, remains fundamentally the same.

Rick: Especially from a financial productivity point of view.

Seth: That's exactly right. Let's take a look at what's happened to the stock market in all of this, because I think it's important if you want to see the future. There's a lot of enthusiasm about the reinvention, and our society as a whole decided to participate. That's a very interesting piece, which hardly anybody really wants to talk about. It isn't just the financial community or the entrepreneurs or the businesspeople. Our entire society—and I don't just mean the United States, but the world—is worried and focused and interested in this reinvention. That caused the investors to do something that never has been done before, or at least for quite a while, and that is to invest speculatively.

Rick: To become an engine of equity for new business generation.

Seth: I think that that would be giving investors a little too much credit. What happened was they could not stand aside. In the old days, five years ago, a large financial institution on Wall Street took risks in small cap stocks by investing in solid small companies with a linear growth and profitability. They bought their stock in the hope that they'd get large. What has happened with the reinvention of the Internet is that the same institutions extended their risk profiles and they extended them to invest in companies without revenues or proven markets or business models. That's a very different game, and the reason they did it was not because they were seeing deep, but because the whole society was interested in it. And if you were managing one of those portfolios, you'd get up at three o'clock in the morning and go, "What's going to happen if I don't get my fair share of this?"

Rick: If I miss this I'm dead!

Seth: Bingo! So not surprisingly from a financial point of view, because ultimately new business creation is about markets functioning, a lot of the companies didn't make it. So we have the fallout that we're sort of in the middle of.

Rick: So this fallout is a natural and healthy part of the new business creation process?

Seth: It absolutely is. That's talking about how the public markets participate in this. As an example, my mother is 74 years old and she watches CNBC. Two years ago she didn't know what an equity was! When I first got into venture capital and said "I'm joining this firm," she asked "What is it?" I said, "You know the Janus fund that manages your money. They buy stocks and sell them later when they go up? Well, I'm going to do that, only I'm going to invest in companies that don't exist." She took a twenty-second pause and said, "Are you sure this is a good idea?" So the piece that's really interesting and important is that there's been this speculative fervor, very valuable and required, and the public markets have participated. And now the public markets have backed away from a certain kind of participation. It's healthy; the system is being refined. But the broad brush, the Internet is dead, the Internet is gone, neither of those is true! What's true now is that we've come through this period and created some unbelievable companies, and the system is learning how to correct and learning how venture capital and private equity can create even more and better opportunities. How do the public markets become a little more selective and not reach too far into the youth of these companies—and still get their fair share of the big winners?

Rick: More of a balance between speculation and prudent participation?

Seth: That's exactly right. We're just entering that phase. We're going to see the continuation of growth and focus on the Internet. We're just in the first inning of this reinvention. We need to get to the second inning. These are deeper, much more complicated, more technical companies, built by focusing on more difficult technologies.

Rick: It's not pantyhose.com anymore.

Seth: Right. We're going to see companies that have business models that have never been seen before—companies that are service providers using the broadband infrastructure delivering high-end applications and third party business relationships and transaction capacity . . . complicated business models with unbelievably valuable businesses . . . technical service provider businesses that will become intertwined with their customers so deeply that they'll be fundamental to their future. Imagine the consultants of the world unified with the good enterprise software companies of the world, but selling their goods as genuine solutions, not just "I can come in and install it." We call that solutioneering, and then the consultants leave and guess what? You still have to have just as many people to maintain it, and the poor clients are not sure they understand the business need.

Rick: It's the old, "Here you go. We installed it; good luck."

Seth: Right, that world is going away. Special services are going to be deeply important, but as a component of long-term service providers who provide highly integrated technology, customized for a given business's needs and integrating them along vertical lines with the important relationships in an industry. That is one major theme of our investment.

Rick: It sounds like a place where consulting and a vertical service provider model and the underlying technology all converge to provide a complete level of integrated partnership.

Seth: That's exactly right. Let me give you a couple of examples. I'm involved with a company called eConvergent. This is an incredibly capable professional services and technical group, out of the CRM space, and they integrate best-of-breed applications and platforms—everything you would think of as CRM and more—and a huge component of their own technology, and deliver it over T1 and DSL. Instead of an onsite business that needs twenty customer service seats and that has to be completely integrated into pre-sales and post-sales and all that stuff. And the prospects look at it and say, "Oh no, this is a $2 million first-wave project plus equipment plus a host of people to run it forever."

Rick: It becomes a whole department. . . .

Seth: Right, eConvergent says, "No, you're going to pay by the month by the seat, and we'll have you up and running in ninety days." And they are doing it today. I'll give you another example, we have a company called AristaSoft.

Rick: I did some research on them for a presentation I gave about the virtualization of the IT department.

Seth: There you go! You're definitely getting the right idea, but now add to AristaSoft's vision. It's not just that virtualization of the IT department, but they're going to deliver third-party business relationships. Imagine if they did what they do for electronics manufacturers, and included specialized platforms and capabilities and maybe even pre-negotiated deals with contract manufacturers, shippers, testing houses, vendor suppliers. This is where the world is going, and this is the piece that we're very focused on.

Rick: Very exciting space!

Seth: We also think that there are businesses that are more horizontal that will turn into service provisioning. An obvious one that I'm very interested in seeing projects on is the storage group, which should also be interesting for your readership. Nobody talks about it because nobody really understands it. As the chairman of Brocade, I'm exposed to the changes there. The storage world is very interesting because the demand for storage is the only thing that's growing faster than the demand for bandwidth. The number of people who can install and manage the storage infrastructure today is woefully small. It's sort of like the early days of multi-protocol networking, where nobody could build a routed network, so specialized service providers emerged. We have one that I can't tell you about yet. We're going to see a marketplace for companies doing storage equipment, like we have just gone through in network equipment. We are front row center in the network equipment space. Virtually every company is a Crosspoint company, and we think the same thing is going to happen in the storage market. I would love it if this interview would cause five people to call me and say I was thinking of a piece of specialized storage gear for a given market. Fifteen years ago network equipment was pretty generic, much like storage equipment is today. As the market has gotten very large, specialization, which looked like niches or product lines, is now a segment that can support a whole company.

Rick: Or an industry. Take the terabytes of storage that you've got in your data center and figure out a way to offer that on a transactional basis, much like the service provider companies we were discussing a moment ago.

Seth: I'm on the board of the company you just described; that's the one I can't tell you about.

Rick: There's a lot of conversation about the startup versus carve-out concept, about the advantages of being two guys in a garage or two guys coming out of Cisco with a great idea, versus an existing company with brand equity and facilities and third-party relationships. Is that a meaningful distinction, and does one have advantages over the other?

Seth: It is a meaningful distinction, but I would cast it a bit differently. One of the ways in which the new business creation and venture capital world has matured in the last five years is that with the invention of the Internet there are many enormous businesses, such as TheSupply.com or Rooster.com (the Cargill grain exchange), for which the intellectual capital is not the dominant theme in the creation of the business. This is not to take anything away from them, but the creation of the business is really about getting all the current players to the table so that you can get this distribution network onto the Internet. The seed crystal to make something happen is critical mass, as opposed to intellectual insight.

Rick: There really is no intellectual property? It's more about relationship capital than it is about intellectual property?

Seth: Again, I would shape it a little bit. Those people have some very hard technological hurdles to cross, but they're mostly about deployment, as opposed to invention. Those are businesses that are very important, and they'll be huge, but they're created by activity that is more like what a merchant bank does. Let's get all the partners together, let's try to work out a very complex deal, let's keep a joint venture on track, and let's go rebuild our industry. These are legitimate, great businesses, but the seed factor, the critical mass, and the economics are very different. There also are enormous opportunities for what has been the mainstay of new business creation in the technology world forever, which is two guys and a dog with a brilliant idea. In the top tier VC firms such as Crosspoint, that's happening every day. It's really about how the future is very different from the past. It's not one or the other. Those people who think that corporate venture capital is going to swamp venture capital, that's a ridiculous notion. The corporations are great at one thing, but really honest business creation is a different world. This kind of critical mass business and the corporate world will play an important role, and so will venture capital, but I think we'll start to see that some firms will be very focused on that kind of business and some will stay focused on the more intellectual capital focused businesses. We're in an era in which firms are doing both. We obviously have done a huge amount of the intellectual capital oriented things, but because of our dominant position in B2B, we've had the opportunity to do these critical mass projects with firms like Cargill and IBM. We, over the long haul, will stick to that deep value creation that comes from technology and intellectual capital. I think you'll see great firms that focus on the critical mass capital.

Rick: Any closing comments that our readership of IT consultants and IT professionals would be interested in?

Seth: There are two things that I'd want to leave them with. One is that the IT professionals of the world are only going to increase in importance and stature. If you think about the service provider model that I described, the people who put this together and run it become very fundamental—even more than they have been around network infrastructure and high-end software. They become very important business leaders, and that's something that I think they should hear. Also, I would love it if your readership would know—let's just challenge them. I have a $20-million check waiting for the group of entrepreneurs who visit me with a brilliant new concept for a new piece of storage equipment or one of these vertical service providers that combine high-tech service provision with a professional services model.[7]

End Notes

1. Helft, M. Reports of the Death of the Dot-Com Have Been Greatly Exaggerated. *The Industry Standard*, Oct. 30, 2000.
2. ibid.
3. ibid.
4. ibid.
5. Venture Capitalists Continue to Fund Companies at Near Record Levels. *Venture Economics News*, Nov. 3, 2000. *www.ventureeconomics.com*
6. Stein, T. Who Wants to Be a Venture Capitalist? *Red Herring*, May 1999.
7. Interview with Seth Neiman. © TechRepublic, Inc. *www.techrepublic.com*. Used by permission. All rights reserved.

BIBLIOGRAPHY

Beckwith, H. (2000). *The invisible touch.* New York: Warner Books.

Bovet, D., & Martha, J. (2000). *Value nets.* New York: John Wiley & Sons.

Carpenter, P. (1999). *E-brands.* Cambridge, MA: Harvard Business School Press.

Carucci, R., & Tetenbaum, T. (1999). *The value creating consultant.* New York: Amacom.

DeMarco, T. (1982). *Controlling software projects.* Englewood Cliffs, NJ: Yourdon Press.

DeMarco, T. (1999). *Peopleware.* New York: Dorset House.

Evans, P., & Wurster, T. (1999). *Blown to bits.* Cambridge, MA: Harvard Business School Press.

Finnie, W. (1994). *Hands-on strategy.* New York: John Wiley & Sons.

Fournier, R. (1998). *A methodology for client server and web application development.* Englewood Cliffs, NJ: Yourdon Press.

Freedman, R. (2000). *The IT consultant: A commonsense framework for managing the client relationship.* San Francisco: Jossey-Bass/Pfeiffer.

Garfinkel, S., & Spafford, G. (1997). *Web security & commerce.* Boston: O'Reilly & Associates.

Godin, S. (1999). *Permission marketing.* New York: Simon & Schuster.

Grant, R. (1991). *Contemporary strategy analysis.* Cambridge, MA: Blackwell.

Hammer, M., & Champy, J. (1993). *Reengineering the corporation: A manifesto for business revolution.* New York: HarperBusiness.

Hartman, A. (2000). *Net ready.* New York: McGraw-Hill.

Highsmith, J. (1999) *Adaptive software development.* New York: Dorset House.

Hughes, A.M. (1994). *Strategic database marketing.* New York: McGraw-Hill.

Killelea, P., & Mui, L. (1998). *Web performance tuning: Speeding up the web.* Boston: O'Reilly & Associates.

Menasce, D., & Almeida, V. (2000). *Scaling for e-business: Technologies, models, performance, and capacity planning.* Upper Saddle River, NJ: Prentice Hall.

Mintzberg, H. (1993). *The rise and fall of strategic planning: Reconceiving roles for planning, plans, planners.* New York: The Free Press.

Mintzberg, H., & Quinn, J. (1995). *The strategy process: Concepts, context and cases.* Upper Saddle River, NJ: Prentice Hall.

Modall, M. (2000). *Now or never.* New York: HarperBusiness.

Negroponte, N. (1995). *Being digital.* New York: Knopf.

Nguyen, H. (2000). *Testing applications on the web: Test planning for Internet-based systems.* New York: John Wiley & Sons.

O'Shea, J., & Madigan, C. (1997). *Dangerous company: The consulting powerhouses and the companies they save and ruin.* New York: Times Business.

Peppers, D., & Rogers, M. (1993). *The one to one future.* New York: Currency/Doubleday.

Peppers, D., & Rogers, M. (1997). *Enterprise one to one: Tools for competing in the information age.* New York: Currency/Doubleday.

Phillips, J. (2000). *The consultant's scorecard.* New York: McGraw-Hill.

Pinault, L. (2000). *Consulting demons: Inside the unscrupulous world of global corporate consulting.* New York: HarperBusiness.

Schaffer, R. (1997). *High-impact consulting.* San Francisco: Jossey-Bass.

Senge, P. (1999). *The dance of change: The challenges to sustaining momentum in learning organizations.* New York: Doubleday/Currency.

Seybold, P. (1998). *Customers.com.* New York: Times Business/Random House.

Shapiro, C., & Varian, H. (1999). *Information rules.* Cambridge, MA: Harvard Business School Press.

Siegal, D. (2000). *Futurize your enterprise.* New York: John Wiley & Sons.

Slywotzky, A. (1996). *Value migration.* Cambridge, MA: Harvard Business School Press.

Stein, L. (1998). *How to set up and maintain a web site.* Reading, MA: Addison-Wesley.

Tapscott, D., Lowy, A., & Ticoll, D. (2000). *Digital capital.* Cambridge, MA: Harvard Business School Press.

Timmers, P. (1999). *Electronic commerce: Strategies and models for business-to-business trading.* Chichester, England: John Wiley & Sons.

ABOUT THE AUTHOR

Rick Freedman is the founder of Consulting Strategies, Inc. (CSI), an IT training and consulting firm. He has eighteen years of experience as an IT consultant, both as an employee of Fortune 500 firms, such as Citicorp and Dun & Bradstreet, and as a principal consultant for Cap Gemini America and ENTEX Information Services. Rick presents seminars on information technology and consulting skills to organizations worldwide.

Consulting Strategies, Inc., trains and coaches IT professionals in corporations and professional services firms in basic consultative skills and behaviors. Through the use of its proprietary training programs, such as *IT Consulting 101, IT Project Management 101,* and *Selling IT Services 101,* CSI helps technicians, engineers, and sales professionals become business advisors. Please visit CSI's website at www.consulting-strategies.com.

You can reach Rick at rickfman@consulting-strategies.com.

INDEX

A

ABCnews, 89
Ace Hardware, 162
Adaptive Development, 14
Adaptive Software Development (Highsmith), 28
AdAuction, 88, 153
Adobe, 223
Adobe Pagemill, 56
Advertising: brand strategy and, 71, 138; impact of Internet on, 138–140; models of banner, 152–153
Aetna Insurance, 192
Agency model: described, 17; questions regarding the, 2–3
Agency.com, 9
Agent's Inc., 137
Aggregation-of-demand model, 66–67
Agile Software, 87, 174
Akamai, 88, 89
Album Advisor (CDNow), 144
Almeida, V., 108, 114
Alta Vista, 83, 145, 150
Altra Energy, 162
Altra Energy Technologies, 80
Amazon.com: auction site developed by, 79; benefiting from eBay's outage, 102; convenience equation used by, 48; customer commitment by, 145; customer interaction with, 70, 109; eRetail business model of, 75; failure of toy division of, 219; Internet time advantage of, 224; new business model demonstrated by, 9; personalized recommendations at, 140; profitability issues of, 76;

rise and fall of stock, 218; strategies competing against, 123, 187
American Airlines, 91
Ameritrade, 118
AMEX Internet Index, 217
Amos Tuck School of Business (Dartmouth College), 53
AMR Research, 93, 174
Andersen Consulting, 17, 201
Andreesen, M., 18
Anheuser-Busch, 44
Antivirus protection management, 124
AOL (America Online), 62, 67, 69, 83, 84, 101, 152, 160, 163
Apple Computer, 67, 142
Application details design, 111, 121–123
Architect of strategy, 24–27
Architecture IT framework, 71
Architecture. *See* IT architecture
Architecture strategy, 108
Ariba, 78, 79, 92, 229, 230, 231
Art Technology Group, 160
Articulating strategic vision, 20–21
Ask Jeeves, 162, 163
ASN (advance shipping notice), 51
ASP (Application Service Provider), 8, 90–97
ASP Industry Consortium, 93
ASP Industry Organization, 212
Astronomy On-line, 152
AT&T, 200
"Atoms to bits" image, 63

Customer value: auction models and, 82; brand based on utility of, 144–145; building IT architectures for, 105; Internet business models on, 74; permission marketers delivery of, 156

Customers: ASP service, 95; brand commitment/awareness by, 144–145; defining the Internet, 148–150; developing website service expectations and, 110, 116–119; forecasting demand by, 67–68; forecasting website behavior by, 109–110, 114–116; Internet business model on creating utility for, 74; Internet business model on selecting, 71–72; meeting the needs of, 223–224; network-based community as, 68–70; partnership through involvement by, 69–70; system crashes/slow download time inconveniencing, 101–103

Customers.com, 159

Customization services: ASP, 94; manufacturing, 54; providing, 159

Cuter Consortium, 189

CVS.com, 169

Cyber Dialogue, 177

D

Daimler-Chrysler, 64

Dangerous Company: The Consulting Powerhouses and the Companies They Save and Ruin (O'Shea and Madigan), 200

Dartmouth College's Amos Tuck School of Business, 53

Data General, 42

Database administration, 125

DataQuest, 211, 220

Delivery. *See* eFulfillment/delivery

Dell Computer, 9, 43, 47, 54, 124, 139

Dells "Partner Pages," 159

Deloitte & Touche, 200

Deloitte Consulting, 220

DemandLine, 67

Demarco, T., 14

Deming, W. E., 59

"Denial of service" attack (February 7, 2000), 102

Diamant, M., 163

Digex, 92

Digital Equipment, 42

Digital Idea, 142

Digital Pulp, 9

Disaster planning/recovery management, 125

Disney's Toysmart, 219

Doerr, J., 228

DoubleClick, 9, 88, 153

Dow Jones, 192

Dowling, T., 212

Durbrow, P., 140

E

E*Trade, 75, 102, 112, 115, 123

Early adoptors, 149

eBay Technology, 9, 78, 79, 101, 102, 118, 224

eBranding: best practices for, 143–144; building, 143; building experience-based, 146–148; customer commitment/awareness of, 144–145; importance of, 142; style over substance mistake in, 140–142

eBrands: Building an Internet Business at Breakneck Speed (Carpenter), 143

eBusiness: applying new methodologies of, 12–14; comparing Big Five methodologies to, 15–16, 17; creating/imparting vision for, 188; customer service/support options for, 176–181; eConsulting Framework guidelines for, 19–28, 20f; eFulfillment/delivery chain of, 97–98, 131–132, 167–176; fall of, 222–225, 232–233; Internet business models for, 8, 71–82, 87, 90–98, 220–222; online toy segment of, 218–220; recognizing Internet opportunity for, 188; The Gartner Group on fallacies of, 168. *See also* Web marketing

eBusiness Team, 128

eBusiness technical design process, 106–112, 109f

eCIs (eCommerce integrators), 199–200

"eCommerce Integrators Exposed" (Forrester Research), 199–202

eCompany Now, 210

eConsultancies, 11

eConsultants: change issue importance for, 183–185; constant development approach by, 213–216; continual research/training of, 165; developing strategic skills, 210–213; Forrester Research report on eCIs by, 199–200; helping organizations migrate, 187–190; impact of Internet on, 1–3; measuring results of, 202–203; outcome communicated by, 206–207; performing a "gap analysis," 121; researching own competitive position, 215–216; self-measurement by, 205; sus-

Venture Capital Resource Library, 212
Venture Economics, 228
Vertical network-based communities, 161
Viacom's Red Rocket.com, 219
Victoria's Secret Website, 112
Vincent, E., 97
Viral marketing, 153–155
Virtual Data Cente, 8
Virtual Emporium, 192
Visibility 2000, 164
Vision, 188
Vividence, 205

W

Wal-Mart, 51, 53, 76
Wall Street Journal, 60, 125, 210, 220
The Wall Street Journal, 64
WalMart.com, 169
Wang Laboratories, 42
"Warehouse-less" retail enterprise, 168, 176
Washington Running report, 70
Web callback options, 177–180
Web development, 104–105
Web DNA, 186, 193–194, 196
Web marketing: advertising and, 138–140; ASP business model, 94–95; defining the customer, 148–150; eBranding and, 140–148; innovative types of "guerrilla," 162–164; Internet business model on, 73–74; to network-based communities, 160–162; new economy marketing models, 150–164; one-to-one marketing introduced to, 159–160; permission (opt-in) marketing, 155–156; traditional marketing compared to, 135–138; viral marketing introduced to, 153–155. *See also* Marketing
Web-based browsers, 84
Webb, M., 102, 118
Webex, 223, 224
WebHeads, 128
Webhouse, 225
WebMD, 160
WebTV, 86
Welch, J., 38, 39, 42, 43, 47, 187
Western Initiative Media, 141
Westinghouse, 39
Whinston, A., 228

Whitman-Hart, 10 (one is misspelled)
Whitmann-Hart, 217
"Who Wants to Be a Venture Capitalist?" (*Red Herring*), 229
"Winner's curse," 80
Witness MarchFirst, 10
World Wide Web Consortium, 213
World Wide Websites: designing application details for, 111, 121–123; designing operational processes of, 111; developing architecture strategy for, 112–114; developing customer service expectations of, 110, 116–119; as eConsulting resource, 212–213; failure of eCIs, 199–200; forecasting customer behavior on, 109–110, 114–116; four-phase hierarchy of, 106–107, 119; maintaining, 112, 127–129; system crashes/hacking attack challenges to, 101–103; testing and prototyping, 126–127. *See also* Internet; IT architecture
W.W. Grainger, 221

X

Xcelerate, 13
Xerox, 61
XML Cover Pages, 212

Y

Y2K, 18
Yahoo: advertising revenue produced by, 67; benefiting from eBay's outage, 101–102; branding strategy by, 143, 147; customer commitment by, 144, 145; "denial of service" attack on, 102; highs and lows of stock, 217–218; infrastructure design quality of, 117; innovative brand marketing by, 162; intellectual property of, 83; "Internet Promotion" category, 153; Internet time advantage of, 224; origin search function of, 150; "Search Engine Placement Improvement" category, 151–152
Yahoo Finance site, 82, 213–214
The Yankee Group, 211
Yourdon, E., 14

Z

Zapolin, M., 141
ZDNet, 102
Zhu, M., 223